SINGING THE SONGS OF THE LORD IN FOREIGN LANDS:
PSALMS IN CONTEMPORARY LUTHERAN INTERPRETATION

DOCUMENTATION 59/2014

THE
LUTHERAN
WORLD
FEDERATION

The views expressed in this publication are those of the authors and do not necessarily reflect the official position of the Lutheran World Federation

SINGING THE SONGS OF THE
LORD IN FOREIGN LANDS:
PSALMS IN CONTEMPORARY
LUTHERAN INTERPRETATION

Edited by
Kenneth Mtata, Karl-Wilhelm Niebuhr, Miriam Rose

EVANGELISCHE VERLAGSANSTALT
Leipzig

Bibliographic information published by the German National Library

The *Deutsche Nationalbibliothek* lists this publication in the *Deutsche Nationalbibliografie;* detailed bibliographic data are available on the internet at http://dnd.dnd.de

© 2014 The Lutheran World Federation

Printed in Germany · H 7807

This work, including all of its parts, is protected by copyright. Any use beyond the strict limits of copyright law without the permission of the publishing house is strictly prohibited and punishable by law.

This book was printed on FSC-certified paper

Cover photo:	NASA, ESA, J. Hester and A. Loll (Arizona State University), public domain
Editorial assistance:	Department for Theology and Public Witness
Typesetting and inside layout:	LWF Communications/Department for Theology and Public Witness
Design:	LWF Communications/EVA
Printing and Binding:	Druckhaus Köthen GmbH & Co. KG

Published by Evangelische Verlangsanstalt GmbH · Leipzig, Germany, under the auspices of
The Lutheran World Federation
150, rte de Ferney, PO Box 2100
CH-1211 Geneva 2, Switzerland

ISBN 978-3-374-03773-5
www.eva-leipzig.de
Parallel edition in German

Contents

Acknowledgments 7

Preface 9
Martin Junge

Foreword 11
Klaus Dicke

Introduction 13
Kenneth Mtata, Karl-Wilhelm Niebuhr, Miriam Rose

I. Hermeneutical Approaches and Challenges

Luther's Early Interpretation of the Psalms and his Contribution to Hermeneutics 19
Hans-Peter Grosshans

"Protect me from those who are Violent." Psalm 140: A Cry for Justice—a Song of Hope 33
Monica Jyotsna Melanchthon

II. Psalms Exegesis: Methodologies Past and Present

Singing, Praying and Meditating the Psalms. Exegetical and Historical Remarks 59
Corinna Körting

From Psalms to Psalter Exegesis 73
Frank-Lothar Hossfeld

III. Difficult Topics in Psalms and their Lutheran Interpretation

The Topic of Violence—A Hermeneutical Challenge in Reading Psalms 81
Jutta Hausmann

Between Praise and Lament. Remarks on the Development of the Hebrew Psalms 91
Urmas Nõmmik

The Vengeance Psalms as a Phenomenon of Critical Justice: The Problem of Enemies in Luther's Interpretation of Psalms 105
Roger Marcel Wanke

IV. Psalms from the Old Testament and Their Reception in the New Testament

Psalms Outside the Biblical Psalms Collection—the Example of Jonah 121
    Karl-Wilhelm Niebuhr

Interpretation of the Psalms in the New Testament: Witness to Christ and the Human Condition 139
    Craig R. Koester

The Christological Reception of Psalms in Hebrews 157
    Anni Hentschel

V. Luther's Interpretation of the Psalms from a Contemporary Perspective

Luther and the Psalms: How Stories Shape the Story 181
    Vítor Westhelle

The Psalms and Luther's Praise Inversion: Cultural Criticism as Doxology Detection 191
    Brian Brock

Theology of the Word in "Operationes in Psalmos" (1519-1521) 213
    Ľubomír Batka

VI. Contextual Approaches to the Psalms

Being 'ādām: A Contextual Reading of the Psalms Today 233
    Madipoane Masenya (ngwan'a Mphahlele)

The Wounds of War: Engaging the Psalms of Lament in Pastoral Care with Veterans Against the Background of Martin Luther's Hermeneutics 245
    Andrea Bieler

Luther's Poetic Reading of Psalms 261
    Dorothea Erbele-Küster

Authors 271

Acknowledgments

The second international hermeneutics conference was made possible through the sponsorship of the Deutsche Forschungsgemeinschaft and the Ministry of Culture of the Free State Thuringia. We extend our appreciation for the official dinner receptions hosted by the Bishop of the Evangelische Kirche in Mitteldeutschland, Ilse Junkermann, and the Official Representative of the Thuringian Ministry of Culture for the Reformation Anniversary, Dr Thomas A. Seidel. The conference participants participated in excursions to famous historical sites in Weimar, Erfurt and Eisenach, thanks to the kind sponsorship of the Wartburgstiftung Eisenach, the Klassikstiftung Weimar and the Augustinerkloster Erfurt. Participants enjoyed the warm welcome by church parishes and leading representatives of the superintendents of Eisenach, Weimar and Erfurt. Last, but not least, we would like to thank the dedicated local organizers of the conference, Dr Karl-Wilhelm Niebuhr, Dr Miriam Rose and their gracious assistants Maria Köhler, Charlotte Reinhold and Anne Puhr.

Preface

Martin Junge

This collection of essays contributes to the ongoing reflection among Lutheran theologians on matters pertaining to interpretive practices and theories within the Lutheran traditions. While the first publication in this series, *"You have the Words of Eternal Life." Transformative Readings of the Gospel of John from a Lutheran Perspective,* focused on the Gospel of John, this book seeks to explore how we read the Old Testament together as Lutheran churches in our different contexts.

The sixteenth-century Reformation was in part the result of a concerted effort to study the Scriptures, informed by rigorous literary and theological analysis, as well as an intentional engagement with the pressing social issues of the day. No book played a more prominent role than the Book of Psalms since it provided a link between the expression of the ordinary Christian's existential quest and the hope for God's deliverance based on God's promises. It was for this very reason that in his first lectures at the University of Wittenberg in October 1512 Martin Luther reflected on the Psalms.

In his 1528 Preface to the Psalms, Luther says;

> Many of the Fathers have loved and praised the book of Psalms above all other books of the Bible...The Book of Psalms has other excellencies: it preserves, not the trivial and ordinary things said by the stains, but their deepest and noblest utterances, those which they used when speaking in full earnest and all urgency to God. It not only tells what they say about their work and conduct, but also lays bare their hearts and the deepest treasures hidden in their souls: and this is done in such a way which allows us to contemplate the causes and the sources of their words and works...The human heart is like a ship on a stormy sea driven about by winds blowing from all four corners of heaven. The Book of Psalms is full of heartfelt utterances made during storms of this kind. Where can one find nobler words to express joy than in the Psalms of praise or gratitude?

In these reflections, Luther affirms the spirit of the Psalms which brings to the fore concrete human experiences such as pain, regret and desperation. But these experiences are not the last word in the Psalms; the last word is, "Out of my distress I called on the Lord; the Lord answered me and set me in a broad place" (Ps 118:5). The message of liberation and deliverance is the final statement for those who in lament find consolation in God's promises.

I commend this collection of essays to teachers at seminaries, teachers, pastors and all those who may want to deepen their understanding of the Psalms in light of the Lutheran tradition and in response to the various contextual challenges.

Foreword

Klaus Dicke

It is a great privilege and pleasure to be able cordially to welcome you to Eisenach on the occasion of the second international hermeneutics conference, "Towards a Lutheran Hermeneutics on Psalms." The University of Jena very much appreciates the fact that the Lutheran World Federation's second consultation on global Lutheran hermeneutical perspectives takes place in Thuringia and that our faculty of theology has the honor to host you on your journey toward the commemoration of the 500th Anniversary of the Reformation in 2017.

Although university presidents worldwide are trained to develop a kind of "my-home-is-my-castle" mentality, I certainly do not regret the one-hour drive from Jena to Eisenach since, for a number reasons, I regard Eisenach to be the right venue for this conference. First and above all, Eisenach is the city where Martin Luther went to school and the Wartburg is where he translated the New Testament into popular German and, among other writings, completed his commentary on the Psalms. Eisenach is therefore not only one of the most prominent Luther cities but also the city where we find both biogeographical evidence for and theological meaning in Luther's hymn *Eine feste Burg ist unser Gott* [A Mighty Fortress Is Our God].

Second, Johann Sebastian Bach was baptized here in Eisenach at St George's church. Bach, whose sacred music comprises more than 200 cantatas and represents a Lutheran hermeneutics of its own, was born 21 March 1685. The fact that Bach's birthday is celebrated annually and that frequently cantatas by Bach, Telemann and others are part of Sunday services at St George's are expressions of the city's spirituality.

Third, the University of Jena, which was founded in 1548 as an academic platform for Lutheranism, closely cooperates with the church of Eisenach and with its senior minister as we approach 2017. For example, a symposium on Luther and Bach was held in 2012, and plans are currently underway for a symposium in 2015 on Nikolaus von Amsdorf who joined Luther on his way from Worms to the Wartburg and died in Eisenach in May 1565. Eisenach is firm and rich Lutheran ground.

In the last weeks, I happened to reread some of Luther's early sermons and writings. It struck me that Luther frequently used the notion of *Erfahrung*, experience. His sermons in particular show that he was a rather sensitive observer of his own inner life as well as that of people surrounding him and that he took a vivid interest in public life and in nature. It seems to me that for Luther in particular the reading of Psalms was a pedagogical exercise and that he recognized the Lord's will in each and every experience. When I prepared this word of greeting I asked myself what Martin Luther would have said to this week's terrible and apocalyptic weather and Johann Sebastian Bach's cantata "Abide with us, for it is toward evening" immediately came to my mind. I took the CD from the shelf and got the answer to my question. The forth movement of the cantata, a bass recitativo, reads:

> Darkness has prevailed in many places.
> But wherefore this has come to pass?
> Simply because the lowly and the mighty have not walked in righteousness
> Before Thee, O God
> And have violated their Christian duty.
> Therefore hast thou removed the candle stick
> Out of his place.

And the final movement of the cantata is Martin Luther's chorale:

> Prove Thy might, Lord Jesus Christ.
> O Thou who art the Lord of Lords;
> Shield Thy poor Christendom,
> That all Christians might praise Thee eternally.

With this prayer by both Luther and Bach I wish you a pleasant and safe stay in their city and in Thuringia, inspiring presentations and discussions and that God may bless your consultation.

Introduction

Kenneth Mtata, Karl-Wilhelm Niebuhr, Miriam Rose

> I will meditate on your precepts, and fix my eyes on your ways. I will delight in your statutes; I will not forget your word (Ps 119:1–16).

On 3 January 1521, Pope Leo X issued the papal bull excommunicating Martin Luther because of his defiance of both the Pope and the Emperor. Emperor Charles V gave Martin Luther the opportunity to recant his theological position by inviting him to the Diet of Worms, which Luther attended on 17 April after having been granted imperial assurance of safe passage. Luther, however, did not recant his teachings; he was declared a heretic and outlawed but allowed safe passage from the Diet. On leaving the Diet, Frederick the Wise, Luther's friend and protector, arranged for Luther to be "kidnapped" and to be brought to the Wartburg Castle for his own safety. It was at the Wartburg Castle (1521–1522) that Martin Luther completed the translation of the New Testament into the German vernacular and from where, in 1522, he returned to Wittenberg to oversee the establishment of the evangelical church. For Luther, the foundation of the church was the Word of God and the Psalms were among those Scriptures that Luther held in high regard.

The essays in this book were first presented at a conference on the Psalms held in 2013 in Eisenach, at the foot of the Wartburg, a symbolic venue for this conference jointly organized by the Lutheran World Federation and the University of Jena. It was the second in a series of hermeneutics consultations organized by the LWF, designed to create a space for the joint exploration of the Lutheran hermeneutical resources among member churches and related theological institutions and the engagement with ecumenical partners as we move toward the 2017 Anniversary of the Reformation.

The first consultation, Nairobi 2011, concentrated on the relationship between the Gospel of John in its context, the readers in their context and the possibility of using the broad Lutheran theological heritage as a reading lens. It was observed that there was the need to strengthen the ecumenical component and to emphasize the readings' relationship to the spiritual renewal of the church and the transformation of society. This interpretive element was built into the Psalms conference, which brought together scholars and church leaders from all seven regions of the LWF as well as ecumenical guests.

The first chapter gives an overview of the spectrum within which the Psalms can be read. One of the essays focuses on the Lutheran hermeneutical perspective while the second relates the Psalms of lament to a contemporary context of violence. The second chapter deals with the methodological challenges posed in reading the Psalms, which are not only a part of the Christian Bible but are also being read as sacred texts in Jewish religious life today. The Lutheran perspective gives priority to the Christological reading of the Old Testament as a crucial point for reading the Psalms in contemporary church settings. A Christological reading of the Psalms implies a deeper understanding of who Christ is for us in light of the Psalms. In this we share the experience of Martin Luther, whose understanding of Jesus Christ was further developed and deepened by the Psalms. In his humanity, Jesus carried in himself the human condition in the presence of God. In this human condition we participate. Such a Christological reading of the Psalms suggests a hermeneutical spiral; the Psalms help us to understand Christ as much as Christ enables us to understand the Psalms. This raises the question what such a reading implies for Christian–Jewish relations. Can Christians read the Psalms without taking into consideration other communities with whom they share this rich resource of faith?

The third chapter deals with a number of difficult themes in the Psalms read from a Lutheran perspective. The scholars highlight some important principles of Lutheran hermeneutics which should be taken seriously when reading the Psalms. One such principle is to take seriously the literary form of the text. Such a reading accepts the sense of God's transcendence, God coming to us without our doing anything. Such a reading is also oriented toward the movement of the reader from despair to faith, from loneliness and distance to community with God and fellow beings. The human community of those who read the Psalms this way also seeks to relate the written word to daily life.

The following chapter discusses the reception of the Psalms in the New Testament. We read the Psalms in the full awareness that there is not only one way of reading a biblical book and that the Psalms have been read in different ways within the Old Testament, in Early Judaism, in the New Testament and later, with each subsequent reading offering significant insights to illuminate further readings. As Christians we read the Psalms both individually and as part of the Psalter, as part of the Old Testament related to the New Testament. We also take into account that Jesus himself and the New Testament writers made use of the Psalter testifying to the unity of two testaments. But we also read the Psalms informed by their historical origins, the history of their reception and theological interpretations and their relevance and meaning for us today.

The essays in the final two chapters relate to Luther's interpretation of the Psalms, with the latter focusing on contextual questions. The Psalms help us to make sense of the human condition by creating a framework for interpreting our experiences. They evince a sensitive description of the human condition addressed in them and are attentive to issues of justice and injustice, violence, conflict, lament and joy. The Psalms celebrate the human condition while they also allow the outburst of yearning for newness of life in God. Especially in the Psalms of lament we recognize the paradoxes of life that we all share despite our different contexts. The lament Psalms are about protest, revenge, anger and a cry for justice emanating from experiences of pain, injustice, suffering, abandonment and rejection. Lament Psalms speak of the experience of the absence as well as the experience of the nearness of God.

The contributions in this book underline the value of reading the Psalms and how the Psalms can contribute to our broader understanding of biblical interpretation. Psalms remain an important section of the Bible through which Christian life can be shaped and challenged. As Christian readers of the Bible we affirm that God speaks to us through the Holy Scriptures of both the New and the Old Testaments. The process of understanding biblical texts reaches its aim when the text becomes effective in the lives of the readers and listeners. Employing Lutheran hermeneutics requires that we pay attention to the manner in which Luther read and subsequent generations of Lutheran interpreters of the Psalms applied them to their contexts while we seek faithfully to speak to our own contexts through the same Scriptures. The Psalms provide both examples and language for individual and communal repentance for sin that alienates humans from God and from one another. In the Psalms we encounter the honest language of concrete human life before God.

I. Hermeneutical Approaches and Challenges

Luther's Early Interpretation of the Psalms and his Contribution to Hermeneutics

Hans-Peter Grosshans

In 1525 Martin Luther added a brief introduction to the German edition of the Psalms in which he outlines how the Psalms should be read in order for them to be helpful. He wrote,

> Compared with others books of the Holy Scriptures, the Book of Psalms has the virtue not only to teach all kinds of good and to propose examples but to show in the choicest way and to point to with distinguished words how we shall keep and fulfill Gods commandments, that is, how a heart should be which has true faith and how a good conscience sticks to God in all incidences, to be comforted and set upright. In sum, the Book of Psalms is a true school, in which we learn, exercise and strengthen faith and good conscience before God.[1]

Luther further suggests that while many Psalms praise God's truth, justice and Word and thus comfort the faithful, many refer to the cross, the lament, the tears and the worry. For Luther it is obvious that faithful Christians have to suffer in this life. The Psalms describe the way in which the Spirit lives, fights, acts and increases in faith through God's Word and truth as well as how the human flesh and earthly life die, suffer, are defeated and diminish.

Luther regarded the Book of Psalms as being highly instructive and worthy of study. After having obtained his doctorate, Martin Luther's first

---

[1] Martin Luther, *Deutsche Bibel*, Bd. 10/I, 588: "Der Psalter hat fur andern buechern der heyligen schrifft die tugent an sich, das er nicht alleyne allerley gutts leret vnd exempel furlegt, sondern auch auffs aller feynest, mit auserweleten worten zeygt vnd weyset, wie man Gottes gepott solle halten vnd erfullen, das ist, wie eyn hertz geschickt seyn sol, das eynen rechten glauben habe, vnd wie eyn gutt gewissen sich halte gegen Gott ynn allen zufellen wie es zu troesten vnd auff zu richten sey, Summa der psalter ist eyne rechte schule, darynne man den glauben vnd gut gewissen zu Gott, lernt, vbet vnd sterckt."

series of exegetical university lectures in the years 1513 to 1515 focused on the Psalms. In other words, he was initially an Old Testament scholar.[2] Throughout his life, Luther continued to work on the Psalms. Notable are his "Operationes in Psalmos" (on the first twenty-two Psalms) from 1519–1521; his second lectures on the Psalms; the "Book of Psalms in German in the Style of the Hebrew Language" edited in 1524; and the various interpretations of the Psalms between 1529 and 1532, such as his interpretation of the first twenty-five Psalms at the time of the Diet of Augsburg during his stay at the Coburg. Furthermore, in 1532 Luther lectured on Psalms 2, 45 and 51; from late 1532 to the end of 1533, he lectured on Psalms 120–134; and from 1534 to 1535 he lectured on Psalm 90. Between 1534 and 1536 he lectured on Psalms 101 and 23, which were to be his last lectures on the Psalms.

Prior to lecturing on the Psalms, Luther had focused on other theologians and philosophers such as Aristotle, Augustine and Peter Lombard as was the usual practice at his time. By 1513, Luther—by now an independent theologian in his own right—while continuing to refer to the writings of other theologians, i.e., Augustine's "Ennarationes in Psalmos," also gave his own interpretation of the Psalms. Furthermore, and maybe even more importantly, he developed his own understanding of hermeneutics.

Whereas in Luther's early exegetical lectures on the Psalms, his new hermeneutics did not correspond entirely to the Protestant principle of Holy Scripture, which he proposed later, the transformation in his understanding of the way in which to interpret biblical texts already becomes apparent.

There is some truth to Karl Bauer's statement that Luther became the reformer of the church through his new hermeneutics.[3] Nevertheless, Bauer did not recognize the new hermeneutics in Luther's first lectures on the Psalms and therefore believed that the lectures during 1513 to 1515 do not show Luther as a reformer. Luther's new hermeneutic becomes obvious in his interpretation of the Psalms in the period between 1519 and 1521 and Bauer therefore believes the major shift in Luther's theology and hermeneutics to have taken place between 1516 and 1519.

Gerhard Ebeling repudiates this claim and has tried to show that already in Luther's first lectures on the Psalms we not only see the roots of his new hermeneutics, but also some new elements of his hermeneutics, which become fully developed in his second series of lectures on the

---

[2] Luther lectured not only on the Psalms but also on other Old Testament books such as Genesis, Isaiah, minor prophets and others.

[3] Luther "became a reformer through his new hermeneutic." Cf. Karl Bauer, *Die Wittenberger Universitätstheologie und die Anfänge der Reformation* (Tübingen: J.C.B. Siebeck [Paul Mohr],1928), 145.

Psalms between 1519 and 1521.[4] According to Ebeling, while Luther only developed his new hermeneutics in the years 1516 to 1519, he already laid the foundations for his reformatory hermeneutics by drawing on traditional hermeneutics in the years 1513 to 1515.[5]

The scope of this essay does not permit me to present my own interpretation of Luther's hermeneutics during the first decade of his teaching career, nor to present Luther's theology on the Psalms. Rather, I shall concentrate on a few elements in Luther's hermeneutics which I understand to be characteristic of Luther's way of interpreting biblical texts in general and his interpretation of the Psalms in particular. When we look at Luther's first lectures on Psalms, these hermeneutical characteristics already indicate the way in which Luther transformed hermeneutics.

SPECIFICITIES OF LUTHER'S HERMENEUTICS

When reading Luther's lectures on Psalms from 1513 to 1515, three dominant elements of interpretation become immediately obvious. Luther follows the traditional scheme of the fourfold sense of Scripture,[6] operates with the traditional difference of letter and spirit (of *litera* and *spiritus*)—the literal and spiritual sense of the biblical text—and practices a strictly Christological reading of the Psalms.

Luther already points to these principles in his preface to the Wolfenbüttel Psalter. He begins his lecture with,

> I will sing praise with the spirit and with the mind also" (1 Cor 14:15). To sing with the spirit is to sing with spiritual devotion and emotion. This is said in opposition to those who sing only with the flesh. And these appear in a twofold sense: The first are those who with an unsettled and weary heart sing only with the tongue and the mouth. The second are those who indeed sing with a cheerful and devout heart but are still enjoying it in a more carnal way, as, for example, taking pleasure in the voice, the sound, the staging, and the harmony. They act as boys usually do, not concerned about the meaning or the fruit of the spirit that is to be raised up to God. In the same way, to sing with the mind is to sing with

---

[4] Cf. Gerhard Ebeling, "Die Anfänge von Luthers Hermeneutik," in Gerhard Ebeling, *Lutherstudien*, vol. 1 (Tübingen: Mohr Siebeck GmbH & Co. K, 1971), 7.
[5] Cf. Ibid., 6.
[6] For this hermeneutical doctrine, see Hans-Peter Grosshans, "Lutheran Hermeneutics. An Outline," in Kenneth Mtata (ed.), *"You have the Words of Eternal Life." Transformative Readings of the Gospel of John from a Lutheran Perspective*, Documentation 57/2012 (Minneapolis: Lutheran University Press, 2019), 23–46.

spiritual understanding. And there are likewise two opposites of these: The first are those who understand nothing of what they sing, as nuns are said to read the Psalter. The others are those who have a carnal understanding of the Psalms, like the Jews, who always apply the Psalms to ancient history apart from Christ. But Christ has opened the mind of those who are His so that they might understand the Scriptures. More often, however, the spirit enlightens the mind, the emotions, the intellect, yes, also vice versa, because the spirit lifts up to the place where the illuminating light is, whereas the mind assigns a place to the emotions. Therefore both are required, but the elevating spirit is better, etc.[7]

After giving some examples, Luther continues,

In the Scriptures, therefore, no allegory, tropology, or anagogy is valid, unless the same truth is expressly stated historically elsewhere. Otherwise Scripture would become a mockery. But one must indeed take in an allegorical sense only what is elsewhere stated historically, as mountain in the sense of righteousness in Ps. 36:6 "Thy righteousness is like the mountains of God." For that reason it is best to distinguish the spirit from the letter in the Sacred Scriptures, for this is what makes one a theologian indeed. And the church has this only from the Holy Spirit, not from human understanding. Thus Ps. 72:8 says: "May He have dominion from sea to sea." Before the Spirits revelation no one could know that this dominion means a spiritual dominion, especially because he adds "from sea to sea" according to the historical sense. Therefore those who interpret this dominion as referring to the flesh and to earthly majesty have the killing letter, but others have the life-giving spirit.[8]

Already in these introductory remarks we can observe how Luther shifts the emphasis of certain aspects of traditional hermeneutics and thus is on the way to transforming hermeneutics.

First, Luther insists on the historical meaning of the biblical texts. When interpreting the Scriptures, no allegory, tropology or anagogy is valid unless, historically, the same truth has been expressly stated elsewhere. This was not a novel insight since, according to the Augustinian tradition, a fourfold spiritual interpretation always had to be based on both the literal and the

---

[7] Martin Luther, "First Lectures on the Psalms I, Psalms 1–75," in *LW* 10, 3.

[8] Ibid., 4–5. Cf. Gerhard Ebeling's penetrating study, "Der vierfache Schriftsinn und die Unterscheidung von litera und spiritus," in Gerhard Ebeling, *Lutherstudien*, I (Tübingen: J. C. B. Mohr, 1971), 51–53, where Ebeling shows how Luther conceived of the entire traditional fourfold interpretation of Scripture as being governed by the overriding approach either of *litera occidens* or of *spiritus vivificans*—of killing letter or life-giving spirit.

historical sense of the text. Since biblical interpretation has to be related to the literal as well as the historical meaning of the text, the spiritual interpretation of biblical texts is limited. Luther later abandoned the theory of the fourfold sense of biblical texts and showed a clear preference for the literal meaning of Holy Scripture. But this is not necessarily the historical meaning of a biblical text, which relates the understanding of the text to its original historical context. The positive use of an allegorical, tropological and anagogical interpretation—in its relation to the historical meaning of the text—in Luther's first lectures on the Psalm stands in stark contrast to his later hermeneutics. But, as we can observe already in his early lectures, Luther is already in the process of transforming his hermeneutics toward a consistent preference for the literal sense of the text. The reason for this is Luther's second obvious hermeneutical emphasis in the preface to his lectures on Psalms.

Second, reading and interpreting Scriptures in historical terms only would be as wrong as ignoring the historical meaning of the biblical text. If we avoid both, then, as a result, we might come directly to the concept of the threefold spiritual sense of the Scriptures. Luther illustrates this by describing the various (inner) modes of singing the Psalms. If we regard the Psalms as spiritual songs, then we come close to the concept of "spiritual understanding," as it was developed in the early church with the concept of the fourfold sense. According to this concept, apart from the literal or historical understanding of a biblical text there is a spiritual understanding that may be allegorical or tropological (moral) or anagogical (eschatological). Spiritual understandings answer specific spiritual questions that may be responded to by the biblical text: What does the text tell us about God's salvific action and history (allegorical)? What does the text tell us that we have to do (tropological)?[9] What, according the text, may we hope for in the life to come (anagogical)? A biblical text should not only tell something about the past and inform us about its historical context (and God's presence there), but should present a divine reality which includes the readers and listeners and their respective contexts and realities, challenging them to understand themselves within this divine reality.

Much of the history of Protestant hermeneutics pertains to how we grasp the spiritual understanding of the biblical text in the sense of being struck and moved by the divine Spirit. Already in his preface to his early lectures on the Psalms, Luther tries to identify the divine Spirit and therefore a spiritual understanding within rather than beyond the biblical texts and their literal interpretation. The reason for this is not a general respect for the Holy

---

[9] The tropological sense of a text questions the reader or listener and challenges them to take a position (in their lives) in respect to the reality presented in the text.

Scriptures, but Luther's awareness that all biblical texts are about Christ. Or, formulated differently and using a term which was later made prominent by the Lutheran Matthias Flacius, Christ is the one and only scopus of the Holy Scriptures. If we assume that all biblical texts, in all their variety, are ultimately about Christ—or at least witness to Christ—then we no longer need different spiritual understandings. Rather, attempts to find various spiritual understandings of a biblical text might result in missing the actual point of the text, namely the witness to Christ. In order to ascertain what a biblical text tells us about Christ it is sufficient to understand the text literally. To avoid misunderstanding: in order to understand a text literally one not only has to read it in its original language but also be aware of all the literary forms (grammatical, semantic, stylistic, poetic, rhetorical).

The fact that Luther understood Christ as the scopus of all biblical texts characterizes his interpretation of the Psalms, even if the Psalms are obviously part of the Old Testament. From the very beginning, Luther's concentration on Christ is clear. To the already quoted preface, Luther added the "Preface of Jesus Christ, Son of God and Our Lord, to the Psalter of David."[10] Referring to a number of biblical witnesses (Moses, Zechariah, Peter, Paul), he suggests some general guidelines for the interpretation of the Psalms.

> From these we draw the following guideline for this dark, yet holy labyrinth: Every prophecy and every prophet must be understood as referring to Christ the Lord, except where it is clear from plain words that someone else is spoken of. For thus He Himself says: "Search the Scriptures, ... and it is they that bear witness to Me" (John 5:39).[11]

Luther links the point of reference of almost all biblical texts, Jesus Christ, to the traditional concept of the fourfold sense of Scripture in order to avoid a merely historical reading and understanding of biblical texts. By referring to Jesus Christ, biblical texts do not only convey historical information but are related to the present and to the individual lives of the readers and listeners and to the communal life of the church, the community of believers. Therefore Luther continues,

> Whatever is said literally concerning the Lord Jesus Christ as to His person must be understood allegorically of a help that is like Him and of the church conformed to Him in all things. And at the same time this must be understood tropologically of any spiritual and inner man against his flesh and the outer man.[12]

---

[10] *LW* 10, 6f.
[11] Ibid., 7.
[12] Ibid.

Luther illustrates this with further examples:

> Let this be made plain by means of examples. "Blessed is the man who walks not, etc." (Ps. 1:1). Literally this means that the Lord Jesus made no concessions to the designs of the Jews and of the evil and adulterous age that existed in His time. Allegorically it means that the holy church did not agree to the evil designs of persecutors, heretics, and ungodly Christians. Tropologically this means that the spirit of man did not accede to the persuasions and suggestions of the inimical flesh and of the ungodly stirrings of the body of sin. Thus also Ps. 2:1 says: "Why do the nations conspire, etc." Literally this refers to the raging of the Jews and Gentiles against Christ during His suffering. Allegorically it is directed against tyrants, heretics, and ungodly leaders of the church. Tropologically it has to do with the tyranny, temptation, and tempest of the carnal and outer man who provokes and torments the spirit as the dwelling place of Christ.[13]

While at this point Luther is still struggling with traditional ways of interpretation according to the threefold spiritual sense of biblical text, he is already on his way to overcome this by directing his understanding of the biblical text toward Jesus Christ.

Third, already in his early interpretation of the Psalms, Luther clearly distinguishes between the killing letter and the life-giving spirit. We already find this terminology at the end of the "Preface to the Glosses" of the *Wolfenbüttel Psalter*, where Luther refers to Psalm 72:8 ("May he have dominion from sea to sea") and points to an historical misinterpretation of this phrase, meaning political dominion ("as referring to the flesh and to earthly majesty") in form of a global theocratic state for instance. Luther says that those people who understand Psalm 72:8 in a political sense use it as a "killing letter" and not as "life-giving spirit."

But in what sense is an historical understanding of Psalm 72:8 "killing"? To seek an historical understanding of this text does not mean relating this text to its past context, but to relate it to history—including past, present and future—as the dimension of human life in which the material conditions of life are organized and social life is structured. This is what is also meant by "dominion." And if the phrase "from sea to sea" is understood only historically then it is also understood politically in the sense that God will install one global political dominion on earth, which is ruled according God's law. Psalm 72 is a song about a king, made just by God, such as people were hoping for.

---

[13] Ibid.

> May he judge your people with righteousness, and your poor with justice. May the mountains yield prosperity for the people, and the hills, in righteousness. May he defend the cause of the poor of the people, give deliverance to the needy, and crush the oppressor. May he live while the sun endures, and as long as the moon, throughout all generations. May he be like rain that falls on the mown grass, like showers that water the earth. In his days may righteousness flourish and peace abound, until the moon is no more. 8 May he have dominion from sea to sea, and from the River to the ends of the earth (Ps 72:2–8).

The young Luther believed that a political interpretation of this text would not only go in the wrong direction but, even worse, lead to death. It is therefore a "killing letter."[14] Clearly Luther would have been highly critical of a theological justification of any global empire of one emperor (even if he would be pious) living according divine law (or of a group of people with good ideology or even divine theology).

But why is such an understanding of Psalm 72 (and similar biblical texts) not only wrong but even killing?

First, history has shown that empires striving for pure und true (even divine) justice remain empires with all the negative aspects implied by the use of force and abuse of power. Moreover, experience has shown that this always implies the killing of people. We must therefore conclude that justice (in its political, economic, cultural dimensions) has to be based on freedom. Others may object that the Western concept of freedom kills in a political, economic and cultural sense, at least outside the Western world.

Reflections of this kind on possibilities of an historical understanding of Psalm 72:8 show that Luther's verdict is correct. Through such understandings of biblical texts we are confronted with "killing letters," despite the fact that in the original historical context people articulated in this song their hopes for a better, peaceful and just life.

It is not, however, because of the consequences (which may imply the killing of people) that Luther thought of Psalm 72:8, which articulates the hopes of people in a vision of a global theocratic empire, as a "killing letter" when understood in historical terms. For Luther, a historical understanding of a text such as Psalm 72 is "killing" because it is not inspired by the "life-giving spirit." Luther understood the "killing" dimension of the pure letter as opposed to the "life-giving spirit." The letter is killing when the reading and understanding of a biblical text is not inspired by the "life-giving spirit." The absence of life is death; and the withdrawal of

---

[14] During Martin Luther's lifetime, Charles V was at the head of a global empire on which the sun never set.

the life-giving power takes away life, that is, it kills. For Luther, the life-giving power is the divine spirit of the biblical texts.

For Luther this divine, live-giving Spirit becomes especially real in the Psalms because he considered David, the author of the Psalms, to be the most illustrious prophet. In the "Preface to the Scholia" in the *Dresdener Psalter* he reflects on this. He tells his audience that he does not want to recite the various interesting aspects of David's life and reign, nor sing the praises of this outstanding prophet, but wants to read and interpret the Psalms of David as the writings of a prophet.

> The man to whom it was appointed concerning the Christ of the God of Jacob, the excellent psalmist of Israel said: "The Spirit of the Lord has spoken by me, and His word by my tongue. The God of Israel spoke to me, the Strong One of Israel spoke, the Ruler of men, the just Ruler in the fear of God, as the light of the morning, when the sun rises, shines in the morning without clouds, and as the grass springs out of the earth after the rain."[15]

On the basis of David's last words Luther concluded that there was a difference between David and the other prophets.

> Other prophets used the expression "The word of the Lord came to me." This one, however, does not say, "The word of the Lord came to me," but he says, in a new manner of speaking, "His word was spoken by me." With this expression he indicates some extremely intimate and friendly kind of inspiration. Other prophets confess that they spoke, but this one declares that in a unique way it was not he who spoke but the Spirit who spoke through him.[16]

Luther therefore regards his role as interpreter of the Psalms as one of passing God's Word, which the divine Spirit spoke through David, on to his own audience.

According to this understanding of the role of the interpreter it is impossible to distinguish preaching from teaching. Theologians have to do both: being a preacher and an academic teacher are inextricably linked.

---

[15] *LW* 10, 9. 2 Sam 23:1-4 reads: "Now these are the last words of David: The oracle of David, son of Jesse, the oracle of the man whom God exalted, the anointed of the God of Jacob, the favorite of the Strong One of Israel: The spirit of the Lord speaks through me, his word is upon my tongue. The God of Israel has spoken, the Rock of Israel has said to me: One who rules over people justly, ruling in the fear of God, is like the light of morning, like the sun rising on a cloudless morning, gleaming from the rain on the grassy land."
[16] Ibid., 10.

Good academic teaching has to be kerygmatic; and a good sermon has to be academically informed.

The emphasis on the divine Spirit is a specificity of the young Luther's hermeneutics and can be found throughout all of his works. By emphasizing the life-giving Spirit already in his first lectures on the Psalms, Luther reorganizes the traditional arrangement in biblical hermeneutics. He adds the fourfold sense to his lectures on the Psalms, which used traditional material.[17] First he uses the traditional example of Jerusalem to illustrate the fourfold sense and then adds the fourfold meaning of Babylon. This was the traditional framework within which the realm of Christ and the realm of the devil are opposed to each other. In allegorical terms, "Jerusalem" means "the good people," in tropological terms the "virtues," and in anagogical terms the "rewards" of the believers. Similarly, in allegorical terms "Babylon" means "the bad people," in tropological terms the "vices," and in anagogical terms the "punishments" of the bad people. Interestingly enough, Luther immediately adds the equally dualistic contradiction of "killing letter" (*litera occidens*) and "life-giving spirit" (*spiritus vivificans*) to this dualistic contradiction.

A second example of the fourfold sense is the meaning of "mount Zion." Seminal here is that Luther gives two explanations of the fourfold sense: first, according to the understanding of the "killing letter" and then, second, according to the "life-giving spirit." The interpretation of "mount Zion" with the fourfold sense is crossed with the distinction of killing letter and life-giving spirit. Historically, in the sense of the killing letter, "mount Zion" then means "the land of Canaan" and, in the sense of the life-giving spirit, "the people living in Zion"; allegorically "mount Zion" means on the one hand "the synagogue or a prominent person in it" or, on the other, "the church or any teacher, bishop or prominent man"; tropologically it means on the one hand "the righteousness of the Pharisees and of the Law" or, on the other, "the righteousness of faith or some other prominent matter"; and anagogically "mount Zion" means on the one hand "the future glory after the flesh" or, on the other, "the eternal glory in the heavens."

What can we learn from this about the hermeneutics in the young Luther's lectures on the Psalms? While it is impossible to identify the historical meaning of a biblical text with the killing letter and the spiritual sense of a biblical text with the life-giving spirit, it is possible to give an interpretation of a biblical text according the fourfold sense ending in a "killing letter" or a "life-giving spirit." For Luther, this last distinction became central and dominant in the interpretation of biblical texts and in hermeneutics and, as a result, the concept of the fourfold sense may be

---

[17] See *LW* 10, 1.

used in a Christ-oriented biblical hermeneutics. It is precisely this model that Luther uses in his first lectures on the Psalms.

Hermeneutical principles in Luther's interpretation of Psalm 1

In Luther's interpretation of Psalm 1 of 1513 one can clearly detect the hermeneutical model that he used in his first lectures on Psalms. His fundamental question is whether the interpretation is one according to the killing letter or according to the life-giving Spirit. This depends very much on the existential situation of the listener, reader and interpreter. Are they living in the Spirit? Are they only living within the horizon of their own desires, longings and needs and the adequate, empirically graspable goods? If they are living in the Spirit, then they will understand the Psalm in its relation to Jesus Christ. And then, in the follow-up, the possibilities of the concept of the fourfold sense may also be used in the interpretation of the Psalm.

Luther translated Psalm 1 from Hebrew into German and in the English version of *Luther's Works* we read,

> Blessed is the man [sic] ... Who has not walked in the counsel of the ungodly, ... Nor has stood in the way of sinners ... nor has sat in the chair of the pestilence. ... But his will is in the law of the Lord, ... And on His law he meditates day and night.... He is like a tree planted beside the running waters, that will yield fruit in its season. ... And his leaf will not fall off. ... And all that he does will prosper.[18]

In his interpretation of verses 2 and 3, Luther's understanding of the difference between killing letter and life-giving spirit becomes clear. The will of the person, who is blessed and has not stood in the way of sinners, is "in the law of the Lord." For Luther such a person does so "without any desire, but he does it with a cheerful and free will"[19] and therefore this Psalm is not addressed to everybody.

> This does not apply to those who are under the Law in a spirit of bondage in fear, but to those who are in grace and a spirit of freedom. Thence Christians are called free ... (Ps. 110:3), spontaneous and willing, because of their Christ, who is the first of this kind. But the Jews are wearisome and unwilling and in the Law only with the hand. For although the Law could restrain the hand through fear of punish-

---
[18] Ibid., 11–22.
[19] Ibid., 13

> ment and provoke to works through the hope of good things, it could nevertheless neither loose nor bind the will inwardly; it could not, I say, loose toward freedom, nor bind its desires. For this happens only by the bonds of love, which not the Law but Christ has given in His own spirit. Thus He Himself says in Ps. 40,8: "I delight to do Thy will, O My God; Thy law is within My heart." "I delight," He says, that is, "it is My desire, and not the compulsion of fear or the hope of gain. And therefore Thy law is not in the outer edges and skin of My heart, but in the inside, in innermost and complete dedication."[20]

The interpretation of the divine law in the Holy Scriptures may go wrong. The "Jews" are the cipher for all those who do not make the divine law their own in their hearts, but obey God's Law because it is commanded, not because they are delighted in their heart and minds about the Law. Pleasure and delight are necessary in order not to read God's Law and commandments as a killing letter. But it is not the presence of pleasure in general, which makes a reading in the life-giving Spirit possible. There may be false pleasures as well, such as when people "want the law of the Lord in their pleasure and not their delight in the law of the Lord."[21] This is always the situation of the interpreter: finding in biblical texts what one is already convinced of. Therefore, while I may be pleased to find biblical arguments supporting my positions in the various areas of life, the pleasure and delight Luther talks about come from the Law of the Lord. In the end, it is delight and pleasure in God.

What kind of model did Luther have in mind? Luther did not presuppose that there is a source of pleasure and delight outside the biblical texts. It is the delight in the process of reading and understanding. This, however, depends on the situation of the individual reader, listener and interpreter. Again Luther thinks in alternatives. Do I see myself in the context of the empirical world, in which I have to act (*coram mundo*), or do I see myself in the context of God's reality (*coram Deo*)? If I see myself as a reader and interpreter in the situation "before God," i.e., being addressed by God via the biblical text, then I will be delighted and receive the biblical text as the life-giving Spirit.

Luther explains the phrase "and on His law he meditates day and night."

> To meditate is to think carefully, deeply, and diligently, and properly it means to muse in the heart. Hence to meditate is, as it were, to stir up in the inside, or to be moved in the innermost self. Therefore one who thinks inwardly and diligently asks, discusses, etc. Such a person meditates. But one does not meditate on the law

---
[20] Ibid., 13–14.
[21] Ibid.

of the Lord unless his delight was first fixed in it. For what we want and love, on that we reflect inwardly and diligently. But what we hate or despise we pass over lightly and do not desire deeply, diligently, or for long. Therefore let delight be first sent into the heart as the root, and then meditation will come of its own accord. It is for this reason that the ungodly do not meditate on the law of the Lord, since as false plants they did not take root. Yet they meditate on other things, namely, on things in which their delight is rooted, things they themselves desire and love, such as gold, honor, and flesh. ... David prays (Ps 119:36): "Incline my heart to Thy testimonies and not to gain!" All of the following do not meditate on the Law, but outside the Law: the greedy, the carnal, and the arrogant.[22]

In the explanation of the phrase "day and night" Luther's work of interpretation becomes very clear. He is taking care of all details of language and tries to ascertain the true meaning of the text.

But what is the meaning of day and night? Here is a large sea. First, literally, it means at all times ... However, time is divided not only into day and night but, second, also into good times and bad times. Thus the day is the time of prosperity, while night is the time of adversity. Third, it is divided into a time of grace and a time of sin. Fourth, into a time of life and of death. ... Fifth, into a time of quiet and of activity, or rest and work. Hence quiet (according to the spirit) is the day, but activity is the night. According to these distinctions there is a variety of uses of these words in the Scriptures. Therefore he who is rooted willingly and spontaneously in the law of the Lord, no matter what time it is, does not go back, does not forget, does not put off meditation on the law of the Lord. The fool, however, and he whose delight is not in His law, changes at every difference in time. And though he may meditate on it sometimes by day, he stops at night, because he has no root (Luke 8:13).[23]

Here Luther believes himself to be in full accordance with the hermeneutical principles of the early church. He refers to Hilary's *"De trinitate"* Book I, ch. 18, where Hilary says:

The best reader is the one who looks for the understanding of the words from the words themselves, rather than imposing his own understanding, and takes something out, rather than bringing something in, and does not force the words to seem to contain what he had assumed must be understood before reading.[24]

---

[22] Ibid., 17
[23] Ibid., 17–18.
[24] Ibid., 18; See Hilary, *De Trinitate,* PL X, 38.

When Luther describes possibilities of reading and using God's Law without considering the situation "before God" it becomes clear that he envisages the situation of the true reader and interpreter to be one of being "before God." The importance of considering the situation "before God" becomes especially clear in the case of a lawyer's reading, who may meditate and delight in the law, but not in the Law of the Lord. Luther was frequently highly critical of jurists who, according to him, delighted in civil and human laws and traditions of the elders, but in the case of God's Law and commandments missed the point, because they did not consider themselves as being addressed by God in the respective biblical texts.

In his explanation of verse 3 "he is like a tree planted beside the running waters, that will yield fruit in its season"[25] Luther further developed his understanding. He applied the image of the "tree planted beside the running waters" to his understanding that the faithful, who delight in the Law of the Lord, have roots. In the image of the "running waters" he found the narrative of Moses hitting the rock in the desert and streams of water running down. For Luther, this narrative illustrates the experience of the faithful with Holy Scripture. "For to those who meditate on the Law the very rock of Scripture gushes forth abundant streams and flowing waters of knowledge and wisdom, and grace and sweetness besides."[26] Here Luther formulated the promise of reading and understanding biblical texts.

> Therefore, whoever desires to be richly educated and, as it were, be flooded with the flowing waters of knowledge, let him surrender himself to meditation on the law of the Lord day and night, and he will learn by experience that what the prophet says in this verse is true.[27]

The whole process of reading, listening and understanding aims at an existential verification, a verification of the biblical texts in the life of those who try to understand.

---

[25] *LW* 10, 19.
[26] Ibid., 20.
[27] Ibid., 20–21.

"Protect me from those who are Violent." Psalm 140: A Cry for Justice—A Song of Hope

Monica Jyotsna Melanchthon

> Every three minutes a woman is beaten, every five minutes a woman is raped/ every ten minutes a little girl is molested...every day women's bodies are found in alleys and bedrooms/at the top of the stairs … . Ntozake Shange[1]

> Place the Book of Psalms in front of you … you will see your own self in it, for here is the true "know thyself," by which you can know yourself as well as the God who created all things. Martin Luther[2]

Pain and distress evoke strong emotions. The experience of suffering is unique to each individual although no individual is sufficiently prepared for suffering. But suffering can initiate a quest for knowledge resulting in new forms of awareness. The psalms of lament demonstrate the personal and individualizing nature of suffering and grief; they throw into sharp relief the sufferers' pain, isolation, vulnerability and fear as well as their doubt and anger. Even in the hurting and agonizing particularity of sorrow and pain, there is a certain universality of experience. As will become evident through our reading of Psalm 140 the individual's experience is also profoundly the experience of humanity as a whole. The Psalter has a significant place in both the individual and corporate lives of people and communities and our task is to wrestle with the theological and social issues arising from these Psalms and to try constructively to relate them to our communities of faith in this century.

For Luther, the value of the Psalms does not lie in their historic setting or in what they seem to be saying about the author or the times in which they were

---

[1] "With No Immediate Cause," at **http://www.ncdsv.org/images/Keynote--with%20 no%20immediate%20cause%20-%20Tucker%205.28.08.pdf**
[2] Adapted from Luther's "Preface to the Psalms," in Martin Luther, *A Manual of the Book of Psalms: Subject-Contents of All the Psalms*, trans. Henry Cole (London: R. B. Seeley and W. Burnside, 1837), 11.

written. Rather, he remarked that the Psalms pointed to Christ in the words of the illustrious prophet David.[3] Therefore, what seems to be important and exciting for Luther is the prophetic nature of the Psalms—the manner in which they point to the future, namely Christ. But the Psalms are also "prophetic" in that they and the laments in particularly unmask and expose the "enemies," those who perpetrate the injustices of the world. Through the cry of the sufferer they emphasize the need for righting this injustice, for the establishment of justice in the world and a return to the world that God had created.

Unfortunately, most ordinary readers do not see justice and injustice as vital expressions within the Psalter. These ancient prayers and hymns have, to a large extent, been tamed and domesticated, their radical and revolutionary potential submerged and suppressed by the genre and cultic focus in Psalm studies initiated by Herman Gunkel and expanded by Westermann. For example, this approach has located the hymns in a festival context (Mowinckel)[4] and the lament in the temple (Schmidt)[5] or a juridical context (Schmidt).[6] As Howard Wallace rightly claims,

> individual psalms have been seen as expressions of personal piety, elements of temple liturgies, part of royal ceremonies or wisdom school practices etc., depending largely on genre determinations and other assumptions made about them.[7]

Yet, the Psalms, especially the laments, are about protest, revenge, anger and a cry for justice emanating from experiences of pain, violence, injustice, suffering, discrimination, abandonment and rejection. As Anderson suggests they wrestle with

> the problems of human existence within the context of this life...they concentrate on the problems of life *now* with a fierce and passionate intensity...for it is only in the context of the *here and now* that the psalmist finds consolation.[8]

---

[3] *LW* 10, 7.
[4] Sigmund Mowinckel, *The Psalms in Israel's Worship*, 2 vols (Oxford: Blackwell, 1962).
[5] Hans Schmidt *Die Psalmen*, HAT (Tübingen: Mohr Siebeck, 1934). So also Walter Beyerlin who suggests that the lamenter is one undergoing a sacral trial in the temple. As one who stands falsely accused he/she utters a Psalm encouraging and provoking YHWH to intervene in judgment and more particularly in his/her favor. Walter Beyerlin, *Die Rettung der Bedrängten in den Feindpsalmen*, FRLANT 99 (Göttingen: Vandenhoeck & Ruprecht, 1970).
[6] Ibid.
[7] Howard Wallace, *Psalms*. Readings: A New Biblical Commentary (Sheffield: Sheffield Phoenix Press, 2009), 3.
[8] B. W. Anderson with Stephen Bishop, *Out of the Depths: The Psalms Speak for us Today*, 3rd edition, revised and expanded (Louisville, Kentucky: Westminster John Knox Press, 2000), 74. Author's own emphasis.

How can we use the Psalter to drive home the necessity and urgency of justice? How can we employ the Psalms to respond to the socioeconomic, political and ecological impulses all around us? How can we transcribe the real problems of the "I" in crisis into social, material, mental or physical categories—dealing with the ultimate conditions of human existence in our day and age? To begin with, it seems essential to give a second thought to the life settings of these laments. It might be helpful to attend to Gerstenberger who identifies the *Sitz im Leben* [life setting] of the individual lament Psalms as belonging to the personal category, addressing the challenges and travails of an individual's life. These laments, he suggests, were used at times of intense personal crisis, illness or bad luck, suffering or danger when the individual would approach the temple or a ritual expert who would give him/her one of these prayers to mediate in the crisis causing the suffering and begin repair.[9] He writes,

> individual complaints belonged to the realm of special offices for suffering people who, probably assisted by their kinsfolk, participated in a service of supplication and curing under the guidance of a ritual expert.[10]

The language of these laments is vague and general and hence they could be used for a wide range of personal distress and suffering.[11] But personal as they might be, they also give voice to the struggle "to build God's world of justice,"[12] by exposing injustice and providing alternate visions of reality. Set and used in the context of worship and the cult, they "penetrate our numbness to human suffering...for the deepest form of worship roots itself in a form of confrontation with the ills and injustices the people endure daily."[13] The "suffering" in the laments and the pain is not always born out of physical illness or personal tragedy alone. There are also instances of personal suffering that arise out of victimization by systems of oppression—institutional violence that can be cultural, economic or even political. These issues of social justice cannot be identified unless one engages the sociopolitical context of these prayers. Once deciphered, they confront us and are "critical to our continued appropriation of the Psalms as living documents."[14]

---

[9] Erhard S. Gerstenberger, *Psalms. Part 1 with an Introduction to Cultic Poetry*, FOTL 14 (Grand Rapids: Eerdmans, 1988), 14.
[10] Ibid., 14
[11] John Day, *Psalms*, T & T Clark Study Guides (London: Continuum, 2003), 29-30.
[12] J. David Pleins, *The Psalms: Songs of Tragedy, Hope and Justice* (Maryknoll, New York: Orbis Books, 1993), 1.
[13] Ibid., 17.
[14] Ibid., 5.

Approaching the Psalms in light of today's context has certainly brought in new and fresh insights and exposed their liberating potential while also exposing another glaring issue. As Gerstenberger writes,

> Hardly one commentary or study of the OT Psalms mentions another important problem of a social nature. The Psalms were composed by men and for men alone, because women (and children) had little to do with ritual affairs or communication with the superhuman.[15]

True! But there where religious traditions have subordinated women by enforcing silence on them, women have engaged in praying and prayer contradicting this expectation. The prayers and songs of Miriam (Ex 15:20-21), Hannah (1 Sam 2:1-10), Deborah (Judg 5), Judith (Jdt 16: 1-17), Mary (Lk 1:47-55) speak loudly and significantly in the praying and oral tradition of Israelite women and ancient Israel. These are perhaps the only traces we have of feminine psalmody (all outside the Psalter) although women are encouraged to praise YHWH along with the rest of creation.

"Young men and women alike, old and young together! Let them praise the name of the Lord, for his name alone is exalted; his glory is above earth and heaven" (Ps 148:12-13). Young girls participated in processions—"the singers in front, the musicians last, between them girls playing tambourines" (Ps 68:25).

One cannot bypass the fact that the language of the Psalter is predominantly masculine and so the only manner in which women can perhaps appropriate the Psalms is to enter into this male world and take on the persona of the male poet. In this regard Kathleen Farmer writes,

> The fact that the tradition handed down to them refers to the God of Jacob rather than the God of Rachel and Leah does not prevent women from claiming the God of that tradition as their own...the God whom our ancestors called the "God of Jacob" becomes the refuge and the strength of women.[16]

Similarly, the masculine language of the lament tradition has not hindered women from using the Psalms in their own praying and personal meditative practice. Hence Farmer writes with regard to the laments,

> The confessional stance of the Psalmists (their willingness to articulate feelings of anger and pain as well as joy in the presence of God, their refusal to submit

---

[15] Gerstenberger, op cit. (note 9), 32.
[16] Kathleen A. Farmer, "The Psalms," in Carol A. Newsom and Sharon H. Ringe (eds), *The Women's Bible Commentary* (London/ Louisville, Kentucky: SPCK/Westminster/ John Knox Press, 1992), 138.

passively to oppressive circumstances, and their confidence in God's concern for their needs) has had and continues to have a significant influence in shaping the theology, the piety, and the lives of many women.[17]

A further issue is whether we can find the particular experiences of women that arise out of their positioning in society within the Psalter. Along with Bail I ask, "Has anyone ever considered whether particular experiences of violence towards women can be located in the Psalms."[18] Do they contain visions of an alternative just society that is inclusive of women? Gerstenberger responds, "Distinctively female topics are all but lacking in the texts themselves. Whenever personal or family life is touched upon, it assumes the typical male and patriarchal perspective."[19] Hence, while it is impossible to detect a historically identifiable distress or female experience within the Psalter, the challenge is to determine whether "the structure of the language used in the Psalms can give space to the specific experience of violence suffered by women."[20]

In the light of the current discussions and widespread exposure given to the issue of violence against women, the question is what language can a rape victim or survivor use to expose the crime, to find strength and consolation, to receive justice and achieve calm? This paper hopes to address this issue by offering an interpretation of Psalm 140 from the perspective of women and their experiences of injustice, violation and sexual assault. I shall use the recent experience of the gang rape of Jyoti Singh Pandey as a second text to derive insights for the understanding of the language of Psalm 140 aided by Luther's comments on the Psalter and the Laments in particular.

METHODOLOGICAL CONSIDERATIONS

The methodology employed here has been informed by the intertextual reading method as employed by Ulrika Bail[21] and Beth Laneel Tanner.[22] Both use "intertextuality" which maintains that every text has imbedded within it "other

---

[17] Ibid., 144.
[18] Ulrike Bail, "O God, Hear my Prayer: Psalm 55 and Violence against Women," in Athalya Brenner and Carole R. Fontaine (eds), *Wisdom and Psalms, A Feminist Companion to the Bible* (Second series) (Sheffield: Sheffield Academic Press, 1998), 242.
[19] Gerstenberger, op. cit. (note 9), 32.
[20] Ibid., 243.
[21] Bail, op. cit. (note 18), 242-63.
[22] Beth Laneel Tanner, "Hearing the Cries Unspoken: An Intertextual-Feminist Reading of Psalm 109," in Athalya Brenner and Carole R. Fontaine (eds), *Wisdom and Psalms*, A Feminist Companion to the Bible (Sheffield: Sheffield Academic Press, 1998), 283-301.

texts," which may be explicit or implicit, such as those "drawn from innumerable centers of culture,"[23] cultures in which the text evolved. I identify these embedded texts and juxtapose alongside them another text that is external to the biblical text, namely the Indian context and the words of the victim, Jyothi Singh Pandey, and her male friend, Awindra Pandey, and verbal impressions and responses of the Indian people as reported and found in various media reports and interviews. I use imagination, embodiment and emotion to translate and interpret the words of the Psalm. My approach is feminist in that I respect and privilege the experiences of women, their capacity to articulate and name their pain and suffering and their agency to effect change. I am sensitive to the Indian culture and context and the Psalm is interpreted in order to subvert and challenge the violent subordination of women within and outside that context. The reader and interpreter is therefore the violated woman who cries for justice and the second "text" placed in juxtaposition to Psalm 140.

THE READER AND THE SECOND TEXT

The brutal attack and gang rape of twenty-three-year-old Jyoti, a physiotherapy intern in Delhi, on 16 December 2012, provoked countrywide angry reactions and foregrounded the issue of increasing incidents of sexual assaults on women in general and rapes in particular. Because rape is considered a crime so unspeakable, so disgraceful and shameful to its victims, the victim was cloaked in protective anonymity. Named *Damini* (lightning), *Braveheart, Amanat* (treasure), *Nirbhaya* (fearless) or simply referred to as *India's daughter* until her name was revealed, Jyothi Singh Pandey, young, ambitious, determined, with a strong resolve to live, succumbed to her injuries and died on 29 December 2012.

Rapes have become a part of the Indian environment and only a small fraction come to light for fear of being stigmatized. According to the *National Crime Records Bureau* (NCRB), "rapes currently take place in India at the rate of one every 22 minutes. The total number of rape cases reported in 2011 was 24,206.[24] From 2,487 in 1971, when the NCRB started to record cases of rape, this spells a rise of 873%."[25] Those that are reported are mostly instances

---

[23] Ibid., 284–85.
[24] "Figures at a Glance–2012," at **ncrb.nic.in/CD-CII2012/cii-2012/figure%20at%20a%20glance.pdf**.
[25] Anand Teltumbde, "Delhi Gang Rape Case: Some Uncomfortable Questions," at **http://roundtableindia.co.in/index.php?option=com_content&view=article&id=6206:delhi-gang-rape-case-some-uncomfortable-questions&catid=118:thought&Itemid=131**. This is a global problem and the most underreported crime.

of what we might call "institutional rape," rape perpetuated by members of repressive state forces, i.e., the police force, army, or such groups as landlords (read dominant caste land owners), upon helpless women of the oppressed classes, often when the women are in custody in police cells or bound by contracts of bonded labor. Rape is therefore understood as the expression of male violence sanctioned by various modes of social power, used as a weapon to maintain the status quo, "a matter of feudal entitlement"[26] rather than of sexual desire. The brutal rape of Jyothi was a "plainly maniacal and criminal act...with none of the complex underpinnings of power and politics."[27]

PSALM 140: A CRY FOR JUSTICE—A SONG OF HOPE

Psalm 140, is one of four Psalms of supplication in Book 5 related to each other by common motifs and language.[28] Scholarly treatment of this Psalm has been generic; it has been mostly considered as an example of the individual lament form[29]— a "prayer for help in first person style;"[30] a prayer of an accused man (Schmidt);[31] or a reflective lament in wisdom style (Lothar Hossfeld);[32] "one of the less pleasing examples of the individual lament without any high spiritual aspirations or sense of personal frailty."[33]

---

[26] Arundhathi Roy Speaks out against Indian Rape Culture, at **www.bbc.co.uk/news/world-asia-india-20826070** .

[27] Shoma Chaudhury, "Rape. And How Men see it," in *Tehelka Magazine*, vol. 10, issue 3, (19 January 2013), at **www.tehelka.com/cover-story-rape-and-how-men-see-it/**.

[28] Erich Zenger notes the fact that all four begin with a petition; the words "trap" and "snare" link 140 and 141; direct speech is evident in 140:7 and 143:10; and Ps 140, 142 and 143 close with the motif of the name of YHWH, in Erich Zenger, "The Composition and Theology of the Fifth Book of Psalms: Psalms 107-145," in *JSOT* 80 (1998), 94.

[29] Arnold Albert Anderson, *Psalms,* vol. 2, NCB (London: Marshall, Morgan and Scott, 1972), 913.

[30] James Luther Mays, *Psalms, Interpretation: A Bible Commentary for Teaching and Preaching* (Louisville: John Knox, 1994), 430.

[31] H. Schmidt argues that the lament Psalm has a setting in a sacral rite where the accused is held in detention in the temple, in H. Schmidt, *Die Psalmen,* HAT (Tübingen: Mohr, 1934).

[32] Frank Lothar Hossfeld and Erich Zenger, *Psalms 3: A Commentary on Psalms 101-150,* Hermeneia: a Critical and Historical Commentary on the Bible, trans. Linda M. Maloney (Minneapolis: Fortress, 2011), 551.

[33] W. Stewart McCullough and W. R. Taylor, *The Book of Psalms,* IB 4 (New York: Abingdon, 1955), 718. The Psalm has also been identified as a Royal Psalm by John H. Eaton, perhaps influenced by the superscription that mentions David and some of the war metaphors. Eaton describes the enemies as the "foreign nations." John H. Eaton, *Psalms* (London: SCM, 1967).

The Psalm is comprised of three sections: verses 2-6 are petitions and a description of distress; vv 7-12 are first a confession to YHWH (vv 7a-8) and then petitions requesting YHWH's judgment upon the enemies (vv 9-12) and verses 13-14 are expressions of assurance or concluding statements of belief.[34] The many rare and archaic words could point to an early date of composition[35] but they have also proven to be a deterrent rendering it impossible to date.[36] Despite this, some have ventured to suggest a date in post exilic times or even the third and fourth centuries BCE.[37]

Commentators have expended much effort on discovering the identity of the speaker in the Psalm, the "I" as related to his/her enemies. But the Psalm lacks any indication which would enable one to posit a precise context. No reasons are given for the hostility that is being experienced. Hence, three major interpretational frameworks, namely, "national," "juridical"' and "personal," based on the motifs of war (vv 3b and 8b), of a hunt (vv 6 and 12b) and of words (vv 4, 10, 12a) respectively have been used to understand this Psalm.[38] Nevertheless, the most prominent of the three frameworks is the personal one with the war and hunt imagery seen to function metaphorically. The sufferer is an individual (v. 7–"I say"; v. 13–"I know") who is confronted with personal problems of a threatening nature. The psalmist turns to YHWH, praying and lamenting—perhaps in the temple—for divine judgment against the enemies who are presented alternately in rapidly shifting numbers—in the singular (vv 2, 5, 9, 12) and in the plural (vv 3, 4, 5c, 6, 10, 11).[39] The lack of detail or specifics or any historical allusions have therefore led some to see this Psalm as part of the Wisdom tradition and a general prayer. Such a rendering in my opinion mitigates the experience of violence and diminishes the anger, force and impact of the plea in the Psalm.

Luther's comments on this particular Psalm are quite general and very brief. He identified it as a "prayer against hypocrites who cause offences and lay nets and snares for them that go the right way." The prayer, he says,

---

[34] Alternately, one can divide the Psalm into 5 sections: vv 2-4; 5-6; 7-9; 10-12; 13-14–the divisions being defined by the structural feature and marker "*selah.*" Hossfeld and Zenger, op. cit. (note 32), 549.

[35] Mitchell Dahood, *Psalms III 101-150: Introduction, Translation, and Notes*, Anchor Bible 17 A (New York: Doubleday, 1970), 301.

[36] Anderson, op. cit. (note 29), 913.

[37] Ibid., 913.

[38] Martin Ravndal Hauge, *Between Sheol and Temple: Motif Structure and Function in the I-Psalms*, JSOTSup 178 (Sheffield: Sheffield Academic Press, 1995), 10.

[39] Hossfeld and Zenger, op. cit. (note 32), 550. Hossfeld and Zenger claim that, "the swift shifting between general and individual means that no particular person, this or that enemy, but the hostile power, the hostile itself is in the foreground."

hopes that the plans of the enemies of the righteous will be thwarted just as the Pharaoh's. The Psalm he says offers "abundant consolation to the godly."[40]

VERSES 1–2[41]

> For the director, a Psalm of David; Deliver me, YHWH, from the evil man, From the man of violence preserve me!

The superscription stating that it is a Psalm of David leads one to construe the "me" as David and draws one into the life and history of David and thereby a "male context." Taking liberty and encouragement from Miller's suggestion that the language of the Psalms is open "to a variety of applications and actualizations,"[42] I am suggesting that the individual in the Psalm is a woman who sees herself as being surrounded by evil and violent men. The individual could very well be a woman who is entreating God for delivery from the "evil man" and the "man of violence" used here in the collective sense, to represent an "enemy constellation."[43] The "man of violence" and the "evil man" are the enemies of the raped/violated woman.[44] There is no opening appeal for YHWH to listen (this comes later in v. 7). The Psalm directly and urgently hastens into an appeal for rescue, for deliverance and preservation for life! The word "deliver"/"rescue" in the imperative "literally suggests pulling someone out from a situation, in this case wresting one from the grasp of the evildoer."[45] The complimentary verb, "preserve"/"guard" is milder, seeking and pleading for protection. This heartrending cry of distress and call for deliverance and rescue as the entry point into the poem is very crucial[46] for it establishes and gives

---

[40] Martin Luther, op. cit. (note 2), 364.
[41] The translation of this verse and all that follow is the author's based on the Hebrew text as found in K. Elliger and W. Rudolph (eds), *Biblia Hebraica Stuttgartensia*, (Stuttgart: Deutsche Bibelgesellschaft, 1984). The verse numbering therefore follows the Hebrew text. Where needed a comparison will be made with the NRSV.
[42] P. D. Miller, "Trouble and Woe (Interpreting the Biblical Laments)," in *Interpretation* 37 (1983): 35.
[43] Hauge, op. cit. (note 38), 25–26.
[44] Contra to Hossfeld and Zenger who claim that that these are generally described acts, and "not acute set of behaviors concentrated particularly on the petitioner," op. cit. (note 32), 550, which in my opinion alleviates the urgency and the seriousness of the plea!
[45] John Goldingay, *Psalms: Volume 3-Psalms 90-150* (Grand Rapids, MI: Baker, 2008), 644.
[46] Karen Cerulo, *Deciphering Violence: The Cognitive Structure of Right and Wrong* (New York: Routledge, 1998), 7, argues that the entry point in a narrative that concerns violence is significant and crucial for the audience to determine whether

us insight into the worldview and the condition of the woman. The cry is shrill, urgent and sorrowful. It is an invitation to us as readers to enter into this world and pay attention to what is being said about the woman, her experience, her relationship with the enemy and with God.

The rescue is needed from evildoers, men of evil and violence. Violence can be structural, psychological or physical. What specific type is being referred to here is unclear. But as Firth suggests, it is not certain that the Hebrew Bible distinguishes between the three and these categories are "not discrete but rather shade into one another."[47] But the Hebrew (*hamas*, translated as "violent" is a significant word for it denotes, "infringement on the personal rights of others, motivated by greed and hate and often making use of physical violence and brutality."[48] Generally described—these are not just bad people, but violent, lawless and outrageous.[49] This mob is evil, violent, uncannily vicious and brutal and brutality is characteristic of all rapes. It reflects an experience of the violent mob as even being demonic. The vulnerability of women when such men are around and on the streets cannot be undermined. The fear generated by this brazen act led to families in Delhi and elsewhere restricting their daughters' freedom because evil lurks on the streets. How these evil men behave is described in the verses that follow.

Verse 3

Those who devise evil in the heart, every day[50] they provoke battle.[51]

---

the violent act is legitimate or not. The progression of narrative events is a primary means by which the narrator imposes her perspective on the information and the hearer interprets the act of violence as legitimate or illegitimate. The sequencing of information in Psalm 140 is what Cerulo would call a "victim sequence" in which the psalmist assumes the role of the victim and "serves as the audience's point of reference," 40. This particular sequencing of events predisposes hearers to judge violent acts *against* the victim as illegitimate and violent acts perpetrated *by* the victim as legitimate.

[47] David G. Firth, *Surrendering Retribution in the Psalms: Responses to Violence in the Individual Complaints*, with Foreword by Donald L. Morcom (Milton Keynes, UK: Patenoster, 2005), 4-5.

[48] H. Haag, smx "hamas" in G. Johannes Botterweck and Helmer Ringgren (eds), *Theological Dictionary of the Old Testament*, vol. 4 (Grand Rapids: Eerdmans, 1980), 482. The word appears only fourteen times in the Hebrew Bible and it is significant that it is used three times in this Psalm (vv 1, 5, and 12). Cf. also Ps 7:17; 11:5; 18:49; 25:19; 27:12; 35:11; 55:10; 58:3; 72:14; 73:6; 74:20.

[49] Cf. Gen 6:11, 13

[50] The LXX reads "all the day." "The latter is a probably a secondary accommodation to a frequent usage in the Psalter," Hossfeld and Zenger, op. cit. (note 32), 549.

[51] "begin a fight," ibid., 549.

> The six accused lured us into boarding the bus on the night of December 16.[52]
> (Awindra Pandey, Jyoti's male friend)

Mays suggests that the violence is verbal on the basis of this and the next verse.[53] Can we limit this to verbal violence? Such a distinction is not, as said above, characteristic of the Hebrew Bible. Whether verbal or psychological violence, it often leads to or "manifests itself in physical violence with roots in existing social structures."[54] Language/speech is "inseparably related to its effect; it has a performative character: it is a 'primary happening'."[55] This is especially so when the female victim reacts or responds verbally or physically. The enemies plan disastrous things in their hearts; they instigate and provoke battle. Plotting and scheming against the victim draws the collective group together as partners and allies. Amity built, their acts of verbal and physical persecution escalate. "Finally, an intoxicating, hallucinatory atmosphere overcomes the mob. Mesmerized, they bond in violent unanimity as they sacrifice the victim."[56]

The woman's experience is not an isolated one. It is something that happens every day, all day—in fact every twenty-two minutes! She recognizes that she shares this experience with many other women. This act was not a random act...it was intentional, premeditated. The six men had been partying, were drunk and they went on a joy ride to lure innocent victims; they were on the hunt for a woman who they could rape. The youngest of the six men presented himself as the conductor and addressed the woman as *Didi* meaning "older sister," inviting her into the bus. Four were sitting on the seats as though they were passengers. Once the bus started moving they began to execute their plan. They provoked her by casting insults on her and her male friend, slighting the relationship they shared and, when they responded in defense, it stirred the anger of the perpetrators and they wanted to punish them. They beat up the man rendering him unconscious and then proceeded, one after the other, to rape her. They really needed no excuse to do so, but they felt justified for a woman is not to talk back to a man! Women are in constant and perpetual

---

[52] "Delhi Gang-rape Victim Wanted Accused to be Burnt Alive: Braveheart's Friend". (published 5 January 2013), at **www.megamedianews.in/index.php/81331/delhi-gang-rape-victim-wanted-accused-to-be-burnt-alive-bravehearts-friend/**.
[53] Mays, op. cit. (note 30), 430.
[54] Firth, op. cit. (note 47). 5.
[55] Bail, op. cit. (note 18), 254. Bail also cites Mieke Bal, who speaks of the extraordinary power of language and its potential to bring death, "for the power to speak is directly related to the power to act," in Mieke Bal, *Death and Dissymetry: The Politics of Coherence in the Book of Judges* (Chicago: Chicago University Press, 1988), 245.
[56] Stephen L. Cook, "Lamentation, Praise and Collective Violence," in *The Living Pulpit* (Oct–Dec 2002), 4.

"defense mode"—struggling to keep safe, to survive—for life becomes a battle for life, for dignity and survival when surrounded by men on the prowl for victims.

VERSE 4

⁴They sharpen their tongue like a serpent, the viper's[57] poison is under their lips, (Selah!)

The woman is confronted by a lynch mob and not a group of reasoning individuals. It is therefore not surprising that she uses animal imagery to categorize them. A serpent's [snake's] tongue moves fast and furious. The language is more than hyperbole.[58] It reflects the experience of one confronted by a violent and demonic mob, later joined by others who do not hesitate to spew out the same poison. They have not only entertained these thoughts about women in their hearts but share them and articulate them. There is no better way to understand this verse than by way of illustrating a few responses to the rape[59]—quick to judge, quick to blame, quick to fan the flames of women's culpability to generate shame, to stress the honor of a culture that is inscribed on women's bodies. Their thoughts are poisonous for they do not engender dignity, humanity or life. They have on their tongue as Luther remarks, "oil, but under their tongue is gall. And snake poison is under their lips, for outwardly they are mild, yet inwardly they brutally kill and poison believing souls."[60] Many young women in India have taken her own lives on account of malicious rumors that have been spread out of spite and anger.

> The root problem for all these crimes is women themselves. The mirror in my auto tells me everything, what young boys and girls are doing behind me. They are willing

---

[57] Qumran reads "spider" instead of "viper"—a vast difference between the two but the latter is perhaps more slippery and dangerous.

[58] The description of enemies using animal imagery is common in the laments. When the pain is intense, both the psalmist and the enemy are dehumanized and can be described only with animal imagery. Conventional modes of communication are lost and the pain experienced is expressed through language that stresses the beastliness of the enemy.

[59] These are cited by Shoma Chaudhury, in "Rape And How Men See It," in *Tehelka Magazine*, vol. 10, issue 2 (19 January 2013). It is perhaps good to take note of what she says in relation to these anecdotes. She writes, "In India—continental as it is in size and plurality—even the most extensive sociological survey can, at best, be only an anecdotal one. This, by every yardstick, is extremely anecdotal and extremely miniscule. But as a dipstick—as an intuition—of what this vast country thinks, it throws up fascinating findings. We expected darkness; we found it. But, gratefully, we also found the unexpected." At **www.tehelka.com/cover-story-rape-and-how-men-see-it/**.

[60] Martin Luther commenting on Psalm 55:2, *LW* 10, 257.

> to pay extra because they want to make love...women flaunt their bodies and provoke men with their dresses, what will he do? (Raju, 45, a migrant auto driver in Delhi)

> Why was the girl out at night? I heard that when she got onto the bus with the man, they started kissing. So it's not the fault of the men who raped her. Why would she want to do such a thing in a public place? (Kishen 33, a farmer from Rajasthan)

> Of course, women's freedom is responsible for the rise in sexual crimes. How can we expect that dry grass with petrol near it under scorching heat won't catch fire?" (Basheer Tawheedi, 40, lecturer from Kashmir)

> Yes women are somewhat responsible for the crimes against them...we know women are easily fooled and lack reason...Men must act as protectors of women because Allah has made one to excel over the other. There can be no equality between the sexes. In Saudi Arabia, there are no rapes because women dress well and don't mingle freely with men. (Tabish Darzi 26, Banker, Srinagar)

While women are frequently blamed for the breakdown of society men are rarely held responsible for their own actions. Apply this to incidents of domestic abuse, child abuse, female feticide, dowry deaths, marital violence, child marriages, divorce, the percentage of working women and the number of honor killings and every fear that India has is blamed on women. Since the debate around rape exploded into public consciousness, there has been a temptation to frame the discourse through every kind of stereotype: a gender war, a class war, a religious war, a culture war, a caste war, a regional war, a war between modernity and tradition, between city and village. Chaudhury writes,

> The hard truth is, there are enough dark voices to justify each of them. If you listen to men across India, you would know enough of them want to keep women in a box or thrust them back if they have escaped. The impulse expresses itself in a myriad ways: as brute misogyny or stifling protectionism. But running common through it all is fear and abhorrence of women who display autonomy over their own bodies and sexuality. Women's clothes, you would imagine, are the greatest internal security threat in India.[61]

The possible violence in the language needs to be noted and it can be construed as the primary form of violence in this Psalm and in the experience of Jyothi and many who experience rape and physical violence. This primary form provides the basis for the response to brutal force and violence.

---

[61] Ibid.

Verses 5-6

> ⁵Guard me, YHWH, from the hands of the unjust, from the man of violence, protect me!—Those who plot to "push my steps." ⁶The proud have hidden a trap for me, with cords they spread out a net, by the wayside they set snares for me. (Selah!)

> The occupants of the bus, which had tinted windows and curtains, had laid a trap for us. They were probably involved in crimes before also. They beat us up, hit us with an iron rod, snatched our clothes and belongings and threw us off the bus on a deserted stretch.[62] (Awindra Pandey)

Guard me/keep me (*shamar*) from the unjust/wicked and from the violent protect me (*naṣar*)[63]—two significant verbs in this petition are known to function as a word pair; as a stock protective formula.[64] This singular rendering (man of violence) is presented in the plural in the following line and verse (those who...). Violence is the work of both individuals and groups of men on the prowl and the woman needs protection from both.

The enemies are described as using several of their body parts to enforce their terror on the victim. Between verses 3 and 6, the heart, the tongue, lips, hands are used. By adding the hands to the heart, tongue and lips she indicates that the assailant's whole person is given to these attacks—to trip the feet/or "push the steps" of the victim, so she might fall both figuratively and physically, a forceful thrusting of the kind that will cast someone down.[65] According to Luther, the "proud," "eminent" people or the "presumptuous"[66] are those

---

[62] Op. cit. (note 52).

[63] The NRSV reads v. 4 "Guard me, O Lord, from the hands of the wicked; protect me from the violent who have planned my downfall; v. 5The arrogant have hidden a trap for me, and with cords they have spread a net, along the road they have set snares for me. (Selah)" The translators have rendered the singular in verse 4 as a plural in an attempt to harmonize it with verse 5 where the plural form of the nouns is used. But to read the singular in verse 4 and plural in verse 5 is important for the psalmist wants to stress that violent acts are performed by both individuals and groups.

[64] Cf. Jeremy D. Smoak, "'Prayers of Petition' in the Psalms and West Semitic Inscribed Amulets: Effacious Words in Metal and Prayers for Protection in Biblical Literature," in *JSOT* 36.1 (2011), 75-92, who suggests that the word pair is perhaps drawn from West Semitic apotropaic religious and magical practices.

[65] Goldingay, op. cit. (note 45), 646.

[66] According to Mitchell Dahood, they are "those that believe that YHWH will not intervene on behalf of his own," op. cit. (note 35), 302. Luther states of such people, "This does not mean that they deny God altogether. For the existence of God is not at issue, and they all acknowledge God. Indeed, the persecutors suppose that God is on their side and that they are offering service to God when they persecute the pious

who have gained the upper hand so completely that they have become smug. They are boasting, rejoicing, singing, and dancing, as though we were done for.[67]

And those

who are arrogant in their hearts but also those who have gained the upper hand by either persecution or deceit (he is talking about both the tyrants and the heretics) and act as though they had already prevailed and smothered the pious. This is also the meaning of our word "proud," those who fly high and soar... .[68]

In the Indian context these would be those who consider themselves superior on the basis of gender, caste, race, class and physical strength. They have a position in the world and therefore have the power to be a greater threat.

The victim is hunted like a wild beast. The metaphor is given precision by the use of hunting language. They set traps, spread cords—the Psalm describes a variety of ways in which someone can be caught with snares of one kind or another. Today these snares and traps are also created out of religious dictums, scriptural sanctions, hierarchical values, neoliberal consumerist ideology and the like that function as traps and snares to confine the woman, to fence her in and to shut her up. If the woman does not fully understand or comprehend the reasoning behind these traps then there will be horrific and violent consequences for her. It is these that she seeks protection from, and only God can do so, for the system and structures of control are too tightly interwoven and unraveling them seems to be beyond the capability of human endeavor.

VERSE 7–8

⁷I say to YHWH: You are my God! Give ear, O YHWH to the voice of my supplications!

⁸YHWH my Lord, the strength of my salvation ! You covered my head on the day of battle.

After throwing us off the bus, they tried to mow us down but I saved my friend by pulling her away in the nick of time. We were without clothes. We tried to stop passersbys. Several auto rickshaws, cars and bikes slowed down but none

---

(John 16:2)," *LW* 14, 247. In the Indian context it would also be those who believe that neither the police nor the legal system will be able to do anything to them.
[67] Luther's comment on Psalm 94:3, *LW* 14, 246.
[68] Luther's comment on Psalm 94:2, *LW* 14, 245. Cf. also his comment on Psalm 94:4, in *LW* 14, 246.

stopped for about 20 to 25 minutes. Then, someone on patrolling stopped and called the police.[69]

Nobody from the public helped us. People were probably afraid that if they helped us, they would become witnesses to the crime and would be asked to come to the police station and court.[70] (Awindra Pandey)

Mother, I want to live![71] (Jyoti Singh Pandey)

The "I" in the Psalm is not gender specific, grammatically speaking, and could be the voice of either a male or female.[72] A performative *qatal*, begins the verse—"I [hereby] say" rather than a recollection of a previous statement.[73] The statement is a declaration of who YHWH is with a plea built into it. It is in this God that the woman takes refuge, a God who is ready to grant power and salvation. When all else fails due to the inefficiency and insensitivity of the police force, the ineffectiveness of the legal system, the incompetence of the political system, the apathy of the public, the profit-driven media, all contributing to a culture of impunity that emboldens men to commit such brazen acts, who do you turn to? There is only God to turn to for help and she hopes that this God is listening, that God hears.

The woman takes refuge in God. Through the use of phrases such as "YHWH, you are my God!" "YHWH my Lord, my powerful salvation," she confesses something about the nature of who this God is to her and to God's people and her loyalty to this God and no one else. These statements affirm the many ways in which YHWH has been committed to her and taken care of her in the past. But she now hopes to stir not just the pity of God and God's saving power but perhaps God's ego as well. These phrases are therefore statements of confession, of trust, of faith but they are also statements that seek to provoke and motivate God to act in her favor and against the enemy. "You have covered my head on the day of battle"—a very protective image here, almost parent-like. You have given me life, brought me this far...please allow me to live it a little longer!

There is no evidence of Jyothi's articulation of faith that parallels the words of the psalmist. But I am sure she prayed and her family and friends

---

[69] Op. cit. (note 52).
[70] Ibid.
[71] Rhythma Kaul, "Delhi Gang Rape Victim Writes on a Piece of Paper, 'Mother I want to Live,'" in *Hindustan Times*, New Delhi (20 December 2012), at **www.hindustantimes.com/india-news/newdelhi/rape-victim-still-critical-writes-to-mother-i-want-to-live/article1-976798.aspx.**
[72] Gerstenberger, op. cit. (note 9), 32.
[73] Goldingay, op. cit. (note 45), 646.

did so too confessing in the healing and the liberative powers of their gods and goddesses. The candle light vigils held in different parts of the country, the pujas and the offerings that were most definitely made to the gods are expressions of this faith in a divine and supreme power. But also inherent in the statement, *Mother, I want to live!* there is faith and a plea—voiced to her mother who was her immediate and present source of courage. Not all who suffer immediately think about God. There may have been some questioning of God and such questioning has a legitimate place in the sufferer's life. In the throes of pain and suffering all Jyothi could perhaps do as far as we know, was to cry out her hurt and pain and longing for life.

VERSE 9-12

> ⁹Grant not, O YHWH, the desires of the unjust, do not prosper his plans! (Selah!)
> ¹⁰Those who surround me lift up their heads. Let the mischief of their lips overwhelm them!
> ¹¹Let burning coals fall upon them. Let them fall into pits and never stand up.
> ¹²The man of tongue shall not stand firm in the land. The man of violence—let evil hunt him speedily down!
>
> Mama, I want them to be burnt alive![74] (Jyoti)
>
> Hang the rapists! Death for the rapist![75] (Protesting crowds)

The concern over evil speech and deceitful words in these verses might indicate that the psalmist is concerned about "the magical power of curses or evil words" alone.[76] Again, I am not too certain that it is helpful to distinguish too strongly between words and action. The "man of tongue"[77] is juxtaposed with the "man of violence," indicating that the wickedness is wider and inclusive of both language/speech and action.

The woman victim/survivor prays to YHWH that the plan of the enemies, those who engage in acts of injustice, may miscarry. The jussives in this

---

[74] Amrit Dhillon, "'Mama, I want them to be burnt alive', my daughter said: Gang-rape victim's mother,'" in *The Daily Telegraph* (Sunday, 13 January 2013), at **www.dnaindia.com/world/report-mama-i-want-them-to-be-burnt-alive-my-daughter-said-gang-rape-victim-s-mother-1788340**.
[75] "Rapists Should be Given Death Sentence," at **www.merinews.com/citizen-debate/rapist-should-be-given-death-sentence/101**; "Delhi Rape Spreads Fear, Women demand Death for Rapists," *The Deccan Herald* (New Delhi, 18 December 2012), at **www.deccanherald.com/content/299351/delhi-rape-spreads-fear-women.html**.
[76] Smoak, op. cit. (note 64), 89.
[77] Could also mean "slanderer."

verse point to the ways in which the psalmist hopes she will be delivered and preserved, guarded and protected now and in the future. The use of jussives instead of imperatives/pleas indicates that the psalmist is perhaps aware of some inbuilt mechanisms in the structure of reality that, if allowed to function effectively, will give her the required justice. Hence the lack of request for divine intervention; rather she requests that these mechanisms of justice or due processes will be allowed to function effectively.

Verse 12b is a curse that is "aimed to accumulate various types of punishment upon the wicked ones."[78] May the wicked not prosper and may they be given their due, namely punishment that befits the crime. They are to be given a taste of their own medicine! The slanderers are not to triumph. Her plea for divine judgment against the enemies includes them being cast into coals of fire.[79] The plea is reminiscent of the many trials by fire that women have to go through to prove their innocence or as punishment for overstepping cultural bounds. But could the request also suggest a rite of purification for these evil men so that they are never to stand up again and able to repeat such crimes? Death was the only way to stop them from repeating such a crime in the face of an inefficient legal system. Such men should have no place in the land; they should be given no asylum, they should be stripped of all power. For only those who honor relationships and justly so are assured of long life in the land (Ex 20:12) and so the sacral principles are maintained and the citizenship of women is honored. The vengeance sought here is understandable.

Two things are important here—what strikes us first is the dominance of the accusation against the enemies. Enemies are not taboos in the Book of Psalms. There is no shame in exposing the enemies; no caution to the psalmist that he/she would be transgressing the Torah by praying for vengeance. Her feelings of vengeance are not repressed. As Bellinger reminds us,

> In these prayers against the enemies, the worshipper does not destroy the enemy, but in a liberating act of faith, places the matter before God, the judge par excellence, God will decide and the psalmist pleads for God to decide against the enemies.[80]

---

[78] Dahood, op. cit. (note 35), 305.

[79] Fire has a very prominent place in Hindu rituals. According to the *Vedas*, a human being is made of five elements—fire being one of them—which are also represented in the Supreme. Therefore, the sacred fire is supposed to signify a communion of the human being with God. As such the offerings made into the ritual fire or *havan*, such as ghee or camphor, symbolize physical attributes (in this case, ego) which are sought to be consumed by the fire to bring about purification. Thus such a ritual purifies the environment by cleansing all impurities in the physical and psychic bodies. In the Hindu religion, all new beginnings are marked by the auspicious fire.

[80] W. H. Bellinger Jr, *Psalms: Reading and Studying the Book of Praises*, 7th printing (Peabody, Massachusetts: Hendrickson, 2009), 54.

Her enemies are presented as enemies of God because they work against the will of God. God is now reminded of what needs to be done. Only those who are innocent before the enemy, and who do not let go of the belief in the justice of God can pray such a prayer trusting their vengeance to God.

Second, I find Fritz Stolz's insights helpful as shared by Roger Marcel Wanke in his paper entitled, "The Vengeance Psalms as a Phenomenon of Critical Justice: The Problem of Enemies in Luther's Interpretation of Psalms,"[81] also included in this volume. Wanke cites Stolz[82] who speaks of two kinds of crises—the cultic and the sapiential crisis. The cult and wisdom are the two sources that provide the psalmist with experiences of God's presence and the knowledge of God. They convey to the psalmist the order, the relationship between God, human beings and the world. When the experiences of the psalmist contradict the tradition or what the cult and wisdom have taught her what is she to do? Stolz calls this the post-cultic and post-sapience phenomenon—one that is experienced when the cult and wisdom can no longer fulfill their roles and reach the objective of establishing order in the life of the psalmist.[83] Even in a post-cultic or post-sapiential crisis (when the experience with God and with people is contradictory to cult and wisdom), the anger and vengeance is voiced and offered as a petition to YHWH. In the case of most women it is also post-law and post-judiciary and failed male authority (for men see themselves as protectors of women)—all systems often fail her. But even in the midst of all this disorientation, the woman holds on to the belief in the justice of God, for justice is found only in God. She would be lost without divine help and rescue. Her own power and resolve to live is useless unless it is rested in divine strength. So, from the next verse, she begins to state her faith in the loving God who liberates the afflicted, the poor, the righteous and the upright.

VERSE 13–14

> [13] I know that YHWH shall judge the afflicted, shall execute justice for the poor.
> [14] Yes, the righteous shall praise your name, the upright shall dwell in your presence.

The "needy" and the "poor" and are now set in contrast to the "unjust," the "man of tongue" and the "man of violence" (vv 9-12). While the enemies

---

[81] Roger Marcel Wanke "The Vengeance Psalms as a Phenomenon of Critical Justice: The Problem of Enemies in Luther's Interpretation of Psalms," in this publication.
[82] Fritz Stolz, *Psalmen im nachkultischen Raum*, Theologische Studien 129 (Zürich: Theologischer Verlag, 1983), as cited by Wanke, ibid.
[83] Stolz, ibid.

make the psalmist fall, YHWH will be responsible for making the evildoers fall. These verses also make clear that the psalmist counts herself as one of the "needy" and the "poor" but she would not articulate this more directly in the form of a self-description. The fact that these are referred to in the third person are indicative of the proverbial nature of these statements.[84]

"I know"[85]—not only bears witness to an event personally experienced but, at the same time, also introduces a confession. She believes that her God is a God of justice who vindicates the sufferer and she is not afraid anymore. As Luther writes,

> You must not fear that the justice of your cause is being defeated, for that is impossible. God loves justice; therefore it must be preserved, and the righteous must not be forsaken. If He were an idol who loved injustice or hated justice, as the wicked men do, then you would have reason to worry and to be afraid. But now that you know he loves justice, why do you worry, why are you afraid, why do you doubt?[86]

In her own experience the petitioner has achieved participation in and access to the fact of divine intervention and salvation. It is an expression of a solid certainty and presupposes that YHWH has intervened and helped. How does she know? In Jyothi's experience, God rises in the form of the protesting and angry crowd to vindicate the victim of sexual assault. Despite the many voices that blamed her, the crowd of women, young and old, of those men who joined them, the many in India and the world over who held vigils, protests and started a discourse and a movement, those who saw her as a survivor rather than as a victim, those who did not blame her, her family who was supportive but, most of all, a nation or a world that is now aware of the issue—it is in and through them that the divine verdict *mishpat* is delivered! The sacral and judicial process is supported with the verb "execute." Justice will be executed and the woman counts herself as among the poor, the righteous and the upright in need of protection and the presence of God. She is confident that she will be vindicated through a just legal system, a vigilant police force, an effective political system, a responsive and compassionate church or religious community, all made possible with God's help!

Luther regards a lack of trust in the grace of God as a fundamental sin. This definition provides space both for the sin of pride and the sin of lacking self-esteem. To trust in God's grace can imply both daring and risking to let one's energy and strength and power be used in the service of God and allowing oneself to be comforted by grace when lacking strength.

---

[84] Hauge, op. cit. (note 38), 30.
[85] Meaning "I have experienced" or "I have been assured of."
[86] Luther's comment on Psalm 37:28, in *LW* 14, 222.

The oppressed and violated woman lacks strength and places her trust in God. This trust and faith is not a lulling opiate but it provides strength and impetus to speak out and to live and to continue to work for the betterment of the world and its people.

> We must overcome afflictions, death and hell. However they will not be overcome by running away or by impatience, but with favor, good will, and love continuing toward God in their presence.[87]

And so Psalm 140 can be sung as the song of an oppressed woman who is bereft of rights in the community. She is confined and surrounded by evil and violence seeking to bring her down and ruin her. Only YHWH can help.

> The petition for God's intervention shows that in the OT there is no other way to real assurance for the righteous which is most critically called into question than a this-worldly demonstration.[88]

While the Psalm gives us no clues as to the identity of these enemies or their institutional affiliation, a reading that takes seriously the experiences of violated women as in this case, will unmask the identity of the enemies. The enemies are those who by virtue of their status in society, those with power derived from caste, class, political affiliation, gender and race prey upon women as an expression of their social power. They represent the evil and evildoer and it is in their language/speech and actions that sin becomes manifest. The enmity between them and the petitioner is unlimited in time and space. It takes place in the land or on earth. This enmity extends from the past verses 7–12; through the present (vv 2–6) and into the distant future (v. 13). The righteous person in this instance is the marginalized and oppressed woman who is dependent on God's intervention and justice (in the form of an effective and just system). Her need and suffering characterize her. But, at the same time, the cry of distress and the petition are characterized by the assurance and trust that YHWH has taken the cause of the poor into YHWH's hands.

When we try to assess the experience of the psalmist, we are struck by the vulnerability of the speaker, who believed that vicious and evil men of violence surrounded her and stalked her every move, but also by her exceptional confidence in divine rescue. The Psalm reveals that the victim of violence/rape is often arbitrarily chosen as was the case of Jyothi who was truly innocent both before humanity and before God. Reading the Psalm as the raped/violated woman "completely shifts our sympathy

---

[87] *LW* 14, 144.
[88] Hans-Joachim Kraus, *Psalms 60-150* (Minneapolis: Augsburg, 1989), 523.

and allegiance away from the majority attitude and toward the victim"[89] and we actually experience the reality of violence through the woman's perspective, violence for which there is no justification.

What the Psalm does not say...

I would like to draw attention to what the Psalm does not say: no reference is made to either shame or dishonor; no reference to personal sin, no expression of anger against God characteristic of other laments. This Psalm is therefore particularly useful and helpful since the ramifications of perceived or ascribed shame, sin and dishonor are immense for women in particular. The lack of any expression of anger against God or doubt in God or even questioning is perhaps indicative of the fact that the psalmist sees no reason to fault God for the suffering but recognizes that she is the victim of human sin and human instituted structures.

For women to "speak" of rape" is itself a measure of liberation, a shift from serving as the object of voyeuristic discourse to the occupation of a subject position as "master" of narrative. By rendering the "I" in this Psalm as the violated woman, the woman is given the opportunity to name the rape instead of clouding and couching it in general terms of suffering. This leads to both personal transformation and self-improvement; for naming the injustice is the first step to transformation. The Psalm short circuits the power of collective violence and

> demystifies the mesmerizing power of scapegoating by ungagging the voice of the victim. We can no longer believe the victim to be subhuman after hearing this personal, human cry of lament. Rather, we come to empathize with the victim as one known and loved by God.[90]

Conclusion: Luther on Lament

The Psalm is a lament and given the fact that the practice of lament has declined within our churches, it is perhaps good to assess Luther's comments on the lament tradition and glean some insights from his comments on other Psalms of lament (e.g., Psalm 6)[91] for an enhanced understanding

---

[89] Cook, op. cit. (note 56), 5.

[90] Ibid. 5.

[91] One of the seven penitential Psalms (6, 32, 38, 51, 102, 130, 143) grouped by the church and recited after the hour of Lauds on the Fridays in lent. Luther himself used these as an "expression of Christian repentance," in *LW* 14, ix.

of Psalm 140. For Luther, suffering and pain are a part of life and a mark of the kingdom. God is prepared and ready to receive the cry of the sufferer. He writes,

> It is a mark of His kingdom that it contains poor, crying, praying people who suffer much on His account. Likewise His way and rule is none other than to help, hear, and end assistance to the poor, the afflicted, the dying and the sinners.[92]

> ...God is so disposed that He gladly hears those who cry and lament, but not those who feel smug and independent. Therefore the good life does not consist in outward works and appearances but in a lamenting and sorrowful spirit, as we read ... (51:17):"The sacrifice acceptable to God is a broken spirit; a broken and contrite heart, O God thou wilt not despise." And again (Ps 34:18): "The Lord is near to the broken hearted." Therefore weeping is preferred to working and suffering exceeds all doing.[93]

This is the nature of a gracious and loving God who is ready to listen to the cry and the pain of a sufferer. Luther encourages people to lament.[94] But Luther is cautious too. Lament within the living context of faith and hope cannot be excessive but moderate for excessive lament and expression of anger and doubt could lead one to blaspheme and fall away from God. Lament is therefore good if it is genuine.

The chief and influential doctrines for Luther's understanding of lament are his understanding of justification by grace through faith, his theology of the cross, and his teaching on affliction.[95] One particular feature of the lament that Luther seems to pay keen attention to is sin and repentance. For example, by citing Psalm 51:17 in his discussion of Psalm 6,[96] Luther seemingly draws attention to "repentance" and the human tendency to sin, both of which are missing in Psalm 6 and Psalm 140. Lament therefore becomes meaningful for Luther only within a framework of a God who justifies and saves, hence the emphasis on sin and repentance. What then would be the case of the sufferer who has not sinned—when the violence is unprovoked? What might the sin of the violated woman be? Some would argue that the woman should not have been out at that time of the day and

---

[92] Martin Luther with reference to Psalm 102:17, *LW* 14, 184.
[93] *LW* 14, 145.
[94] Kathleen. D. Billman and Daniel L. Migliore, *Rachel's Cry: Prayer of Lament and Rebirth of Hope* (Cleveland: United Church Press, 1999).
[95] Ibid., 54.
[96] *LW* 14, 145.

she should not have gotten into the bus. Was this her sin? Can the type of rape she experienced be justified?

Luther would perhaps respond by citing his position on "inherited" sin[97] or original sin. This universality of sin is problematic, for the faults of the powerful and the proud are embedded in the language of universal sin. The poor and women who do not have the capacity to commit such sins are also called to repentance and responsibility. It would be helpful therefore to draw attention away from personal sin and to attend to structural sin rooted in political, economic and social life for the sake of the raped and violated victim. The exercise of freedom on the part of a woman is not sin. Sin is the exercise of coercive power to reinforce structures of oppression, be it gender, race, caste or class.

Luther might suggest that the woman like Job is both a sinner and righteous—a justified sinner, one who is oppressed "along with Christ." Just as Jesus Christ went through suffering and humiliation to exaltation so must the woman suffer affliction in this sinful world. The woman therefore is unified with Christ through a shared experience. In doing so she experiences the grace of God for Christ is the embodiment of "God's grace, mercy, righteousness, truth, wisdom, power, comfort and salvation, given to us by God without any merit on our part."[98]

From the perspective of women who experience oppression and pain far more intensely than their male counterparts, the fact that Christ suffers along with them is a source of empowerment and hope. The cross is a symbol of God's solidarity with her and freedom from all suffering and pain.

> A God capable of suffering brings hope into hopeless situations. By embracing the suffering of all those who suffer, God gives hope for a transformation of all suffering and death through the resurrection.[99]

God is therefore present in the midst of her suffering and after and reveals Godself in the disturbing questions and issues raised by Jyothi's experience. This God evokes hope and evokes a response, and action for change and transformation of all structures that subjugate and suppress women. The woman did not choose to suffer; it is not to be spiritualized or valorized but one to be noted/acknowledged, named and confronted.

---

[97] *LW* 37, 363.
[98] *LW* 14, 204.
[99] Arnfriður Guðmundsdóttir, *Meeting God on the Cross: Christ, the Cross, and the Feminist Critique* (New York: Oxford University Press, 2010), 57.

II. Psalms Exegesis: Methodologies Past and Present

SINGING, PRAYING AND MEDITATING THE PSALMS. EXEGETICAL AND HISTORICAL REMARKS

Corinna Körting

Introduction

Over the last hundred years, one of the main questions arising in research on the Psalms has been to ask what the *Sæfær haT^ehillîm*, the Book of Praise, has been used for. At first sight, the answer appears to be simple: this collection of texts was used as the songbook during the Second Temple period. This is how Hans-Joachim Kraus would have defined it in the 1960s.[1] While such scholars as James Limburg view the Psalter as a worship book—at least initially[2]—others point to its strictly literary character and purposeful composition. Today, the Psalter is referred to as a book of meditation and a witness to Jewish piousness which has its setting in teaching and not in the service of the Second Temple.[3]

Why did the assessment of the Psalter change so dramatically? How can we explain the shift from a songbook for the community to a book of meditation for the individual?

In what follows, I shall try to answer this question, provide a brief overview of some major positions in research regarding this problem and

---

[1] Hans-Joachim Kraus, *Psalmen I*, BK.AT XV/1 (Neukirchen Vluyn: Neukirchner Verlag², 1961), XVIII.
[2] James Limburg, "Psalms, Book of," in *ABD* 5, 522-36, here 524-25.
[3] Cf. Notker Füglister, "Die Verwendung und das Verständnis der Psalmen und des Psalters um die Zeitenwende," in Josef Schreiner (ed.), *Beiträge zur Psalmenforschung: Psalm 2 und 22*, FzB 60 (Würzburg: Echter, 1988), 355-79; Christoph Levin, "Das Gebetbuch der Gerechten: Literargeschichtliche Beobachtungen am Psalter," in *ZThK* 90 (1993), 355-81, here 358; Manfred Oeming, *Das Buch der Psalmen: Psalm 1-41*, Neuer Stuttgarter Kommentar AT, 13/1 (Stuttgart: Katholisches Bibelwerk, 2000), 23. Klaus Seybold, *Poetik der Psalmen*, Poetologische Studien zum Alten Testament 3 (Stuttgart: Kohlhammer, 2003), calls it a Torah-like reader ("Lesebuch") (ibid., 364-73).

refer to the importance of the Psalms for Martin Luther himself and the Lutheran tradition.[4] Against the background of current Old Testament research, one must question whether Luther's emphasis on singing the Psalms remains relevant to scholarly work on them or if it is a welcome challenge to the work done in exegesis.

Before looking more closely at research on the Psalms, I briefly point to some aspects of Luther's position regarding the singing of the Psalms.

Luther's letter to Georg Burkhardt Spalatin of 1523 is an important witness. Luther's major concern was writing the Psalms in German and he asked Spalatin if he would be a Heman, Asaph or Yedutun.[5] The reason is that the Word of God shall dwell among the people through chant.[6] According to Inka Bach and Helmut Galle, Luther used the term "*psalmus*" to refer to Psalm songs, which are paraphrasing the biblical Psalms, and not as independently written hymns.[7] The songs had to be as true to the biblical text as possible.

One of the reasons given for this is the recommendation that God's Word shall be present among the people through chant. Still, why singing? What does Luther see in the biblical texts and especially in the Psalms that leads him to stress their singing? Four reasons are mentioned by Luther in the form of catchphrases:

1. **Following an example.** Luther stresses that kings and prophets sang songs and played music to praise God. Paul encouraged the Colossians to do the same.[8]

---

[4] Cf. Susan Gillingham, *Psalms Through the Centuries*, vol. 1, Blackwell Bible Commentaries (Oxford et al: Blackwell Publishing, 2008), 141.

[5] Cf. *WAB*, 3, 220; Inka Bach and Helmut Galle, *Deutsche Psalmendichtung vom 16. bis zum 20. Jahrhundert: Untersuchungen zur Geschichte einer lyrischen Gattung*, Quellen und Forschungen zur Sprach- und Kulturgeschichte der germanischen Völker, 95 (219) (Berlin and New York: de Gruyter 1989), 89.

[6] "... quo verbum dei vel cantu inter populos meneat," *WAB* 3: 220.

[7] Bach and Galle, op. cit. (note 5), 90. Cf. also Günter Bader, *Psalterium affectum palaestra: Prolegomena zu einer Theologie des Psalters*, Hermeneutische Untersuchungen zur Theologie 33 (Tübingen: Mohr Siebeck, 1996), 165. Bader points out that the inner praise of the Psalter should get an equivalent through the production of new hymns.

[8] In this way the Word of God shall be heard and learned. Cf. Luther's preface to the *Gesangbuch* of 1524: "Das geystliche lieder singen gut und Gott angeneme sey, acht ich, sey keynem Christen verborgen, die weyl yderman nicht alleyn das Exempel der propheten und koenige ym allten testament (die mit singen und klingen, mit tichten und allerley seytten spiel Gott gelobt haben) sondern auch solcher brauch, sonderlich mit psalmen gemeyner Christenheyt von anfang kund ist. Ja auch S. Paulus solchs 1 Cor. 14 eynsetzt und zu den Collossern gepeut, von hertzen dem

2. **Being part of the community of saints.** In his second introduction to the Psalter, Luther mentions this aspect. The individual becomes part of the community of saints because all who believe sing one song due to the fact that everybody finds the right words befitting their situation.[9]

Another "community" is of importance when it comes to the question of who is allowed to sing during the service. For Luther, it is not the choir but the whole congregation who should be encouraged to sing, because participation elicits the understanding of the words.[10]

3. **Singing the Psalms as a school for heart and temper.** After his exegesis of Psalm 1, Luther claims that "we" should sing and read the Psalms so that "we" may be comforted and "our" faith may be strengthened.[11]

The three aspects mentioned above are relevant for singing as well as praying the Psalms. This is not the case with my last point:

4. **A school for affects.** What Luther says about the Psalms and music comes together here. Music governs all movements of the heart, as does

---

Herrn singen geystliche lieder und Psalmen, Auff das da durch Gottes wort und Christliche leere, auff allerley weyse getrieben und geuebt werden," *WA* 35, 474. He also mentions the aspect of "following an example" in the second preface to the Psalter. Cf. Heinrich Bornkamm (ed.), *Martin Luther: Vorreden zur Bibel*, 4th edition, Kleine Reihe 1550 (Göttingen:Vandenhoeck & Ruprecht 2005), 68.

[9] Cf. Bornkamm, ibid., 68. "Die Erfahrung des Einstimmens lässt sich vielmehr folgendermaßen beschreiben: Ich finde meine eigene Stimme getragen vom Zusammenklang der anderen Stimmen, der entweder für mich ausspricht, was ich (noch) nicht selbst sagen kann, oder mir hilft auszusprechen, was ich erst im Begriffe bin zu begreifen. So ist das Einstimmen in ein Kirchenlied ein Zusammenstimmen mit den Gläubigen im Glauben: ὁμο-λογεῖν, wie das griechische Wort für 'bekennen' lautet. Und tatsächlich ist es dem gemeinsamen Sprechen des Credos nicht unähnlich, in welchem es zum Übereinstimmen und Zusammenstimmen im synchronen wie diachronen Sinn kommt: mit den aktuell Versammelten sowohl als auch mit den früheren Generationen von Gläubigen, die auf diese Weise ihren Glauben bekannt haben." Cf. Bernd Wannenwetsch, "Singen und Sagen: Zur musisch-musikalischen Dimension der Theologie," in *NZSTh* 46 (2004), 330–47, here 331.

[10] Cf. Gillingham, op. cit. (note 4), 140–41.

[11] Cf. Christian Gottlieb Eberle (ed.), *Luthers Psalmenauslegung*, vol. 1 (Stuttgart: Verlag der Evangelischen Bücherstiftung 1873), 21; Wolfram Adolph, "Zu Luthers Verständnis der Musik und seine Haltung zum Recht der Orgel im reformatorischen Gottesdienst," in Karl Heinz Nestle (ed.), *Faszination Orgel: Beiträge zur neuen Orgel der Katharinenkirche in Oppenheim* (Oppenheim: Verlagsbuchhandlung am Markt Oppenheim, 2006), 23–37, here 25-26.

the Psalter.[12] The underlying idea here was formulated by Melanchthon as follows: "*affectus affectu vincitur*," an affect can only be subdued by another, even stronger, affect, but not by reason.[13] The aspects Luther mentions are all present in the exegesis of Psalms. This is due to the fact that following an example or being part of the community as well as singing as a school for the heart is broached in the texts. But what does this say about the use of the Psalter from a historical perspective? To what extent is Luther's emphasis on singing the Psalms and the Psalter supported by the exegesis of the Psalms?

Research on the Psalms

Throughout the last century the question of whether the Psalms were a part of the liturgy of the temple, or even the basis for the reconstruction of ancient liturgy, has been widely discussed. In his commentary of 1900 Frants Buhl combined some of the major arguments for and against the use of the Psalms in public services. He wrote that the Psalms were a spiritual song collection for the public service of Israel. Yet, he distinguishes between

---

[12] "...das nach dem heiligen wort Gottes nichts nicht so billich vnd so hoch zu rhuemen vnd zu loben, als eben die Musica, nemlich aus der vrsach, das sie aller bewegung des Menschlichen hertzen (denn von den vnuernuenfftigen Thieren wil ich jtzt nichts sagen) ein Regiererin, jr mechtig vnd gewaltig ist, durch welche doch offtmals die Menschen, gleich als von jrem Herren, regiert vnd vberwunden werden. DEnn nichts auff Erden krefftiger ist, die Trawrigen froelich, die Froelichen trawrig, die Verzagten hertzeuhafftig zu machen, die Hoffertigen zur demut zu reitzen, die hitzige vnd vbermessige Liebe zu stillen vnd dempffen, den neid vnd hass zu mindern, vnd wer kan alle bewegung des Menschlichen hertzen, welche die Leute regieren, vnd entweder zu tugend oder zu laster reitzen vnd treiben, erzelen, dieselbige bewegung des gemuets im zaum zu halten vnd zu regieren, sage ich, ist nichts krefftiger denn die Musica." Preface to the Symphoniae iucundae from 1538, German translation by Johann Walter 1564, WA 50:370-71. "Denn ein menschlich Herz ist wie ein Schiff auf einem wilden Meer, welches die Sturmwinde von den vier Orten der Welt treiben. ... Was ist aber das meiste im Psalter anders als solch ernstlich Reden in allerlei solchen Sturmwinden?" Bornkamm, op. cit. (note 8), 67. Cf. Bader, op. cit. (note 7), 170-82.

[13] Philipp Melanchthon, *Loci Communes* 1,44; cf. Horst Georg Pöhlmann (ed.), *Philipp Melanchton. Loci Communes 1521: Lateinisch-Deutsch*, 2nd ed. (Gütersloh: Gütersloher Verlagshaus, 1997), 36. Regarding affects discussed by Luther or Melanchthon, see also Bernd Wannenwetsch, "Affekt und Gebot: Zur ethischen Bedeutung der Leidenschaften im Licht der Theologie Luthers und Melanchtons," in Johann Anselm Steiger et al (eds), *Passion, Affekt und Leidenschaft in der frühen Neuzeit*, vol. 1, Wolfenbütteler Arbeiten zur Barockforschung 43 (Wiesbaden: Harrassowitz, 2005), 203-15. Cf. Wannenwetsch, op. cit. (note 9), 337-38.

the role of the Levitical singers, who had to sing the major part, and the congregation that had to answer with "amen," "hallelujah" or "thanks to the Lord."[14] Buhl recognized that some of the Psalms were not very useful in liturgy and he opened up his definition of the purpose of the collection as one that includes Psalms for teaching and edification.[15]

We find this pattern, such as Buhl presents it, throughout research over the past one hundred years. The discussion has shifted mainly between four, maybe six, positions that have been combined in different ways: (1) the Psalms were songs used during services; (2) the Psalms were used for teaching and edification; (3) individual Psalms were used liturgically but the Psalter as a whole served for "private" concerns; or (4) the whole Psalter was used as songbook during the Second Temple period; 5) the Psalms were sung by the community; or 6) the Psalms were sung by professional singers while the congregations answered with liturgical formulas (*Gebetsrufen*).

In the following, I shall refer to two representatives of the main positions before the 1980s. One, Hermann Gunkel, stands at and towers over the beginning of a century of Psalm research. The other, Hans-Joachim Kraus, stands at a peak and at the same time at the turning point of twentieth-century Psalm research as genre critique.

Although describing a living context (*Sitz im Leben*) is essential for genre description, Gunkel was rather wary of describing a concrete liturgical setting. Perhaps he was simply more interested in language and poetic style than in cultic function, as some critics would put it.[16] And yet, Gunkel noted that the different characteristics of the texts point to different purposes or settings. He found hints at edification or teaching and texts deriving from cultic use. Looking at headlines that point to various cultic occasions[17] or terminology of cultic performance, he argued that the hints for music and performance might belong to smaller collections but have nothing to do with the usage of the Psalter as a whole.[18] His conclusion was thus that the Psalms were composed partially for cultic and partially

---

[14] Cf. Frants Buhl, *Psalmerne oversatte og fortolkede*, 2nd edition (Köbenhavn: Glydendaske Boghandels Forlag, 1900/1918). Here 2nd ed., VIII.

[15] Ibid., XI. This was especially Duhm's point. Yet Duhm drew the conclusion that this kind of composition of texts from varying settings might have been composed after the destruction of the temple and was therefore not meant for use during the temple service (Psalmen, IX–X).

[16] Cf. Sigmund Mowinckel, *The Psalms in Israel's Worship*, vol. 1 (Oxford: Blackwell, 1962), 31; Fritz Stolz, *Psalmen im nachkultischen Raum,* ThSt 129 (Zürich: Theologischer Verlag, 1983), 12.

[17] Cf. like the dedication of the temple (Ps 30), the Sabbath (Ps 92).

[18] Cf. Hermann Gunkel, *Einleitung in die Psalmen: Die Gattungen der religiösen Lyrik Israels* (Göttingen: Vandenhoeck & Ruprecht, 1933). Here 4th edition, 442–44.

for non-cultic spiritual use. As a whole collection, the Psalter follows non-cultic purposes. The collection shall serve as an *Andachts- und Hausbuch für den frommen Laien.*[19]

I shall now take a rather big step in chronological terms by going from 1933 to the 1960s and 1970s and the voluminous commentary on the Psalms written by Hans-Joachim Kraus. Kraus is convinced that the Psalms, including those composed far from the temple (he mentions Ps 42-43 as an example), would need a cultic context in order to exist. To him, a term like private poetry (*Privatdichtung*), as used by Gunkel, is therefore completely wrong.[20] The reason for the diverse character of the collection, according to Kraus, is based on the aim of collecting, canon-like, old Psalms and prayers and providing them as a songbook for the Second Temple community.[21]

The question of whether or not the Book of Psalms has a liturgical use has also been vital for Qumran research. Again, opinions range from private use for personal edification[22] to liturgical use. Yet, for our question, it is interesting to see that smaller combinations of biblical and non-biblical Psalms have been found that differ from the order of the Masoretic text.[23] This might support the idea that smaller units of Psalms or single Psalms did have a liturgical use while the Psalter did not.[24] An interesting example is Psalm 91. It has been found as the closing text for a collection of exorcist Psalms (11QPsAp^a). There are very few differences between the Masoretic Psalm and the Qumranic version. It is therefore striking that the direct divine speech is missing in the Qumranic version. This has been taken as a hint that "these changes were introduced in order to adapt the biblical

---

[19] Ibid., 452; cf. 446-52.

[20] Cf. Kraus, op. cit. (note 1), LXI. Cf. Erhard S. Gerstenberger, "Psalmen und Ritualpraxis," in Erich Zenger (ed.), *Ritual und Poesie: Formen und Orte religiöser Dichtung im Alten Orient, im Judentum und im Christentum* (HBS 36; Freiburg et al: Herder, 2003), 73-90, here 74; Egbert Ballhorn, "Zur Pragmatik des Psalters als Lehrbuch und Identitätsbuch Israels," in Albert Gerhards et al (eds), *Identität durch Gebet: Zur gemeinschaftsbildenden Funktion institutionalisierten Betens im Judentum und Christentum* (Studien zu Judentum und Christentum; Paderborn: Schöningh, 2003), 241-59, here 249-50.

[21] Cf. Kraus, op. cit. (note 1), XVII-XVIII.

[22] H. -J. Fabry is of this opinion. Unfortunately he does not discuss the problem deeply but only states that we do not know enough about Second Temple or early synagogue liturgy in order to prove that the Book of Psalms has been used there. "Der Psalter in Qumran," in Erich Zenger (ed.) *Der Psalter in Judentum und Christentum*, HBS 18 (Freiburg et al: Herder 1998), 137-63, here 151.

[23] Cf. Peter W. Flint, *The Dead Sea Psalms Scrolls and the Book of Psalms*, STDJ 17 (Leiden et al: Brill, 1997); Eva Jain, "Les manuscripts psalmiques de la Mer Morte et la réception du psautier à Qumran," in *RevSR* 77 (2003), 529-43.

[24] Cf. Ballhorn, op. cit. (note 20), 256.

Psalm for use as an apotropaic prayer."[25] Other collections of texts found in Qumran like the Songs for the Sabbath Sacrifice[26] or various regular praises at their fixed times,[27] point to the fact that songs existed for liturgical use at least beside the Masoretic Psalter and perhaps instead of it. [28]

Another important aspect to be mentioned is the fact that the Masoretic Psalter has been treated in Qumran in the same way as the prophetical books.[29] *Pesharim* and *Midrashim* were written on both groups of texts.[30] In the *Pesharim*, the Psalter was treated as scripture whose hidden sense needs to be revealed.[31]

It seems therefore that the Qumran findings again teach the necessity of differentiating clearly between Psalms and Psalter.

From a historical research perspective, the Qumran findings have taught us far more. Their influence on Psalm research in general cannot be underestimated. Many aspects, like the compositional character of the Psalter or the specific position of wisdom texts that could only with difficulty be ascribed to a liturgical place, have been seen before. Still, with Gerald H. Wilson's work during the 1980s on the Psalm scroll 11QPs^a and his observation "of a purposeful, editorial activity"[32] the door has finally been opened for a *"Psalterexegese."* One of the major insights also vital for our question is the instructive position of Psalm 1. Wilson writes: "[T]he hymnbook analogy ignores the fact that, in the

---

[25] Cf. Esther Eshel, "Apotropaic Prayers in the Second Temple Period," in Esther G. Chazon (ed.), *Liturgical Perspectives: Prayer and Poetry in Light of the Dead Sea Scrolls*, STDJ 48 (Leiden et al: Brill, 2003), 69-88, here 84. See also Corinna Körting, "Text and Context—Psalm 91 and 11QPsAp^a," in Erich Zenger (ed.), *The Composition of the Book of Psalms*, BEThL 238 (Leuven: Peeters, 2010), 67-77.

[26] Cf. Bilhah Nitzan, *Qumran Prayer and Poetry*, STDJ 12 (Leiden et al: Brill, 1994), 282-318. "The recitation of these praises leads to an experience of identification with the heavenly model of praise to God, and strengthens the recognition by the worshippers that through their song they perform the will of God, which will be received on high as a 'free-will offering'," 318.

[27] Cf. ibid., 49-87.

[28] Cf. Ulrich Dahmen, *Psalmen- und Psalterrezeption im Frühjudentum: Rekonstruktion, Textbestand, Struktur und Pragmatik der Psalmenrolle 11QPs^a aus Qumran* (STDJ 49; Leiden et al: Brill 2003), who points to the liturgical function of several collections and regards a liturgical use of the Psalms scroll 11QPs^a as possible. He uses the term "sekundäre 'Liturgisierung'," 274-76.

[29] Cf. Flint, op. cit. (note 23), 218-19; Levin, op. cit. (note 3), 358.

[30] 1Q16; 4Q171; 4Q173 and 4Q174; 4Q177. Cf. Flint, op. cit. (note 23), 45-47; Ballhorn, op. cit. (note 20), 253-54.

[31] He adds that the Psalter has also been treated the same way in the New Testament and the early churh. The Psalter has been seen as a prophetical book pointing to Christ, cf. Ballhorn, op. cit. (note 20), 253-56.

[32] Gerald H. Wilson, *The Editing of the Hebrew Psalter*, SBLDS 76 (Chico: Scholars Press, 1985), 199.

final analysis, the canonical Psalter has become a book to be read and meditated upon (Psalm 1) rather than music to be sung."[33] Like the Torah, the Psalter consists of five divisions. Torah Psalms such as Psalm 1 therefore contain the central clue to the interpretation of the Psalter. James Luther Mays claims that the Torah Psalms define the hermeneutical principle that the Psalms should be read as instruction.[34] To Mays, the Book of Psalms is no longer the songbook of the Second Temple community but, still in communal use, a composition of texts with the pedagogical intention of teaching about God. Erich Zenger links the observation of a purposeful arrangement to the central role of the Torah and wisdom Psalms and formulates the consequences of this approach: recognizing it as an elaborate arrangement of texts unhinges it from concrete cultic use and allows it to be seen as a prayer book, teaching for prayer and/or for the sanctification of everyday life—outside the temple and synagogues.[35]

THE PSALTER AS A SONGBOOK—STILL A POSSIBILITY?

All this knowledge regarding the compositional character of the Psalter and its use have to be taken seriously and it is not my intention to ignore what has been discovered to date. Yet, we have many hints on singing, praise and music for musicians, Psalm singers and writers.[36] The Septuagint may even challenge the careful distinction between the use of Psalms and Psalter. What is mentioned in a rather understated way in the Masoretic Psalter, i.e., the concrete liturgical situations, has been added in the Septuagint version.[37] It would be difficult to explain this only by reference to the use of smaller units.

I would like to approach the challenge given by hints for music and singing in two different ways. First, I shall apply the "program" of reading

---

[33] Gerald H. Wilson, "Shaping the Psalter: A Consideration of Editorial Linkage in the Book of Psalms," in J. Clinton McCann (ed.), *The Shape and Shaping of the Psalter*, JSOTSup 159 (Sheffield: Sheffield Academic Press, 1993), 72–82, here 72.

[34] James L. Mays, "The Question of Context in Psalm Interpretation," in McCann, ibid., 14–20; cf. also Ballhorn, op. cit. (note 20), 251.

[35] Cf. Erich Zenger, "Psalmenforschung nach Hermann Gunkel und Sigmund Mowinckel," in André Lemaire and Magne Sæbø (eds), *Congress Volume*, VTSup, 80 (Leiden et al: Brill, 2000), 399–435, here 435. Levin, op. cit. (note 3), 358.

[36] Cf. John A. Smith, "Which Psalms were sung in the Temple?," in *Music and Letters* 7 (1990), 167–86; Frank-Lothar Hossfeld, "Musik und Gebet im Alten Testament," in Winfried Bönig et al (eds), *Musik im Raum der Kirche* (Stuttgart and Ostfildern: Carus-Verlag and Matthias-Grünewald-Verlag, 2007), 44–50.

[37] Cf. Joachim Schaper, "Der Septuaginta-Psalter: Interpretation, Aktualisierung und liturgische Verwendung der biblischen Psalmen im hellenistischen Judentum," in Erich Zenger (ed.) *Der Psalter in Judentum und Christentum*, HBS 18 (Freiburg et al, 1998), 165–83.

the Psalms as a book to the question of meditation related to praise; second, I shall bring thoughts deriving from the so-called "material approach,"[38] important especially in social and cultural sciences, into the discussion.

PSALM 150 AS CLOSURE AND GOAL OF THE PSALTER

As I have pointed out above, Psalm 1 has been understood as one of the major keys to understanding the Psalter as a book of meditation and/or instruction. The emphasis put on Psalm 1 is understandable regarding its function as an opening for the whole Psalter. Yet, we need to ask how to connect this to the closure of the Psalter and its emphasis on praise. Psalm 150 is just the final text of a crescendo of praise beginning in Psalm 146. The individual (Ps 146:1), the congregation (Ps 147:2) and the whole creation (Ps 148) are called to praise God while the final demand in Psalm 150:6 is "Let everything that breathes praise the Lord! Praise the Lord!" Is this still just a text for meditation? Is Psalm 150 nothing more than a theologically inspired verbal and literary image of a cosmic liturgy, perhaps inspired by the actual use of instruments during temple service?[39]

Walter Brueggemann sees the development from Psalm 1 to Psalm 150 as moving from obedience to praise.[40] Whether one accepts his reading of Psalm 1 or is critical of it, the advantage of his reading is that the Psalter is seen as a book with an opening and a goal.[41] If praise is the goal, such praise as Psalm 150 calls for that includes not just the individual or some nations but the whole of creation, then this has something to say about our reading of the whole book. We could thus conclude that everything to be studied, learned and understood about God and God's righteous judgment over Israel and the nations, about God being close to or hidden from the individual, that all this is intended, finally, to lead to praise.[42]

---

[38] Dick Houtman and Birgit Meyer, *Things: Religion and the Question of Materiality* (New York: Fordham University Press, 2012), esp. 1-23.

[39] Frank-Lothar Hossfeld and Erich Zenger, *Psalmen 101-150*, HThK (Freiburg et al: Herder, 2008), 874.

[40] Cf. Walter Brueggemann, *The Psalms and the Life of Faith*, ed. by Patrick D. Miller (Minneapolis: Fortress Press, 1995), 189-213.

[41] Hossfeld and Zenger describe the composition as a movement from lament to praise at first. Op. cit. (note 39), 874. Yet the Psalter does not open with lament (this begins in Ps 3) but with the life of the righteous and meditation on the Torah. The connection between Psalms 1 and 150 becomes clearer later when they write that there is a movement: "Von der *Tora* zur *Tehilla*," ibid., 885.

[42] YHWH loves the righteous, not just according to Psalm 1, where the righteous are called blessed but esp. according to Psalm 146:8–the Psalm that opens the final doxology of the Psalter. Cf. Levin, op. cit. (note 3), 362-63.

This reading is a theological one and does not at first say anything about liturgical use or any other life context; it might at first simply say something about the movement of the heart towards God in meditation. Yet, if we are so careful about Psalm 150 in our analysis, how about being just as wary of Psalm 1, thus mitigating the emphasis on studying and meditation?

However, instead of questioning the overemphasis on Psalm 1 as the key for the reader of the Psalter, I would like to emphasize the importance of Psalm 150 and the whole final doxology of the Book of Psalms. To this end, I shall cite some important remarks made by Frank-Lothar Hossfeld and Erich Zenger on Psalm 150 as the final Psalm of the Psalter:[43] Psalms are court music of the heavenly king; they are exercise (*Einübung*) and anticipation (*Vorwegnahme*) of the cosmic festival celebrating the completion of the world; while singing/praying the Psalms, humans realize their specific kinship with God and express community with God initiated through praise.[44] The last point in particular goes beyond theological evaluations of the Psalter as a "temple of words" that can be entered.[45] Community with God initiated by praise needs active realization. What has just been said is an evaluation of music and praise at a theological level. It should be an answer to the question of how a specific terminology shapes the theology of the Psalter.

Now, I would like to turn to real (material) things.

THE "MATERIAL APPROACH" IN RESEARCH AND HOW IT CAN BE MADE FRUITFUL

Aside from the many approaches we can find in research (especially in the social sciences and humanities) such as the "spatial" or the "linguistic" approaches, we can also find a "material" approach. What makes this approach interesting for the specific question treated in this paper is its focus on real things, including not just objects or materials but also sounds, silences, smells, gestures or colors. The shift to a focus on the material is based on the

---

[43] Cf. Hossfeld and Zenger, op. cit. (note 39), 885.

[44] Cf. the full German quotation: "Im Singen/Beten der Psalmen realisiert 'aller Atem', d.h. der Mensch, seine spezifische Gotteskompetenz und Gottesverwandschaft, insofern er der Gottesgabe seines 'Atems' die ihr mögliche höchste Ausdrucksgestalt gibt, nämlich die Gestalt der im Gotteslob realisierten Gottesgemeinschaft," Hossfeld and Zenger, op. cit. (note 39), 885; Hossfeld, op. cit. (note 36), 45.

[45] This is not a critique of this portrayal of the Psalter used e.g. by Zenger, op. cit. (note 35), 434–35. On the contrary, my remark only points to the necessity that the theological world described needs realization in singing and praying.

> dissatisfaction with approaches that take ideas, concepts, ideologies or values as immaterial abstractions that are regarded as prime movers of history. Privileging the abstract above the concrete reduces material culture (as well as words and gestures) to expressions of an underlying meaning or to the status of "mere" signs.[46]

Or, to express it positively

> Materializing the study of religions means asking how religion happens materially... A materialized study of religion begins with the assumption that things, their use, how they are valued and their appeal are not something added to a religion but rather inextricable from it.[47]

At first these statements do not seem to be unexpected. Studies of the ancient Israelite cult specifically, or of Israel's religious life in general, take up these questions. Yet, as I have shown above, the connection between the single Psalm and cultic life seems to be lost. For the Psalter, this connection might never have existed. The emphasis lies on teaching and studying. Taking up the questions of music and singing coming from a different angle than genre critique, or studies of literary history or composition might provide some new insights.

What this might look like has been shown, for example, in an article by Friedhelm Hartenstein.[48] He combines knowledge about instruments, their construction and their sound with the information the texts give about their use. The short answer is that sounds, music and instruments as they are mentioned in the Psalter do not just symbolize something, for instance God's presence, but they (also) evoke it. Instrumental music and singing are media of religious communication.[49]

The first example: Psalm 57:7-8 [Ps 57:8-9 MT]

> My heart is steadfast, O God, my heart is steadfast. I will sing and make melody. Awake, my soul! Awake, O harp and lyre! I will awake the dawn

---

[46] Houtman and Meyer, op. cit. (note 38), 5.
[47] Cf. Birgit Meyer et al, The Origin and Mission of *Material Religion*," in *Religion* 40 (2010), 209.
[48] Cf. Friedhelm Hartenstein, "'Wach auf, Harfe und Leier, ich will wecken das Morgenrot' (Psalm 57,9) – Musikinstrumente als Medien des Gotteskontakts im Alten Orient und im Alten Testament," in M. Geiger et al (eds), *Musik, Tanz und Gott*, SBS 207 (Stuttgart: Verlag Katholisches Bibelwerk, 2007), 101-27. It should be noted that Hartenstein does not follow what has been claimed by researchers promoting the "material approach" in a strict sense. Yet his way of starting with "things" and how they matter provides useful insights.
[49] Cf. Hartenstein, ibid., 102.

The music of harp and lyre produces an effect; they wake up the dawn and prepare the coming of YHWH.

As a second example, I would like to mention the shofar. It is especially interesting because it is not known as an instrument that makes a beautiful sound, and still it is among the instruments mentioned in Psalm 150. It can be used in profane as well as cultic contexts in order to make a loud noise (terû'āh) that draws attention.[50] Taking different texts into account, we find that the sound catches YHWH's attention that YHWH might remember YHWH's people and might act on behalf of them.[51] The sound is sent to God like a prayer.[52]

Things matter.[53] They are not mere symbols. The examples of musical instruments and their sounds provide an insight into religious practice, experience[54] and how music forms the experience of reality.[55]

Coming back to Luther again, the last point—the question of how music forms the experience of reality, of belief—should be stressed. He is arguing for creating an affect, an emotion. The Psalms are not simply an expression of faith; they make the experience of faith possible.[56] Bernd Wannenwetsch explains this with, for example, the singing of *"In dulci jubilo"* [In Sweet Rejoicing] in a Christmas service. Singing this song allows the singers to experience rejoicing. The logic of a dictum of faith [*Glaubensaussage*] that the song puts on the lips of the singers is understood later.[57]

---

[50] Cf. Corinna Körting, *Der Schall des Schofar: Israels Feste im Herbst*, BZAW 285 (Berlin and New York: de Gruyter, 1999), 157–62; Edo Škulj, "Musical Instruments in Psalm 150," in Jože Krašovec (ed.) *Interpretation of the Bible* (Sheffield: Sheffield Academic Press, 1998), 1117–30.

[51] In Leviticus 23:24 this kind of noise is connected with remembrance (*zikkārôn*); cf. also Numbers 10:9–10 where the sound of an instrument (in this case a trumpet) causes remembrance. Cf. Joachim Braun, *Die Musikkultur Altisraels/Palästinas*, OBO, 164 (Göttingen and Freiburg Schweiz: Vandenhoeck & Ruprecht and Universitätverlag Freiburg Schweiz, 1999), 209–18.

[52] Cf. 2 Chronicles 13:12-16; cf. Jacob Milgrom, *Numbers*, JPS Torah Commentary (Philadelphia and New York: Jewish Publication Society, 5750/1990), 75.

[53] This expression is based on Houtman and Meyer, op. cit. (note 38), 4–5.

[54] "Die Musik vermochte auf Personen und Dinge einzuwirken, die hintergründige Wirklichkeit zu berühren und konnte selbst etwas von dieser in der Tiefe erfahrenen Welt offenbaren." Hans Seidel, "Israel und Juda," in Ernst H. Meyer, *Geschichte der Musik I: Musik der Urgesellschaft und der frühen Klassengesellschaften* (Leipzig: Dt. Verlag für Musik, 1977), 262; Hossfeld, op cit. (note 36), 50.

[55] Cf. Hartenstein, op. cit. (note 48), 101.

[56] Wannenwetsch, op. cit. (note 9), 332; Adolph, op. cit. (note 11), 24–25.

[57] Wannenwetsch, ibid., 333.

Conclusion

Singing and praise are major subjects of the Psalms and the Psalter. Luther saw this and connected his exegetical insights with his own convictions on the importance of singing the Psalms in Christian congregations. Yet research has shown that this does not say anything about the actual use of the Psalter during the Second Temple period. Besides the observations of composition techniques that make the Psalter a book of studies, to my mind it is important that the Psalter be treated in the Qumran community in the same way as the prophetical books, namely as prophetical, authoritative literature that needs to be explained. In addition, we must consider that new compositions of Palms for liturgical use were possible—which means that the Masoretic Psalter was by no means the only source for liturgical prayer and praise.

Music and song should not disappear from Psalm research. Theologically, Psalm 150 sets the goal for either singing, praying or studying the Psalter because it is in praise that community with God is initiated. And even if we regard the Psalter solely as a book of meditation, disconnected from temple service and music, we have to admit that reading these texts evokes the world of temple service with music and shouting and singing. Then it again becomes evident that things matter, that music and sounds matter.

From Psalms to Psalter Exegesis

Frank-Lothar Hossfeld

Since 1980, the so-called newer exegesis of Psalms has increasingly complemented classical twentieth-century *Formkritik* [form criticism] and *Gattungskritik* [genre criticism] and developed its own dynamics. As Erich Zenger stated at the 2008 Leuven Psalms congress:

> Compared to Gunkel's lack of interpretative interest in the literary context in which a Psalm is situated in the Book of Psalms, recent research on the Psalms has been increasingly interested in individual Psalms as *part of a collection or, rather, as part of the whole text*. Furthermore, more recent research has attempted to illuminate the genesis of the Psalter as a book. At the same time, this endeavor is connected to questions that have already been controversially discussed by Gunkel and Mowinckel, i.e., For which purpose was the Psalter compiled? Which circles created the Psalter and for what target group? Even if compared to other books the Psalter finds its specific profile in the fact that its single texts *are marked as such*, it is, at the same time, a textual whole ... which like most other biblical books was gradually formed and, in the first place, also has to be read or rather heard as a book. ... With regard to the Psalter it has to be emphasized that the bringing together of individual Psalms in groups of Psalms or rather part Psalters and the gradual formation of the Psalter as a whole is the work of temple singers and priests and wisdom teachers, who were "experts" with regard to poetry as well as literature.[1]

In his research report, "Continuing the Engagement. Psalms Research since the Early 1990s," J. Kenneth Kuntz reaches the following conclusion,

> Presently, as scholars reflect of the Psalms, literary and theological concerns prevail over historical concerns. That trend is likely to continue. Clearly the final form of the text remains prominent on the scholarly radar. ... Moreover, it is inconceivable that conversations about the shape and shaping of the Psalter will abate. It would be salutary, however, if new ventures on this front were as much the product of disciplined investigation as the outcome of a fertile imagination. If

---

[1] Erich Zenger, "Psalmenexegese und Psalterexegese. Eine Forschungsskizze," in Erich Zenger (ed.), *The Composition of the Book of Psalms*, BEThL, 238 (Leuven, Paris, Walpole: Peeters Publishers, 2010), 17–65, here 24, 26, 27 (emphasis in the original).

we are justified in claiming that Psalms scholarship boasts a rich recent history, we are no less justified in anticipating its promising future.²

In his postscript to the 2010 Oxford conference, "Jewish and Christian Approaches to the Psalms. Conflict and Convergence," organized and conducted by S. Gillingham, John Barton states,

> A second theme [after the interrelation of Jewish and Christian use and study of the Psalter] is the Psalter as a book: a collection of individual Psalms that is more than the sum of its parts: This has a historical dimension concerned with ... both ends of the process: the original formation of Psalms within the ancient Near East and the collection of the Psalms into a finished whole. The latter has, again, two aspects—the historical process of collection, and the interpretation of the collection as a book or "work." Both will continue to be of interest, but my strong impression is that it is the last that is the point of growth in biblical studies at the moment. How did Jews and Christians in the past read, not just individual psalms, but the Psalter: and how should Jews and Christians nowadays read the complex book. A sort of consensus seems to be emerging that the Psalter is not a random collection, but is planned to convey certain theological ideas.³

The tension between the individual Psalm and the Psalter corresponds to the relationship between the diachronic and synchronic ways of reading the Book of Psalms. As F. Hartenstein elaborates,

> The perspective of an exegesis of the Psalter is of particular relevance for the understanding of the Psalms and their literary and historical contexts there where the complexity of the text in terms of form and content is perceived not only at the level of the final text. Furthermore, a canonical reading of the Psalter and the Psalms is a (necessary) addition in as far as it makes visible the tightly woven net of possible allusions to Old Testament texts. However, also here there is a considerable risk that the perspectives of the modern reader are incorporated. Control in terms of methodology is most likely to yield success there where the compositional reading of the Psalter is always combined with the question regarding its genesis.⁴

---

[2] J. Kenneth Kuntz, "Continuing the Engagement. Psalms Research Since the Early 1990s," in *Currents in Biblical Research 103* (2012), 321–78, here 364.

[3] John Barton, "Postscript," in Susan Gillingham (ed.), *Jewish and Christian Approaches to the Pslams. Conflict and Convergence* (Oxford: Oxford University Press, 2013), 260–61.

[4] Friedhelm Hartenstein, "Schaffe mir Recht, JHWH!" (Ps 7,9). Zum theologischen und anthropologischen Profil der Teilkomposition Psalm 3-14," in Zenger, op. cit. (note 1), 229–58, 234–35 (author's own translation).

In the following, I shall illustrate the interconnection between diachrony and synchrony using three examples from the macrostructure of the Psalter: (1) the main caesura of the Psalter after Psalm 89 (cf. 3.); (2) the singular colophon of the Psalter in Psalm 72:20 (cf. 4.); and (3) the division of the Psalter into five books by the four doxologies Psalm 41; 14:72; 19:89; 53:106; 48 (cf. 5.)[5]

With regard to the complete Psalter it has become common practice in the exegesis of the Psalter to refer to the main caesura after Psalm 89 since it splits the Psalter into two, i.e., the first half, Books 1 to 3, and the second, shorter, half, Books 4 and 5. Modifications refer to the genre of the Psalms, the actual disappearance of the sign Sela in the second half (except for Psalms 140 and 143) and the changes in the system of headings and superscriptions.[6]

The first half of the Psalter focuses on lamentation and prayer while praise, thanksgiving and hymns predominate in the second half. If we were to interpret the sign Sela in terms of music, then we would probably notice a shift in the way in which the Psalms are performed; in any case, the disappearance of the sign Sela in the second half is irrefutable proof of a change.

In the first half there are only five (respectively six) Psalms without headings (Ps 1-2; 10; 33; 43; 71). In the second half, the number of these Psalms (Ps 91; 93-97; 99; 114; 119; 137) increases; here, certain laudatory set phrases take over the function of headings and arrange the Psalms into smaller groups (cf. "Bless the Lord, O my soul" in Ps 103; 104; the *hodu*-formula "O give thanks to the Lord, for he is good" in Ps 106; 107; 118; 136; then the *alleluiah*-Triads in Ps 104-106; 111-113; 115-117).

The headings in the first half are highly complex: they consist of the specification of genre, the attribution to a person or a group (cf. David: seventy-three times; Moses: once; Solomon: twice; Asaph: twelve times; Korah: eleven times), the cultic-liturgical remarks (cf. "to the chorusmaster": fifty-four times), the specification of melody and the biographical situation attributed to David (thirteen respectively fourteen times in the first and second and once in the fifth Psalter of David).

The main caesura draws attention to two specifics: the combination of text (prayer) and music as well as the dynamics from lamentation to praise,

---

[5] Cf. Erich Zenger and Frank-Lothar Hossfeld, "Das Buch der Psalmen," in Christian Frevel (ed.), *Einleitung in das Alte Testament*, KStTh 1,1 (Stuttgart: Kohlhammer, [8]2012), 428–52, here 436.

[6] Also Bernd Janowski: "It is generally acknowledged that the 117 superscriptions to the Psalms belong to the more difficult and somewhat unresolved problems that exist in Psalms research." (in print)

whether with regard to the individual Psalm (cf. the so-called change of atmosphere in Ps 3:8 and Ps 22:22 or Ps 17:15 and Ps 13:6), or subgroups (cf. the hymns Ps 8; 19; 29 at the center of moaning subgroups) or to the five books of Psalms with the final doxologies or the concluding Hallel in Psalms 146–150 and finally with regard to the entire Psalter.[7]

Praise is a human condition before God which expands in time and space within the Psalter. It spreads from the individual via the groups to the people and from there to humankind (cf. Ps 96; 98; 100; 150). It expands in time (cf. the selective vow of praise of the individual at the end of the lamentations, e.g., Ps 26:12; 27:6), it can encompass the entire life of an individual (e.g., Ps 71:24; 104:33; 145:1, 21) and may finally culminate in the eternal praise of humankind (cf. Ps 145:21).

The individual metatext of the Psalter is of great significance, namely the Colophon Psalm 72:20 "The prayers of David the son of Jesse are ended."

In light of the first and second Psalter of David, Psalms 3–41; 51–72, which predominantly contain laments, the genre "rogations" is clearly comprehensible. More difficult to understand, however, is the assumed conclusion of the rogations, since Psalm 86 continues with the designation of genre: "David's rogation," there are a further three Psalters of David (Ps 101–103; 108–110; 138–145) in the complete Psalter and in total 73 Psalms are attributed to David in the Hebrew Psalter (LXX: 88 or rather 89 Psalms). Here, we face the phenomenon of the so-called "Davidization" of the Psalter, a process that ends in the total assignment of the Psalter to David (2 Macc 2:13; 11QPs[a] David's Compositions; Lk 20:42; Acts 4:25–26). The attribution to David is the only one running through the whole Psalter, which underlines the enormous importance of David as a historic king, prophet, writer, musician and prototype of a human being.

Starting from the designations of David besides the references to David as "king" and "the anointed one" in the corpora of the Psalms and continuing with the considerable interest in the classic type of form and genre criticism in the royal Psalms, the exegesis of the Psalter has established the structural significance of the eleven royal Psalms (cf. Ps 2; 18; 20; 21; 45; 72; 89; 101; 110; 132; 144). They are the central or prominent corner stones of groups of Psalms or partial Psalters. They witness to the general interest of the Psalter in the figure of the king as the concrete mediator of the kingdom of YHWH. In the process of reading they testify to the metamorphoses in the image of the king in relationship to the kingdom of God (in heaven above), and the historical reality of Israel (cf. Ps 2; 89; 132; 144 connected with 145).

---

[7] Cf. Frank-Lothar Hossfeld, "Von der Klage zum Lob. Die Dynamik des Gebets in den Psalmen," in *BiKi* 56/1 (2001), 16-20.

Since the mid-1990s, the structurally relevant royal Psalms, combined with the study on the beginning and ending of the five books, have been the impulse to shed light on the history of how the Psalter has been read.[8] Books 1 and 2 reflect the founding era of kings David and Solomon, followed by the decline until the Babylonian exile in Book 3. Book 4 segues from the exile to expectations of homecoming and the reunion of Israel. Book 5 concentrates on the reestablishment of Israel. In the fifth book, Psalms 126:1-3, 136:23-24 and 137 look back at the period of exile and the reversal of Zion's/Jerusalem's fortunes. At the same time, Psalm 147:2-3 indicates that the process of reestablishing Israel is yet to be concluded, while Psalm 149 implies the future enforcement of YHWH's kingdom by a judgment on the nations.

Thus, with its division into five books, the Psalter follows the history of Israel and thus responds to YHWH's acts of salvation in history, which is yet to be completed by means of prayer.[9]

The three examples relevant to the macrostructure of the Psalter prove the interconnection between the diachronic and synchronic ways of reading the Psalter. In addition, David's and, consequently, Solomon's central importance prove that the Psalter itself draws on biblical literature outside the Psalter such as the books of Samuel (cf. the biographical information in thirteen of the Psalms of David and the adoption of Ps 18 in 2 Sam 22) and also serves as a model or source for the reception through the Chronicles (cf. 1 Chr 16 and 2 Chr 6:41-42).

Martin Luther treads the paths of the early church fathers by highly esteeming the Psalms. In addition to classical questions regarding the translation of the texts three issues catch the commentator's eye:

- In his "Prologue to the Psalter (1524)" Luther distinguishes between the "Psalter" as the designation for the whole Book of Psalms and the "Psalm" respectively the "Psalms" as the designation for individual texts. This corresponds to the main concern of more recent exegesis of the Psalms.

---

[8] Cf. R. G. Kratz, "Die Tora Davids. Psalm 1 und die doxologische Fünfteilung des Psalters," in *ZThK* 93 (1996), 12-34; Nancy de Claissé-Walford. *Reading from the Beginning. The Shaping of the Hebrew Psalter* (Macon, GA: Mercer University Press, 1997).

[9] Cf. Frank-Lothar Hossfeld, "Dejinné zastavenia Izraela ako ráz tiahnuci sa Žaltárom. Abstrakt prednášky v tézach," in *Studia Biblica Slovaca* 4/2 (2012), 72-81.

- For Luther, the Psalter was the book of books of the whole Bible. It is the "little Biblia"[10] of the Old and New Testaments. It is the Enchiridion, the handbook for the entire Holy Scripture. The historical-critical exegesis seeks to investigate the function of the handbook in the context of the Old Testament. With regard to the New Testament the function of the Psalter as a handbook assumes the prophetic character of the Psalter and emphasizes the exceptional dignity the Psalter has for the New Testament, because in spite of the appearance of the incarnated son of God the New Testament does not create a new Psalter.

- Martin Luther contributed to setting the course for a history of reception. On the one hand the Psalms are turned into texts for reading and meditation, on the other, the Psalter serves as a basis for new musical settings of literary work.

---

[10] "Vnd sollt der Psalter allein deshalben thevr vnd lieb sein / das er von Christus sterben vnd aufferstehung / so klerlich verheisset / vnd sein Reich vnd der gantzen Christenheit stand vnd wesen vurbildet. Das er wol möcht ein kleine Biblia heissen / darin alles auffs schönest vnd kürtzest / so in der gantzen Biblia stehet / gefasset vnd zu einem feinen Enchiridion oder Handbuch gemacht vnd bereitet ist." Martin Luther, *Vorrede auf den Psalter, Die gantze Heilige Schrifft Deudsch*, Wittenberg 1545, Bl. 288b.

III. Difficult Topics in Psalms and their Lutheran Interpretation

THE TOPIC OF VIOLENCE—
A HERMENEUTICAL CHALLENGE
IN READING PSALMS

JUTTA HAUSMANN

Accounts of violence in Old Testament texts constitute a severe provocation for many readers of the Bible as well as for biblical scholars.[1] A look at several texts published over the last twenty years indicates that not only Old Testament scholars but scholars in different fields are dealing with this subject.[2] Interpersonal conflicts and violence are not very often placed in theological perspective by biblical authors. In the Bible, both men and women experience violence in some form. They partly accept it as a way of resolving problems,[3] but are mostly unable to tolerate it when they themselves are the victims.[4] Thus we often find laments and accusations in Psalms about the violence suffered at the hands of enemies.

We are often told that a plea for violent intervention is not allowed from a Christian perspective, being contradictory to the command to love even one's enemies. It appears at odds with the New Testament injunction that if anyone strikes you on the right cheek, you should turn the other cheek. Beyond that, we can see a "Christianizing" of the Psalters, for example, in the addition of the Trinitarian formula in liturgical use, or by a Christological interpretation. Such treatment can be retraced to the New Testament.

---

[1] See Roger Wanke's contribution in this volume.
[2] See Bernd Janowski, *Ein Gott, der straft und tötet?* (Neukirchen-Vluyn: Neukirchener Verlagsgesellschaft, 2013). In addition amongst others, Thomas Römer, *Dieu obscur. Cruauté, sexe et violence dans l'Ancien Testament* (Geneva: Labor et Fides, 2009); André Wénin, *La Bible ou la violence surmontée* (Paris: Desclée de Brouwer, 2008); Gerlinde Baumann, *Gottesbilder der Gewalt im Alten Testament verstehen* (Darmstadt: Wissenschaftliche Buchgesellschaft, 2006); Jonneke Bekkenkamp and Yvonne Sherwood (eds), *Sanctified Aggression. Legacies of Biblical and Post-Biblical Vocabularies of Violence*, JSOTS 400 (London/New York: T&T Clark, 2003); Walter Dietrich and Christian Link, *Die dunklen Seiten Gottes*, vol. 1, *Willkür und Gewalt*, vol. 2, *Allmacht und Ohnmacht* (Neukirchen-Vluyn: Neukirchener Verlagsgesellschaft, 1995/³2000).
[3] Especially in case of war, Numbers 31; 1 Kings 12:26-30.
[4] 1 Kings 19:1-4; Jeremiah 18:18-23; Psalm 83.

But, however they have been treated, these accounts of violence have often been received in the same manner over time.

Until today, we can experience in our churches—mainly in the reality of parish life—an alienation from the Hebrew Bible and therefore from Jewish theological thinking. In our Lutheran tradition, we can go back to Martin Luther and his comments marked by anti-Judaism.

Besides the—for Luther important and characteristic—Christological approach to the Old Testament there is also his already much-discussed anti-Judaism[5] that, regrettably, also characterizes his interpretation of Psalms. There is in all likelihood a connection between these two approaches, especially in Luther's later period. Kaufmann has indicated a distinction between an earlier, more lenient, and a later more hostile attitude toward Jews. This, however, is theologically incorrect. In fact, the Jewish refusal to commit to Christ has rendered the recognition of Judaism and its tradition impossible for Luther and his followers.[6] We find an example of this in Luther's interpretation of Psalm 58 (which we will examine more closely later). Let us now simply look at some lines of thought in it:

Relating to verse 3: "...the prophet accuses them [=the heretics] of practicing hypocrisy and of magnifying their own righteousness. These two were and are in the Jews, then and now." The Jews "are, first, unrighteous and hypocrites, and then also evil, by establishing and regarding unrighteousness and iniquity."[7] Relating to verse 6 and Augustine:

> *God will break in pieces their teeth*, that is, their biting and slanderous accusations. According to Augustine, this happened first when Christ refuted the Jews on the basis of their own words ... Second, this will happen when at the end of the world and in the hour of death He will justify and condemn each one on the

---

[5] Cf. Walter Bienert, *Martin Luther und die Juden* (Frankfurt am Main: Evangelisches Verlagswerk, 1982); David G. Singer, *Baptism or Expulsion: Martin Luther and the Jews of Germany*, JES 44 (2009), 401–408; Thomas Kaufmann, *Luthers "Judenschriften"* (Tübingen: Mohr Siebeck, 2011); James E. McNutt, *Luther and the Jews Revisited: Reflections on a Thought Let Slip*, CThMi 38 (2011), 40–47; Folker Siegert (ed.), *Kirche und Synagoge. Ein lutherisches Votum*, (Göttingen: Vandenhoeck & Ruprecht, 2012); Dorothea Wendebourg, *Jews Commemorating Luther in the Nineteenth Century*, LuthQ XXVI (2012), 249–70.

[6] Kaufmann, ibid., 128. Cf. Kaufmann, ibid., 3: „daß er [Luther] vor allem einer Lesart alttestamentlicher Traditionsbestände verpflichtet war, die er infolge einer christologischen Deutung als Anklage gegen die Judenheit auslegte," and Duane H. Larson, "Jewish-Christian Relations," in Günther Gassmann, Duane H. Larson and Mark W. Oldenburg, *Historical Dictionary of Lutheranism* (Boston/Folkstone: Scarecrow Press, 2001), 161–62.

[7] *LW* 10, 268.

basis of his own words. Third, when in goodness He causes someone to keep his biting slanders to himself before he puts them forth. ... But He also breaks their teeth in this way, that he deprived the Jews of the power to harm Christ and the Christians by their slanders.[8]

According to Luther, the Jewish approach to the Bible is unacceptable and leads them to ruin; they themselves are responsible for their fate. Strongly emphasizing that only a Christological interpretation, that is, an interpretation based on the New Testament, is acceptable for a Christian reading of the Old Testament that understands the New Testament as an antithesis to the Old, this position obviously requires a refusal of the Jewish approach. In any case, the *Wirkungsgeschichte* [history of reception] of both—the rejection of the Jewish approach as well as the idea of the unique truth of the Christological interpretation—had and continue to have problematic effects today.[9] Fortunately, this form of a very frank anti-Judaism seems anachronistic and is rarely found now except among a number of representatives of radical positions present in all Christian denominations. But beside this open anti-Judaism, we often find other forms, such as attributing a higher (moral or theological or both) quality to the New than to the Old Testament in our churches. Or they deny the fully-fledged revelation of God to the Jewish people and/or raise the question of truth, citing John 14:6 and other similar texts.[10]

Concerning Psalms, the Roman Catholic scholar Erich Zenger[11] nearly twenty years ago resolutely sought a different understanding of those texts that ask for God's intervention by violence or that describe the experience

---

[8] Ibid., 268f. Cf. Volker Weymann, „Luthers Schriften über die Juden. Theologische und politische Herausforderungen," in *Texte aus der VELKD*, Nr. 168 (2013), at **http://velkd.de/downloads/Texte_168_Luthers__Schriften_ueber_die_Juden_download.pdf**, 7f.

[9] Cf. Christian Danz, *Grundprobleme der Christologie* (Tübingen: Mohr Siebeck, 2013), 230ff.; Kaufmann, op. cit. (note 5), 134ff.; Robert Rosin, *Reformation Christology: Some Luther Starting Points*, CThQ 71 (2007), 147–68; David G. Horrell and Christopher M. Tuckett (eds), *Christianity, Controversy, and Community*: New Testament Essays in Honor of David R. Catchpole, SNT 99 (Leiden: Brill, 2000); Donald J. Dietrich, *God and Humanity in Auschwitz: Jewish-Christian Relations and Sanctioned Murder* (New Brunswick, New Jersey: Transaction Publishers, 1995).

[10] See the examples from the research history by Erich Zenger, *Ein Gott der Rache? Feindpsalmen verstehen* (Freiburg: Herder, 1994), 27ff.

[11] Obviously, it was not an accident that a Roman Catholic scholar brought a new perspective. The official document *Nostra aetate*, which suggests quite another approach to Judaism than that adopted in earlier times was certainly a reference for him.

of violence performed by God.[12] In this, he was influenced, as were many other scholars, by the experiences of Christian-Jewish dialogue. Since then, a lot of literature has been published and we can see some progress at a scholarly level. But working with students and parish members and in discussion with colleagues, different faculties and different theological chairs, it is evident that attempts to provide another understanding are often far from being accepted. So it seems worthwhile again to deal with the subject of Psalms and violence.

TWO EXAMPLES FOR A POSSIBLE UNDERSTANDING OF PSALMS DEALING WITH THE EXPERIENCE OF VIOLENCE

PSALM 58

In Psalm 58, violence occurs at two different levels: 1) violence between human beings, and 2) violence being performed by God. The first level refers to violence committed by evildoers. The rhetorical question at the beginning (v. 2) shows that the main problem is harmful words, not physical violence. The physical aspect only appears once in verse 2 where the mention of the hands points to physical action. However, we return to the semantic field of language—and of hearing—in the following verses: verse 4 refers to speaking lies and the closing of ears. And the metaphor of poison recalls the poisoning effect of words. When the psalmist asks for help from God, the tooth in the mouth in verse 7 is to be understood in the context of the snake's poison (v. 5). The metaphor "teeth of the young lion" evokes the destructive power in the language of the evildoers and is part of the wish that God shall liberate the psalmist from it.[13] In addition, we find some comparisons to natural phenomena to underline the appeal to God to destroy powerful aggressors (vv 8,9). In between, a metaphor for destructive speech appears again in verse 8: the arrow motif is clearly combined with speech in Psalm 57:5, but occurs in other Psalms too in combination with abusive language.

---

[12] Zenger, op. cit. (note 10).

[13] Peter Krawczack, *"Es gibt einen Gott, der Richter ist auf Erden!" (Ps 58,12b)*, BBB 132 (Berlin: Philo, 2001), 248: "Somit wird Gott in V 7 um ein eingreifendes und destruierendes (Gerichts-)Handeln gebeten, das auf der Bildebene der Giftzähne der Schlange, die Neutralisierung der als Waffe des Un-Rechts eingesetzte Sprachmächtigkeit der Frevler erwünscht." And Bernd Janowski, "Ein Gott der Gewalt?" in Ilse Müllner et al (eds), *Gottes Name(n). Zum Gedenken an Erich Zenger*, HBS 71 (Freiburg: Herder, 2012), 11-33, 24.

The use of harmful language is clearly a form of aggression against the psalmist. Hence we are dealing mainly with psychological terror. The Psalm belongs to a group of Psalms where violence is not the experience of physical aggression but found in the use of words. [14]

A special challenge can be seen in verse 11. The drastic picture seems to testify to a brutal desire for vengeance. But if we note that all the metaphors used before do not seem to relate to real bloodshed, we may see in this verse another metaphor to predict the expected fate of the evildoers—a sign of hope for the psalmist and of warning for the evildoers: their actions will rebound upon themselves.[15] In his article, Hossfeld directs our attention to the headline of the Psalm, which is the same in Psalms 57 and 59 and shows that the request for the destruction of the enemies has been toned down, at least as far as the psalmist is concerned.[16] Here, we can see an example already in Old Testament times of the wish to avoid an impression of brutal vengeance.

The chiastic structure of the Psalm puts verse 7 at its center: in this way, the cry for help from God marks the aim of the Psalm. The focus is clearly on the desire that enemies will thereafter be unable to use their destructive language against the psalmist.

Psalm 137

In contrast to Psalm 58, in Psalm 137 we find a popular lament that can be dated to the time after the Babylonian exile. Again, the suffering caused by words pronounced by the people's enemies is the constitutive motif. The oppressors' invitation to sing songs of joy about Zion as the people grieve about their deportation from Jerusalem (v. 3) can only be understood as mockery.[17] But in this Psalm, we are confronted with more serious physical violence than was the case in Psalm 58,[18] especially in relation to the destruction of Jerusalem—of the city, its buildings, the land and its inhabitants—and the experience of deportation. The memory evoked at the request of the sons of Edom in verse 7 is again a reminder of physical violence.

---

[14] See among others Psalm 35:21; 52:4.

[15] See Janowski, op. cit. (note 13), 25.

[16] Frank-Lothar Hossfeld, "Das göttliche Strafgericht in Feind- und Fluchpsalmen: der Psalmenbeter zwischen eigener Ohnmacht und dem Schrei nach göttlicher Parteilichkeit," in Andreas Holzem and Bernd Wegner (eds), *Krieg und Christentum* (Paderborn: Schöningh, 2009), 130.

[17] For this phenomenon of mockery, cf. Psalm 79:10; 115:2.

[18] See Psalm 149:6, where we find the combination of physicall and psychological violence (in the form of harsh words) in one verse!

We also encounter some indirect violent language in this Psalm. This already begins in verse 1 with the mention of crying, assuming its reason. Verse 8 speaks about Babel in the Masoretic version as *hasch^{e}dudah*. The use of this grammatical form of the passive indicates that Babel itself is destroyed at the time that it was most powerful. As in Amos 5:2, we find the expected fate of Babel anticipated here.[19]

The *'aschre* in verses 8 and 9 formally indicates congratulation. The semantic connotation in verses 8 and 9 however suggests that it is being used ironically, as at the start of a curse. A similar case is the use of *schillem* and *gamal* in verse 8. The originally neutral words become expressions of violence because of their context. The same thing occurs in verse 7 with the verb *sachar*. The memory is to be understood as an active one leading to God's action against Edom. The sentence is therefore an indirect curse.

The request in verse 9 however is very direct. On the surface, it seems very cruel, but when we take a look at the hidden aim, the focus shifts. Young children represent the future of a people. Their annihilation is equivalent to the annihilation of the actual oppressors' power.[20] It seems that the psalmist saw this instrument as the only sure chance for the safe survival of his own people.

Also in Psalm 58 and other Psalms, the psalmist asks for help from God. We see no invitation to violence in self-defense. The call for violence is not the same as its execution. It may be that the request will avoid further excesses of physical as well as psychological violence.

Conclusion

We have met with quite different reactions to experiences of violence recounted in Psalms. My own approach as well as that of most of modern scholars neglect anti-Judaism and avoids a Christological interpretation. But is it a Lutheran one?

In modern Western Protestant tradition, the scholarly interpretation of the Bible has been and is until now mainly part of scholarly historical work

---

[19] See Norbert Rabe, *"Tochter Babel, die verwüstete!" (Psalm 137,8)-textkritisch betrachtet*, BN 78 (1995), 84-103. Therefore it is not necessary to change the text in active *haschod^{e}dah* as is sometimes proposed.

[20] Cf. Andreas Michel, *Gott und Gewalt gegen Kinder im Alten Testament*, FAT 37 (Tübingen: Siebeck Mohr, 2006) 197: "Bei der 'Totalvernichtung' von Ps 137,9 liegt, ebenso wie bei jener von Jer 51,20-23, der Akzent auf der rhetorischen Vermittlung der Aussage, nicht so sehr auf der geschichtlich nachprüfbaren Realisierung ... Intendiert ist die Annihilierung des Gegners als Gegner."

looking at (the historical) development of texts and at how they and their authors were rooted in their own times. This is not necessarily connected with the question of normative validity. As long as Christians think about the great historical gap, especially between Old Testament and contemporary times, the phenomenon of being affected existentially—as individuals as well as groups—by difficult biblical texts is clouded.[21] Parallel to these approaches, we have a tradition of reading the Bible in our churches which suggests that the reader is being directly addressed by God. Problematic texts, especially those dealing with violence, are often omitted from the canon of texts used in parishes. So, a thoughtful reading of these texts is often lacking, sometimes combined with prejudices. There is often a lack of knowledge about scholarly work, its implications and results.

In most cases, discussion of violence in connection with the Old Testament—including divine violence—has physical violence in mind. A close look at Psalms, however, reveals that in many—I think even in most—cases, the topic of experienced violence is focused on the psychological terror exerted by violent language.[22] The plea for God's intervention against the enemies is often, as in Psalm 58, a request to destroy the tools of speech. There is no doubt that the aim is not to destroy the enemy itself but to make sure that with God's help, the enemy can no longer harm the psalmist by his/her language. Seen from a textually pragmatic perspective, these Psalms give a sort of hope to desperate people who no longer see a possibility of saving themselves from the—verbal—attacks of their enemies.

Violence is a topic which occurs astonishingly often in the Book of Psalms, whether it is the experience of violence and/or requests for violence to be practiced. Both are connected to each other. The plea for God's violent intervention is consistent with the fact of people having been themselves the victims of violence.

Violence is evoked mainly in individual and group laments in the form of complaints and/or requests rooted in a desperate situation from which there is no way out. These expressions are much more human reactions

---

[21] Whereas scholars like Rolf Rendtorff who regard themselves as committed to the canonical approach, not only offer less problems when considering the historical gap but are closer to the traditional Jewish approach of the Hebrew Bible. The recent proposals within and beyond the exegesis also enable a more significant re-presentation of the biblical texts, such as can be found in Luther's emphasis on the *pro nobis*. Cf. amongst others, Volker Leppin, "Vorlesungen," in Volker Leppin and Gury Schneider-Ludorff (eds), *Das Luther-Lexikon* (Regensburg: Bückle & Böhm, 2014), 728–34.

[22] See the discussion on the relation between language and violence amongst others in Burkhard Liebsch, *Subtile Gewalt. Spielräume sprachlicher Verletzbarkeit* (Weilerswist: Velbrück Wissenschaft, 2007).

to people's own catastrophic situation than God's words to men or women. The canonization of these texts accepts them as one way of speaking to God, as one expression of despair about one's enemies. This did not end with the canonization of the Bible. This context should not be forgotten in judging the texts. We are far from a decrease of violence in our times therefore texts like these are a great gift to bring all the suffering and bad feelings resulting from it before God.

The difficulty in attributing an (exact) date to most of the Psalms lets us see on the one hand that the Psalms often underwent a gradual process of formation. We can never exactly determine their social and historical context. On the other hand—and this is more important for me—most Psalms are not connected to a concrete place and/or time and therefore express a broad spectrum of the experiences of human beings over time and space. This insight supports Luther's approach to the Psalms as prayers that are given to us, to people, as has been understood since his "Operationes in Psalmos."

Psalms take human beings as a whole seriously, with the whole reality of their experiences and feelings in the here and now[23]—as do other biblical texts in the Old Testament. It seems that the psalmists had more insights into psychological processes than did many of our Christian brothers and sisters who, over centuries of church history, judged that thoughts and words on violence in the Psalms were inappropriate to Christian thinking and ethics. The anthropological perspective should not be forgotten, nor be played off by a Christological or New Testament approach.[24]

The New Testament writers also understood the anthropological background, the suffering from injustice, unfair attacks and situations with no way out, Like the psalmists, they did not envisage salvation in human actions but trusted in God's mighty action (see the apocalyptical texts in the New Testament, which are not free from expectations of violence either) (Mt 24; Rev 9; 12).

An important point concerning the approach in the perspective of the New Testament is the danger that, by stating that only this New Testament perspective is adequate for real understanding of the Psalms (and other Old Testament texts), Israel, that is, the Jewish people, is abandoned and replaced. The first readers and speakers of the Psalms were Jewish men

---

[23] See Hossfeld, op. cit. (note 16), 131: "Der manche Christen so irritierende konkretgeschichtliche Immanenzbezug."

[24] Ralf Koerrenz, "Hermeneutik des Lernens. Der anthropologische Wirklichkeitsbezug der biblischen Überlieferung," in Ingo Baldermann et al, *Biblische Hermeneutik*, JBTh 12, (Neukirchen-Vluyn: Neukirchener Verlagsgesellschaft 1998), 221–42, here 222.

and women; the first followers of Christ were Jewish men and women living in the world of the Psalms, hearing them, using them to express their own experiences and feelings. When Luther—and often his followers over the centuries until today—speaks in his interpretation of the fifty-eighth Psalm of the Jewish people as generating their own end by denying Christ, comparing the Jews with evildoers, he does not take the form of the Psalm seriously. In his interpretation, a lament about a situation of personal despair over enemies' attacks becomes a statement on Jews, their theology and God's guaranteed punishment. It seems that it is easier to denounce the Jews, to represent the dubious thesis that the church replaces Israel as God's people than to ask God to destroy them. It is obvious that this assessment of their *Wirkungsgeschichte* did much to prepare the lack of resistance in many regions during the Nazi period and perhaps may help to inspire other forms of hate-speech relating to other nationalities, sexual orientations and so forth, partially inspired by misunderstanding texts such as Psalm 58.

The role and effect of language are of special importance in such cases of discrimination and racism, and Luther himself frequently emphasizes the destructive power of language.[25] It would be misguided to focus only on Luther's anti-Jewish statements in relation to the topic of violence in the Psalms. On the contrary, we could apply this criticism to Luther's overall approach to the Psalms, from his "Dictata super Psalterium" to his "Operationes in Psalmos."[26] As his approach developed, it shifted its emphasis from a firmly Christological interpretation to one that let the reading turn into personal prayer. That shall be particularly clear in the interpretation of Psalm 6.[27]

When we take Scripture seriously as a yardstick of our theological reflection,[28] we should not forget its critical potential that allows and even forces us to question our previous approaches. In this perspective, it is really a necessary form of Lutheran hermeneutic that links us to Luther's own critical insights, based on taking Scripture itself seriously, seeing the aforementioned development in his hermeneutical approach to Psalms from a more Christological approach to one which is rather reader-orientated (*pro nobis*). His own freedom *vis-à-vis* given exegetical and theological au-

---

[25] See Albrecht Beutel, "Sprache/Sprachverständnis," in op. cit. (note 21), 652-55.
[26] See Gerhard Hammer and Manfred Biersack, *Operationes in Psalmos 1519-1521: Historisch-theologische Einleitung* (Köln: Böhlau, 1981), 413f.
[27] Cf. Archiv zur Weimarer Ausgabe der Werke Martin Luthers 2, 362,12.
[28] Marianne Grohmann, *Aneignung der Schrift. Wege einer christlichen Rezeption jüdischer Hermeneutik* (Neukirchen-Vluyn: Neukirchener Verlagsgesellschaft, 2000), 10.

thorities, referring among others to the principle of *sola scriptura*, invites us to question the interaction between seemingly contrary texts such as Psalm 58 and the command to love our enemies (Ex 23:4f; Mt 5:43f.) as well as the challenges of our time.[29] In this context, Luther' approaches to ethical questions play an important role.[30]

---

[29] See Weymann, op. cit. (note 8), 24ff.
[30] Cf. Antti Raunio, "Ethik," in op. cit. (note 21), 204–211.

Between Praise and Lament. Remarks on the Development of the Hebrew Psalms

Urmas Nõmmik

Lament or complaint Psalms belong to the most important biblical genres, particularly because of their potential to address people in different times and places, not to mention their role in bringing together the Old and New Testaments (cf. Psalm 22).[1] As lament Psalms, they often offer evidence that lament and praise belong closely together. For some time, scholars have been discussing the reason for the change of mood in the complaint Psalms. This, in turn, is related to the place of the lament Psalms in Israel's cultural and religious history. In order for us to discuss this and to pave the way to reaching hermeneutical conclusions relevant for us nowadays, it is appropriate to take a look at the *Sitz im Leben* [life setting] of the Psalms, both in the monarchic period of Israel and Judah and in the Second Temple period. We will draw attention to some new insights from the study of ancient Near Eastern texts as well as the perspective of diachronic research that might help us to clarify or at least broaden the spectrum of the use of lament Psalms in various situations today.

The monarchic period

Critical scholars unanimously agree that the Psalm literature of the Israelite and Judahite monarchies is fragmentary and often difficult to identify and analyze. Nevertheless, the existence of two Psalm genres—hymns and individual laments—in pre-exilic times is certain. Several pre-exilic hymns have been detected and, in a number of cases, the debate concerns only details, not their general dating. Regarding the individual lament Psalms, it is generally agreed that the roots of this genre can be traced back to the monarchic period, possibly even further, but the problem that

---

[1] See Anni Hentschel and Craig R. Koester (also Ps 69) in this volume.

has been discussed at length and which I would like briefly to focus on in the following, is the question of their original setting.

One can be sure about the general cultic framework of the lament Psalms since several of their constitutive elements, such as the petition for God's help, suggest a ritual or at least a prayer. In a nutshell, according to the most popular theories the Psalms of individual lament have been applied in the case of definite distress: certain Psalms for certain situations of acute distress. Furthermore, most studies on the complaint Psalms have focused on the change of tone at the end of many lament Psalms, the so-called *Stimmungsumschwung* [mood swing]. According to one theory this can be explained from the psychological perspective as an immanent change to confidence during the prayer or, according to another perspective, by the provoking effect of some cultic ritual, an offering, receiving an oracle of salvation, etc.[2]

The fact that the available texts are unfortunately not accompanied by liturgical agendas has been problematic for all theories. Almost every kind of cultic explanation that does not directly contradict the Psalm text is possible. Why then do we not look for further alternatives?

Some preliminary critical observations concerning the Psalm literature of the monarchic era are in order. First, the contexts of the court and the temple suggest that that which was recorded was of considerable significance for the cult. Secondly, it is most probable that everything was written either by the court or temple scribes and not by independent or semi-independent religious groups as it was possible during the Second Temple period. During the monarchic era, it is probable that the cultic texts were used in a stable and regular context. An institutionalized cult itself, as it is the case in the monarchic surroundings, presupposes a regular usage of religious literature. Significant texts in regular contexts do not exclude their use to help certain persons in definite situations of distress but calls for additional theories about their application.

---

[2] Cf. the standard lexica, e.g., Rainer Albertz, "Gebet. II. Altes Testament," in *Theologische Realenzyklopädie* 12 (Berlin, New York: de Gruyter, 1984), 34–42, here 35: "... hier zeigt sich ein Transzendieren der Notsituation im Verlauf des Betens: Indem der Leidende seine Not vor Gott bringt, streckt er sich in die Zukunft hinein auf die Wende seiner Not hin aus ..." (cf. 39f.). Or, Henning Graf Reventlow, "Gebet. II. Altes Testament," in *Religion in Geschichte und Gegenwart*[4] 3 (Tübingen: Mohr Siebeck, 2000), 485–88, here 486: "Konkreter Anlaß sind Nöte wie Krankheit, Anfechtung durch Feinde, Schuld. Entscheidende, ursächliche Not ist die Beklagte Ferne Gottes." And in a more differentiated way, Friedhelm Hartenstein, "Psalmen/Psalter. II. Altes Testament. b) Gattungen," in *Religion in Geschichte und Gegenwart*[4] 6 (Tübingen: Mohr Siebeck, 2003), 1763–66, here 1765. It should not be forgotten that the secondary, often very late Psalm titles suggest a distinct *Sitz im Leben*.

It can be maintained that hymns, particularly YHWH's kingship Psalms, could be used regularly, as is the case with hymnic texts at our weekly church services. Several regular annual, monthly and weekly feasts can be reconstructed for the Second Temple period (Deut 16; Lev 23; Num 28, etc.)—the vestiges of some of which certainly date back to the monarchic era. Contrary to hymns, it is difficult to imagine that lament Psalms were used in a regular context but their considerable scope compared to other forms of pre-exilic literature suggests their active application. They are increasingly significant when considering the problem of prayers and pleas—a phenomenon that indisputably belonged to the life of pre-exilic communities. At the textual level, they are not represented to a comparable extent: prayer and plea mostly belong to lament Psalms, or at least can be found in the vicinity of longer complaint texts. Was complaint often regarded as organically belonging to the prayer and vice versa? Were complaints then performed regularly as prayers most probably were?

Perhaps a reference to Job's dialogue would help to clarify our question. Already in its earliest form, the Joban poem made extensive use of other genres, particularly the complaint (Psalms).[3] The ancient Near Eastern parallels of "Joban literature" demonstrate the equally prestigious position of the complaint. However, despite the fact that we do not know the setting of this skeptical complaint and wisdom literature, it would be rather complicated to maintain a situation of actual distress when its purpose is performance. A theatrical drama is possible, but everybody agrees that Job's poem cannot be handled as simple entertainment—if it were a drama to be performed in front of an audience, then because of the need to consider and discuss existential matters. Death and suffering were far more important than monarchic ideology that is nowadays sometimes considered the only trigger for the emergence of early texts in Israel and Judah. Even the standard Epic of Gilgamesh, which undoubtedly participated in the royal ideologies of the ancient Near East, in its second half engages with the problem of death.

Should we then look for a more existential *Sitz im Leben* of the lament Psalms? Was human life considered as permanent hardship, and were complaints addressing this problem? Those questions are accompanied by the

---

[3] Cf. especially Claus Westermann, *The Structure of the Book of Job. A Form-Critical Analysis* (Philadelphia: Fortress Press, 1981), 31-70, and also Georg Fohrer, *Das Buch Hiob*, Kommentar zum Alten Testament 16 (Gütersloh: Gütersloher Verlagshaus Gerd Mohn, 1963), 70, 68-86; regarding the speeches of the friends, Urmas Nõmmik, *Die Freundesreden des ursprünglichen Hiobdialogs. Eine form- und traditionsgeschichtliche Studie*. Beihefte zur Zeitschrift der alttestamentlichen Wissenschaft 410 (Berlin, New York: Walter de Gruyter, 2010), 218-23, 292.

critical observation that the distress described in the lament Psalms is often not unambiguous; traditional phrases, conventional word-pairs and metaphors are strung together in order vividly to describe the distress in a rather exemplary way. To compare it once more with countless descriptions of misery in Joban literature, distress as such is significant, not its specific character.

Alternatives can be found in the scholarly works on Mesopotamian texts or comparing them with the Old Testament Psalms. I would like to mention only a few but relevant impulses from the studies of the last decades.

As demonstrated by Stefan M. Maul and Annette Zgoll, certain texts, including the complaint Psalms, were used in apotropaic rites. The *eršahunga* prayers fulfilled the purpose of calming the heart of an angry deity.[4] The gigantic series of *namburbi* texts were composed for respective rituals of a judicial procedure against a sinister omen or omen indicator or, put briefly, for counter-rituals against evil fate.[5] King Assurbanipal applied those rites and texts extensively in order to influence the future in his favor.

> Believing that he [the king—U.N.] had already eliminated all possible future evil before it could even take shape surely bolstered the king's self-confidence, strengthened his resolution, and steeled his will to fight. In this sense, "release rituals" were by no means a hindrance born of superstition. Instead, they were a stabilizing factor in the history of the Assyrian Empire.[6]

Annette Zgoll noticed a similar need for appeasing and channeling divine anger through the complaint parts of the *ninmešara* songs,[7] which in line 99 call themselves *šir kuĝakeš* "the song of determining fate."[8] She further suggests that the *šu'ila* prayers also serve to cope with the unpredictability

---

[4] Cf. Stefan M. Maul, *"Herzberuhigungsklagen." Die sumerisch-akkadischen Eršahunga-Gebete* (Wiesbaden: Harrassowitz, 1988), 27.

[5] Stefan M. Maul, "How the Babylonians Protected Themselves against Calamities Announced by Omens," in Tzvi Abusch and Karel van der Toorn (eds), *Mesopotamian Magic. Textual, Historical, and Interpretative* Perspectives, Ancient Magic and Divination 1 (Groningen: STYX Publications, 1999), 123–29, here 123.

[6] Ibid., 129; cf. Stefan M. Maul, *Zukunftsbewältigung. Eine Untersuchung altorientalischen Denkens anhand der babylonisch-assyrischen Löserituale* (Namburbi), Baghdader Forschungen 18 (Mainz am Rhein: Philipp von Zabern, 1994), 225.

[7] Annette Zgoll, *Der Rechtsfall der En-hedu-Ana im Lied nin-me-šara*, Alter Orient und Altes Testament 246 (Münster: Ugarit-Verlag 1997), 116, cf. 435: "Die Funktion des Textes *NMS* ist also nicht Prophylaxe gegen den göttlichen Zorn, vielmehr Erregung und Kanalisierung dieser Zornesmacht."

[8] Ibid., 137.

of the future[9] and pointed to the prophylactic function of the lament ceremonies from the Ur III period, "Weeping and lamenting are functionalized also here, are a means of appeasing the divine anger /.../."[10] In Mesopotamia the apotropaic rituals seem to have been widespread.

Relying on Maul's and Zgoll's studies, particularly those based on *namburbi* texts, Oswald Loretz[11] interpreted individual lament Psalms as representative of the so-called *rîb* pattern. He suggests a judicial procedure between the complainer and the omen indicator, with an oracle from some important deity such as the sun-god, accompanied by ritual prophylactic activity against distress and the omen indicator. In the ancient Near East, a bad omen required quick counteraction, since the person targeted by the omen was excluded from the deity's custody or even threatened by it.

Chances of proving claims such as Loretz's are slight since the narrow text basis does not allow definite conclusions.[12] A further finding of Stefan M. Maul helps us to take a step further. He edited a fragment of a Babylonian cultic calendar from the sun sanctuary in Sippar (BM 50503 [82-3-23, 1494]) together with data on recited songs and prayers, including the lament Psalms.[13] The context of the cultic calendar underlines the regular cultic performance of the lament Psalms and, as Erhard S. Gerstenberger suggests, this kind of "analogy of Babylonian incantation prayers embedded

---

[9] Cf. Annette Zgoll, *Die Kunst des Betens. Form und Funktion, Theologie und Psychagogik in babylonisch-assyrischen Handerhebungsgebeten an Ištar*, Alter Orient und Altes Testament 308 (Münster: Ugarit-Verlag, 2003), 268: "Diesem Gebet [Ištar 1 – *U.N.*] liegt die allgemeine Erkenntnis eigener Machtlosigkeit und Verwiesenheit auf die Gottheit zugrunde. [...] Beten heißt gegenüber der Zukunft, sich vorzusehen vor dem Unvorhersehbaren, ist ein Versuch, die Zukunft zu terminieren."

[10] "Weinen und Klagen sind auch hier funktionalisiert, sind ein Mittel, den Gotteszorn zu beruhigen /.../" Zgoll, op. cit. (note 7), 116, note 486; transl. – *U.N.*). Cf. Maul, op. cit. (note 4), 27.

[11] Oswald Loretz, *Psalmstudien. Kolometrie, Strophik und Theologie ausgewählter Psalmen.* Beihefte zur Zeitschrift für die alttestamentliche Wissenschaft 309 (Berlin, New York: de Gruyter, 2002), 131-170, and Oswald Loretz, *Götter–Ahnen–Könige als gerechte Richter. Der "Rechtsfall" des Menschen vor Gott nach altorientalischen und biblischen Texten*, Alter Orient und Altes Testament 290 (Münster: Ugarit-Verlag, 2003), 9-210.

[12] Cf. William S. Morrow, *Protest Against God. The Eclipse of a Biblical Tradition*, Hebrew Bible Monographs 4 (Sheffield: Sheffield Phoenix Press, 2007), 47-48.

[13] Stefan M. Maul, "Gottesdienst im Sonnenheiligtum zu Sippar," in Barbara Böck et al (eds), *Munuscula Mesopotamica. Festschrift für Johannes Renger*, Alter Orient und Altes Testament 267 (Münster: Ugarit-Verlag, 1999), 285-316, especially 309-11. I am grateful to Dr Amar Annus for pointing this article out to me.

in extensive ritual prescriptions" should not be disregarded.[14] Whereas distress seldom comes upon people regularly, the performance of laments had some other function. In some way, it was probably prophylactic, but it also relates to existential confidence. It is no coincidence that the complaint to the sun god Shamash dominates; Maul explains this with the rising of the sun from the netherworld that was especially prayed for by the people of the ancient Near East.[15] If we add the fact that the morning was (and is) the moment of overcoming chaos and threat, we can fully understand that sunrise is also the moment that instills confidence for the whole day.[16]

A door to another hermeneutical perspective can be opened: what matters here is not acute distress but potential distress that should be dealt with prophylactically. According to the above observations on complaint Psalms, Joban literature and Mesopotamian complaint literature, it is likely that distress was and can be handled as something constantly threatening human life, as one of the existential issues, since distress in the lament Psalms emerges from an immediate threat to life. Maul puts it as follows:

> The psychological effects which the forecasting of the future had on those who believed must by no means be underestimated: an ill-defined apprehensiveness in the face of the menaces of an uncertain future wherein at its worst one is at the mercy of every chaotic power imaginable, gives way to a delimited fear of a known and hence understandable threat. Such fear can be controlled since it refers to a concrete, familiar, perhaps even already experienced events.[17]

For ancient religions, an obvious way to solve existential anxiety was a ritual, in many cases an apotropaic ritual. Those rituals needed texts and the lament Psalms certainly suggest themselves for similar rituals in Israel. The alternative way was a drama, a provocative performance of a distress

---

[14] Erhard S. Gerstenberger, "Modes of Communication with the Divine in the Hebrew Psalter," in C. L. Crouch et al (eds), *Mediating Between Heaven and Earth. Communication with the Divine in the Ancient Near East*, Library of Hebrew Bible/Old Testament Studies 566 (London, New York: T&T Clark, 2012), 93–113, here 95, note 7.
[15] Maul, op. cit. (note 13), 310.
[16] Cf. especially Bernd Janowski, *Rettungsgewißheit und Epiphenie des Heils. Das Motiv der Hilfe Gottes "am Morgen" im Alten Orient und im Alten Testament*, Band I: Alter Orient. Wissenschaftliche Monographien zum Alten und Neuen Testament 59 (Neukirchen-Vluyn: Neukirchener Verlag, 1989), 184: "Die Welt ist nach alttestamentlicher Auffassung nicht eine Welt prästabilierter Harmonie, sondern eine Welt, die besonders in der Nacht, aber auch in den kritischen Lebensmomenten wie Krankheit, Feindbedrängnis, Rechtsnot und Todesgeschick ins Chaos zurücksinken kann, die aber jeden Morgen von Jahwes Schöpferwirken neu gefestigt wird."
[17] Maul, op. cit. (note 5), 123.

situation, through which the persons taking part either as performers or immediate audience experience a distress situation and consciously or unconsciously reflect it. This reflection is of immeasurable value for one's life and coping with a real distress situation. In general, it has a certain stabilizing effect on society.[18]

Important at this point is the affirmation of trust and praise often expressed in hymnic terms in the second part of the Hebrew lament Psalms. After having experienced the dramatized distress situation or performed ritual, participants leave the sphere of anxiety. Perhaps it can be compared to the rituals involving a clay image of the harbinger in the *namburbi* ritual:

> The fears had become a concrete object with which one could deal and which one could treat as an opponent while respecting the gods' decision to apportion a bad fate. /.../ The harbinger on the other hand was to be condemned and thereupon destroyed.[19]

Those who participate in rituals experience a specific intimacy with God. Trust and praise cement existential confidence. It is self-evident that the past tense is used while mentioning distress and assuring the fact of being heard by God in lament Psalms. Psalms 3:5-6 [numbers according to Masoretic text 6-7] says:

> Me, I lay down and slept;
> I woke again, for YHWH sustains me.
> I am not afraid of tens of thousands of people
> who have set themselves against me all around.[20]

THE SECOND TEMPLE PERIOD

Hundreds of years of evolution of the complaint Psalms and changing historical-religious contexts might suggest that the complaint Psalms have not always been applied in the same way. We should recall that many lament Psalms are not precise enough in describing distress; therefore, we

---

[18] Cf. once more with *namburbi* rituals, see note 6 above.
[19] Maul, op. cit. (note 5), 125-26.
[20] Modified translation of NRSV. Cf. Maul, op. cit. (note 13), 310: "In dem regelmäßigen Götterkult in Sippar ist freilich nicht die Angst vor einem realen Feind vorherrschend. Vielmehr steht die dunkle, fast archetypisch zu nennende Furcht im Vordergrund, daß der Gott, der schützend seine Hand über das Gemeinwesen legt, die ihm anvertrauten Menschen auf immer verlassen könne."

are not able to reconstruct their exact contexts. Sometimes the description is too general or a cluster of rather different calamities appears, and an attempt to visualize the distinct situation behind the text fails.

Furthermore, the research on Psalms in recent decades, starting with Fritz Stolz, has revealed the post-cultic milieu of several or most of the Psalms.[21] Notwithstanding the debates and given the complexities of reconstructions,[22] many earlier lament Psalms have been reworked for different settings. Some ritual accompanying the reciting of such reshaped Psalms is not excluded, but decisive is the new phenomenon of repetitive distress descriptions within the framework of one and the same Psalm, the phenomenon of pessimistic Psalms with reluctant expressions of praise (i.e., Psalm 39), and the phenomenon of "lament" Psalms that use the traditional elements in an unconventional order.

These observations suggest a different setting and attitude toward distress. Psalm 22, which has been intensively studied from a form-critical perspective, can serve as an example of such a text. It consists of several parts that do not originate from the same hand and none of which is likely to date from the pre-exilic period. The second part, occasionally called Psalm 22B,[23] is younger than the first.[24] The first half of the Psalm

---

[21] Fritz Stolz, *Psalmen im nachkultischen Raum*, Theologische Studien 129 (Zürich: Theologischer Verlag, 1983).

[22] Cf. e.g., Erhard S. Gerstenberger, *Psalms, Part 1 with an Introduction to Cultic Poetry*, The Forms of the Old Testament Literature 14 (Grand Rapids: Eerdmans, 1988), 9-21, and Katherine J. Dell, " "I Will Solve My Riddle to the Music of the Lyre" (Psalm XLIX 4 [5]): A Cultic Setting for Wisdom Psalms?," in *Vetus Testamentum* 54 (2004), 445-58.

[23] So Bernhard Duhm, *Die Psalmen*, Kurzer Hand-Kommentar zum Alten Testament 14 (Freiburg i.B.: J.C.B. Mohr [Paul Siebeck], 1899), 68ff. and others. It is not excluded that instead of verses 23ff. there was originally some kind of hymnic text but it cannot be reconstructed any more.

[24] Concerning the date of Psalm 22A, cf. Hermann Gunkel, *Die Psalmen*, 5. Auflage [Nachdr. 1926] (Göttingen: Vandenhoeck & Ruprecht, 1968), 95; Hartmut Gese, "Psalm 22 und das Neue Testament. Der älteste Bericht vom Tode Jesu und die Entstehung des Herrenmahles," in *Zeitschrift für Theologie und Kirche* 65(1968), 1-22, here 13, note 24; Fritz Stolz, "Psalm 22: Alttestamentliches Reden vom Menschen und neutestamentliches Reden von Jesus," in *Zeitschrift für Theologie und Kirche* 77(1980), 129-48, here 133; Marko Marttila, *Collective Reinterpretation in the Psalms. A Study of the Redaction History of the Psalter*, Forschungen zum Alten Testament II 3 (Tübingen: Mohr Siebeck, 2006), 85ff. However, dating into the pre-exilic time or maintaining its strong influence is popular, cf. Herrmann Spieckermann, *Heilsgegenwart. Eine Theologie der Psalmen*, Forschungen zur Religion und Literatur des Alten und Neuen Testaments 148 (Göttingen: Vandenhoeck & Ruprecht, 1989), 252; Fredrik Lindström, *Suffering and Sin. Interpretations of Illness in the Individual Complaint Psalms*, Coniectanea Biblica, Old Testament

is likely to have existed for some time as an independent text, but it can be divided into an earlier Psalm and its extrapolation. The text can be reconstructed as follows:[25]

1b [2]	<u>My God, my God</u>, why have you forsaken me?
	Why are you so far from helping me, from the words of my groaning?
2 [3]	<u>O my God</u>, I cry by day, but you do not answer;
	and by night, but find no rest.
3 [4]	<u>Yet you</u> are holy, enthroned
	on the praises of Israel.[26]
4 [5]	In you our ancestors trusted;
	they trusted, and you delivered them.
5 [6]	To you they cried, and were saved;
	in you they trusted, and were not put to shame.
6 [7]	<u>But I</u> am a worm, and not human;
	scorned by others, and despised by the people.
7 [8]	All who see me mock at me;
	they make mouths at me, they shake their heads:
8 [9]	"*He trusted on*[27] Yhwh; let him deliver–
	let him rescue the one in whom he delights!"
9 [10]	<u>Yet</u> it was <u>you</u> who took me from the womb;
	from my safety[28], my mother's breast.
10 [11]	On you I was cast from my birth,
	and since my mother bore me you have been my God.
11 [12]	Do not be far from me,
	for trouble is near!
	– and there is no one to help.
12 [13]	Many bulls encircle me,
	strong bulls of Bashan surround me;
13 [14]	they open wide their mouths at me,
	[like][29] a ravening and roaring lion.

Series 37 (Stockholm: Almqvist & Wiksell, 1994), 77; Frank-Lothar Hossfeld, in Hossfeld and Erich Zenger, *Die Psalmen I. Psalm 1-50*, Die Neue Echter Bibel 29 (Würzburg: Echter, 1993), 145. As regards Psalm 22B, the majority places it in the Hellenistic period.

[25] Translation adapted from NRSV, slightly modified; verse numbers according to NRSV, the Masoretic verse numbers in [].
[26] It is not sure that the verse is complete; cf. especially Duhm, op. cit. (note 23), 68f; Gunkel, ibid., 95.
[27] Imperative is emended to perfect; so a number of commentaries.
[28] Ancient translations and Cairo geniza fragments presuppose this emendation (BHS).
[29] Preposition "like" is added (BHS).

14 [15]	I am poured out like water,
	and all my bones are out of joint;
	my heart is like wax;
	it is melted within my breast;
15 [16]	my *mouth*[30] is dried up like a potsherd,
	and my tongue sticks to my jaws.
16 [17]	For dogs are all around me,
	a company of evildoers encircles me;
	they bind[31] my hands and feet,
15b [16b]	*they*[32] lay me in the dust of death.[33]
17 [18]	I can count all my bones,
	they stare and gloat over me;
18 [19]	they divide my clothes among themselves,
	and for my clothing they cast lots.
19 [20]	<u>But you</u>, Yhwh, do not be far away!
	O my help, come quickly to my aid!
20 [21]	Deliver my soul from the sword,
	my life from the power of the dog!
21 [22]	Save me from the mouth of the lion!
	From the horns of the wild oxen – you answer me.

Two layers differ slightly in their poetic form and content. Four strophes (vv. 1b-11 [2-12], 19-21 [20-22]) of mostly three bicola (vv. 3-5 [4-6], 6-8 [7-9], 9-11 [10-12a];[34] 19-21 [20-22]), with an anacrusis at the beginning (underlined above), form the earlier Psalm. A number of keywords used repeatedly support this reconstruction of the first layer. Its aim has been lament and plea, but it attracts attention that strophes complaining distress (vv. 1b-2 [2-3], 6-8 [7-9]) alternate twice with strophes expressing confidence (vv. 35 [4-6], 9-10 [10-11]), and that there is no hymn at the

---

[30] The word "my strength" is emended to "my mouth"; so the majority of scholars.
[31] Cf. Hans-Joachim Kraus, *Psalmen. 1. Teilband. Psalmen 1-59*, 7. Auflage, Biblischer Kommentar zum Alten Testament 15/1 (Neukirchen-Vluyn: Neukirchener, 2003), 323.
[32] The subject is emended; cf. Duhm, op. cit. (note 23), 71; Stolz, "Psalm 22", op. cit. (note 24), 130.
[33] Even if the rearrangement of the cola is sometimes speculative, v. 15-16 [16-17] demand a solution in this direction, taking into account the parallelism; cf. esp. Duhm, op. cit. (note 23), 70f. Many consider the possibility of glosses; cf. especially Spieckermann, op cit. (note 24), 240.
[34] For several reasons, the third colon belongs to the second layer, or is a gloss; cf. Klaus Seybold, *Die Psalmen, Handbuch zum Alten Testament 1/15* (Tübingen: J.C.B. Mohr [Paul Siebeck], 1996), 96; Marttila, op. cit. (note 24), 85ff.

end, or it cannot be reconstructed. Instead, an invocation stands at the end: ʿănītānī "you answer me!"[35]

The extrapolation in vv. 12-18 [13-19] is a longer commentary and description of "trouble" ṣārā in v. 11 [12], shaped in four shorter strophes (vv. 12-13 [13-14], 14-15a [15-16a], 16+15b [17+16b], 17-18 [18-19]). Its distinct character is revealed by a number of keywords (especially in vv. 12a[13a], 14a·[15a·], 16a·[17a·], 17a[18a]), by the vice versa use of calamities (bulls, lion, dogs, enemies) from the older layer, and by a number of sound figures. The accumulation of several distresses raises the question whether an acute distress situation can imply all those elements. It seems to be a longer period of distress. And permanent distress introduces the basic problem of distance from God; cf. particularly v. 19 [20]. This seems to have been a very prominent issue in the Second Temple period, since the emergence of many Psalms and the popularity of constant editing and extrapolating of the Book of Job for instance would not be explicable. Hence, the lament in the Second Temple period is particularly conscious of the problem of permanent suffering.[36] Distress is acute and never ending.

One can speculate that the background to the Second Temple lament Psalms was a difficult socioeconomic situation, or that a severe crisis triggered a distinct shift in Psalm (and wisdom) literature. There could have been an economic downfall of many worthier, literate people,[37] combined with an emerging opposition of religious conceptions and groups in Jewish society. More likely perhaps is another social shift—if the context of the pre-exilic Psalms was the temple and court, including their ideas and problems, the setting of the post-exilic Psalms certainly excluded the royal context, and the temple background can definitely be maintained only by certain Psalms, not by all of them. The perspective of the poor and needy—and deeply religious—people reveals itself. Permanent distress is also clearly more significant here than some acute calamity.

This brings us to the question, How does one cope with the never-ending suffering in those Psalms? In Psalm 22, the statements of confidence in vv. 3-5 [4-6] and 9-10 [10-11] keep their position at the beginning of the Psalm, before the longer description of calamities starts, and carry on the vein of older lament Psalms. Secondly, it is YHWH who is addressed here, not any other god; the text even takes a more personal approach, since God is twice addressed

---

[35] With optative connotation, so Otto Kaiser, private communication.
[36] Concerning Psalm 22 especially underlined by Stolz, op. cit. (note 21), 137.
[37] Cf. the fact of many "poor" and "needy" in the Psalms, also in Psalm 22. Cf. Hossfeld, op. cit. (note 24), 145, and cf. Johannes Un-Sok Ro, "Socio-Economic Context of Post-Exilic Community and Literacy," in *Zeitschrift für die alttestamentliche Wissenschaft* 120 (2008), 519-617.

as *'attā* "You / Thee" (vv. 3[4[, 9 [10]). Only this God, and no one else, even if insufferably distant from the petitioner, dominates the world and affects human fates. In proceeding in this way, it will soon be of no importance whether distress is acute or not; much more important is a trustful relation to God and one's alignment with distress. Resignation is certainly not the ideal, but peace in confidence is. Contact to the highest God, a dialogue with God, is possible.

The most suitable means of defining one's relation to God, whether in trouble or not, is praise of God. The genre of the lament Psalm strongly suggests this. Many hymns and their fragments that can be detected from the monarchic time and short praise at the end of lament Psalms belonging already to its oldest layers are crucial elements. This was essential for both Hebrew and Mesopotamian lament texts.[38] In the later development of the lament genre, the aspect of praise becomes even more important—distress is not eliminated but overcome by praise. Hand in hand with the growth of distress descriptions and transience complaints in Hebrew Psalms, hymnic parts also increase, often within the same text. The above example of Psalm 22 provides a symptomatic case. Some time after the longer extrapolation on calamities in vv. 12-18 [13-19] and during the Second Temple period, the Psalm started growing at the end where traditionally praise ought to be found, so that probably in two or three steps communal and universal hymnic verses 22-31 [23-32] have been added.

This kind of merging of lament and praise flavored with the growth of two extremes—transience laments and universal hymns—can be particularly well shown with the help of observations about the literary development of the Book of Job. It should be noted that whereas the original dialogue of Job sharply contrasted Job's speeches with a high proportion of lament elements (e.g., Job 3) and YHWH's speeches with their hymnic tenor (38-39), during the redaction history of the book, large portions of hymns (e.g., 12:7-13:2; 26; 28) noticeably changed the dialogue. What has been underestimated in the studies on the Book of Job are the secondary parts that underline the transient nature of human life.[39] Those passages can even belong to the youngest redactions, together with the lowliness redaction, e.g., in 4:12-21, 40:3-5 and 42:1-6.[40] Furthermore, several Psalms can be evaluated as representative of

---

[38] Cf. observations on the literary development of the Akkadian versions of the prayer addressed to Ištar by Anna Elise Zernecke, "How to Approach a Deity: The Growth of a Prayer Addressed to Ištar," in Crouch et al, op. cit. (note 14), 124-43.

[39] E.g., in Job 7 and 14 there are long passages on transience but with slight shifts compared to the usual tone of Job's speeches, hence potential candidates for secondary additions.

[40] Cf. especially Jürgen van Oorschot, "Die Entstehung des Hiobbuches," in Thomas Krüger et al (eds), *Das Buch Hiob und seine Interpretation. Beiträge zum Hiob-Symposium auf dem Monte Verità vom 14.-19. August 2005*, Abhandlungen zur Theologie des Alten und Neuen Testaments 88 (Zürich: Theologischer Verlag, 2007), 165-84.

similar movements in the Psalm literature, once more, hand in hand with extensive praise in neighboring Psalms. It is particularly true of Psalm 90 which introduces the fourth book of Psalms (Ps 90–106). By specifically underlining the transient nature of all humans, the Psalm is exemplary in the whole Book of Psalms. Nevertheless, the following sixteen Psalms consist almost entirely of hymns. Among them are well-known songs of praise, such as Psalm 99, including the triple formula of holiness (vv. 3, 5, 9), and Psalm 104, probably the most beautiful hymn of divine creation in the Bible.

Conclusion

Praise and lament belong to the oldest cultic phenomena and literary genres in the ancient Near East and in the Bible. Furthermore, they have existed side by side since the earliest times. When examining the relationship between praise and lament in the Hebrew Psalms, then some critical questions concerning the setting of the pre-exilic lament Psalms and observations about the later development of lament and praise elements in Psalter lead us to conclusions which might affect the reading of Psalms today.

Taking into consideration the insights that Mesopotamian literature has revealed, the critical questions posed above in regard of the context of lament Psalms from the time of Israelite and Judahite monarchies open a door for understanding the lament Psalms in more existential terms. Distress in general, fear of being abandoned by God, overcoming of this fear, prophylaxis against calamities (not understood as part of magic) and one's preparedness for potential acute distress situations are the aspects that should be considered beside the application of lament Psalms in acute distress situations.[41] However, in all cases, praise at the end of the lament Psalm is an adequate answer to distress and existential issues. According to the nature of the Bible, the solution is of course theological: existential issues in general can be solved only through a certain relation to God. In the Old Testament, it is the trustful relationship with God and the hope that grows out of it. There is no other option than the only God, since YHWH is the creator, the only one who qualitatively differs from creatures and thus is the only possible solid basis of trust and hope.

Regarding the development of the lament Psalms one can conclude that the descriptions of the calamities grew longer and merged with transience complaints suggesting an emphasis on permanent distress, while proportionally praise became more important. Thus, in the Old Testament Psalms, human existence between praise and lament is tangible in word.

---

[41] Cf. Andrea Bieler in this volume.

One's relationship to God is already dichotomic in traditional forms of lament Psalms and increasingly ambivalent in later times. The ambivalence is not a paradox to be solved mentally but to be lived through. In the New Testament and Christianity, the existence between praise and lament will be experienced anew—for Christ, distress, acute and existential at the same time, is radicalized in death and overcome by resurrection. Gospels explicitly make use of the model of distress of Psalm 22 (cf. esp. Mk 15:24, 29-30, 34, 39 and parallels, or Mt 27:43-44, or Lk 23:35), while describing Christ's passion and death on the cross. Together with the epistles they are certainly aware of the praise at the end of the Psalm (cf. Mt 27:51-54; 28:17-20).[42] Praise comes after lament.

With regard to Lutheran hermeneutics nowadays, there is a chance to take seriously the tension between lament and praise in complaint Psalms and in larger Psalm compositions. More space could be given to the very dichotomy itself, by stressing it in sermons, readings of Psalm texts or in exegesis, whether in academic contexts or not. Being aware of how significant the struggle with anxiety was in ancient Israel and the Near East the understanding of the human condition can be deepened. The next step, God's answer to deep existential issues through Christ, can be prepared in a responsible and stimulating way. As our conclusions above stressed the significance of the dichotomy of lament and praise in ancient rituals—literally, living through the anxiety together with the emergence of hope in praise, strengthened by the interdependence of word and ritual action—we become aware of the potential of the tension between praise and lament, if performed in a way that worship attendants are mentally as well as physically involved.[43]

Particularly in the globalizing world subject to numerous challenges and the intense interchange of experiences, universal models of addressing existential issues such as in the complaint Psalms and praise of the universal God as in their hymnic parts become almost inevitable. Lutherans all over the world are encouraged to read and literally experience the complaint Psalms together in happiness or in distress.

---

[42] Refer to Anni Hentschel in this volume.

[43] A simple example would suffice: while reading complaint Psalms, together or alone, already a longer pause marking the transition from lament to praise is stimulative; cf. the meaning and function of pause in the music of Arvo Pärt.

The Vengeance Psalms as a Phenomenon of Critical Justice: The Problem of Enemies in Luther's Interpretation of Psalms

Roger Marcel Wanke

Despite his doubts and fragilities, Luther was motivated by his faith in Jesus Christ to break out of paradigms. He opposed the deformation in the church of his day and, through the transformation of the Gospel of Jesus Christ, helped to form and inform the common people and the nobles about the uniqueness of God's Word and salvation through grace and justification by faith alone. He thus set the right tone for the Protestant Reformation and the right form for a decisively evangelical church.[1]

Luther's preoccupation with the Psalms, especially at the beginning of his career, led him to the Letter to the Romans and, from there, to rediscovering the gospel and to the Reformation. Scholars agree that among the books of the Old Testament, the Book of Psalms is the one most received, accepted and interpreted in the context of the Christian community.[2]

In the following essay, I shall first examine the hermeneutics of the so-called vengeance Psalms, which are part of the Psalter. How are we to understand them? Why are they in the Psalter? Second, I shall present the vengeance Psalms as part of a phenomenon which I will refer to as critical justice. How does the psalmist remain firmly *coram Deo*, even when he does

---

[1] Roger Marcel Wanke, "Lutero—Reforma: 500 anos—Biografia," in *JOREV* (Ano 41, Jan/fev 2012 nº 747), 8-9.

[2] Cf. Erich Zenger, "Das Buch der Psalmen," in Erich Zenger et al (eds), *Einleitung in das Alte Testament*, 6. Auflage (Stuttgart: Kohlhammer, 2006), 348-70; Hans Jochen Boecker, *Das Lob des Schöpfers in den Psalmen* (Neukirchen-Vluyn: Neukirchener, 2008), 10; Siegfried Kreuzer, "Die Psalmen in Geschichte und Gegenwart. Aspekte der Erforschung und der Bedeutung der Psalmen," in Thomas Wagner, Dieter Vieweger and Kurt Erlemann (eds), *Kontexte. Biografische und forschungsgeschichtliche Schnittpunkte der alttestamentlichen Wissenschaft. Festschrift für Hans Jochen Boecker zum 80. Geburtstag* (Neukirchen-Vluyn: Neukirchener, 2008), 327-48, especially 327-28.

not experience God's justice in the face of his enemies? In a third step and concentrating on selected texts, I shall present how Luther interpreted the vengeance Psalms and attempt to understand his interpretation of them. I shall conclude by presenting some perspectives and tasks that I see as necessary and interesting for the research around Luther's hermeneutics—not only with regard to Pslams, but also to biblical interpretation in general.

How do we understand the vengeance Psalms?

If we agree with Dietrich Bonhoeffer's affirmation that "the Psalms in the Bible are also the Word of God,"[3] and with Christoph Levin, who claims that the Book of Psalms is the prayer book of the just,[4] then we must ask how we may understand the vengeance Psalms which, at first, do not look like God's Word, much less part of a prayer book of those who find themselves justified by God! For example, we read, "O God, break the teeth in their mouths; tear out the fangs of the young lions, O Lord" (Ps 58:6), or "O daughter Babylon, you devastator! Happy shall they be who pay you back what you have done to us! Happy shall they be who take your little ones and dash them against the rock!" (Ps 137:8-9). If we read these verses, we are confronted with the terrible weight of our words before God and before our enemies.

The vengeance Psalms pose one of the major hermeneutical problems in the Old Testament. How to reconcile these Psalms with Jesus' teaching in the Sermon on the Mount (Love your enemies and pray for those who persecute you [cf. Matthew 5:43-48])? Already the Torah (cf. Ex 23:4-5; Lev 19:17-18) as well as the sapiental books of the Old Testament (Prov 25:21) teach the People of Israel to deal differently with their enemies (cf. Ex 23:4-5; Lev 19:17-18), as do the sapiental books of the Old Testament (Prov 25:21) that teach us that helping the enemy is better than seeking revenge.

However, vengeance appears already on the first pages of the Bible. Cain and Abel are presented as the prototypes of human beings and their relationship is marked by hostility and vengeance. Hans Walter Wolff posits that the narrative of Cain and Abel seeks to clarify the universal problem of human interaction. Even as an assassin, Cain is protected by

---

[3] Dietrich Bonhoeffer, *Die Psalmen. Das Gebetbuch der Bibel*, 13. Auflage (Bad Salzuflen: MBK-Verlag, 1989), 9.

[4] Christoph Levin, "Das Gebetbuch der Gerechten. Literargeschichtliche Beobachtungen am Psalter," in Christoph Levin, *Fortschreibungen: Gesammelte Studien zum Alten Testament*, BZAW 316 (Berlin, New York: de Gruyter, 2003), 291-313.

God against arbitrary blood revenge.[5] The human being, created by God, is determined to love and overcome all hate.

Yet when we open the Book of Psalms, we are confronted with the prayers that really wish for vengeance and destruction of all enemies. Enemies are almost constantly present in Psalms and can be classified as enemies per se, the so-called *reša'ym*, unfaithful friends or relatives and even wild animals.[6] In general, Psalms approaches the question of enemies in two different ways: in some, the psalmist cries to God for liberation from his enemies and, in others, already experiences God's intervention; his lamentation turns into gratitude and praise of God. In others, essentially those of lament, the psalmist calls for vengeance and asks God for liberation without, however, experiencing the awaited liberation (cf. 94, 109, 137).[7]

To be surrounded by enemies is not only the lot of the People of Israel and the psalmists, but also a universal phenomenon recorded in the ancient Orient. Othmar Keel has contributed much to this reflection, especially in relation to the Psalms.[8] Drawing parallels to Babylon, Keel characterizes the vengeance Psalms as extermination prayers (*Vernichtungsgebete*), which express human impotence in the face of insecurity and injustice caused by enemies. For Keel, these Psalms are not an expression of a malevolent search for revenge, but of a situation in which the psalmist is defenseless, terribly fearful and calls on God to defend him by destroying his enemies.[9]

What remains clear is that enemies are not a taboo but openly referred to in the Book of Psalms. The psalmist openly acknowledges that he has enemies and is not cautioned that he would transgress the Torah by praying for vengeance. His desire for vengeance is not suppressed in the name of ethics, morality, or the principles that govern what today would be called politically correct behavior. Maybe it is for this reason that we are scandalized by the vengeance Psalms. Maybe this is why they are not a part of our liturgies, our church service agendas or our lectionaries. Few take the risk of preaching vengeance Psalms. This was not so in the Old Testament context. Bernd Janowski affirms that "In Israel, it was taught that the sufferer should expose his fears in prayer and not leave conflicts with enemies out of his relation with God. In this way, the 'God of justice'

---

[5] Hans Walter Wolff, *Anthropologie des Alten Testaments*, 7. Auflage (Gütersloh: Kaiser, 2002), 274-75.

[6] Cf. Bernd Janowski, *Konfliktgespräche mit Gott, Eine Anthropologie der Psalmen*, 2. durchgesehene und erweiterte Auflage (Neukirchen-Vluyn: Neukirchener, 2006), 105-108.

[7] Zenger, op.cit. (note 2), 361-62.

[8] Othmar Keel, *Die Welt der altorientalischen Bildsymbolik und das Alte Testament. Am Beispiel der Psalmen*, 5.Auflage (Göttingen: V&R, 1996), 68-97.

[9] Ibid., 85-86.

was confronted with human suffering."[10] I agree with Bernd Janowski when he writes, "We should take the problematic of enemies more seriously than by superficial reference to the commandment from Matthew 5:43 to love thy enemy."[11]

Vengeance Psalms are always laments and reflect the experience of God's absence. The lament reflects fundamental dimensions of human experience: suffering, horror, infirmity and agony as well as the desire for vengeance in the light of injustice. We only rarely find a separate approach to the vengeance Psalms in secondary literature. They are classified and presented solely as laments, either individual or collective. Some Psalms contain only brief verses in a tone of vengeance (cf. Ps 3; 139:21-22). Others, however, are long, and their content is strongly marked by such a tone (cf. Ps 12; 35; 58; 59; 69; 70; 83; 109; 137; 140). Vengeance Psalms are also prayers. The psalmist knows that he cannot do justice alone and thus delegates all the vengeance to the one who is responsible, namely God.

For modern scholars, the vengeance Psalms do not contradict the gospel and the Great Commandment. For Erich Zenger, they are expressions of faith in God's justice that delegates vengeance to God, while waiting for God's intervention.[12] For Gordon Fee and Douglas Stuart for example, these Psalms, which they call "imprecatory Psalms," are legitimate[13] not contradictory to Jesus' teachings in the Sermon on the Mount precisely because the "biblical commandment is to practice, not to feel love; they help us not to practice rage when that is what we are feeling,"[14] William Bellinger affirms,

> In these prayers against enemies, the worshipper does not destroy the enemy, but in a liberating act of faith, places the matter before God, the judge *par excellence*. God will decide, and the Psalm pleads for God to decide against enemies.[15]

---

[10] Janowski, op.cit. (note 6), 133: "In Israel hat man den Leidenden also gelehrt, seine Ängste im Gebet auszusprechen und die Konflikte mit dem Feind nicht aus der Gottesbeziehung herauszulassen. Der 'Gott der Gerechtigkeit' wurde auf diese Weise mit dem Leiden seiner Geschöpfe konfrontiert."
[11] Ibid., 101.
[12] Erich Zenger, *Ein Gott der Rache? Feindpsalmen verstehen* (Freiburg/Basel/Wien, 1994). Cf. Erich Zenger, "Fluchpsalmen," in *LThK³* 3 (1995), 1335s.
[13] Gordon Fee and Douglas Stuart, *Entendes o que lês? Um Guia para entender a Bíblia com o auxílio da Exegese e da Hermenêutica* (São Paulo: Vida Nova, 1989), 191-93. English title: *How to Read the Bible for All its Worth: A Guide to Understanding the Bible* (Grand Rapids: Zondervan, 1982).
[14] Ibid., 193.
[15] W. H. Bellinger Jr., *Psalms. Reading and Studying the Book of Praises*, 7th edition (Peabody: Hendrickson Publishers, 2009), 54.

In his booklet, *Praying with the Psalms*,[16] Dietrich Bonhoeffer, one of the great interpreters of Luther's writings especially in reference to Psalms hermeneutics, draws attention to the danger of looking solely for the possible motivation with which the psalmist prayed for vengeance. His concern was the content rather than the motivation for the prayer, and he thus affirmed that the enemies described in the vengeance Psalms are God's enemies, who attack the psalmist because of God's work. Based on the assumption that the vengeance Psalms are prayers that ask God for the fulfillment of God's justice in the judgment of sin, Bonhoeffer affirms that because of sin, no one escapes God's judgment. Bonhoeffer also interpreted the vengeance Psalms Christologically,[17] for the "divine vengeance did not strike the sinner, but only the one who did not have any sin, who entered sin's place: Jesus Christ." Thus, says Bonhoeffer, "the vengeance Psalm takes us to the cross and God's love, which forgives enemies. I cannot forgive God's enemies. Only the crucified Christ can do it [...] In Jesus Christ the fulfillment of vengeance is transformed, bestowed on all humanity."[18]

While agreeing with Bonhoeffer regarding the importance of the content of the vengeance Psalm, I nonetheless believe that the question of motivation should not be neglected. What motivates people who feel justified but abandoned by God, especially when they see justice not being done, to pray for vengeance over their enemies? These psalmists do not cease to believe in and await God's justice. For this reason, says Bonhoeffer, it is not only the innocent victims who can trust their vengeance to God, but also those who continue to believe in and await God's justice, even against all odds and faced with multifold injustice. Applying a Christological hermeneutic of the vengeance Psalms here, as Bonhoeffer did, is helpful. In the Old Testament, the psalmist did not have this Christological perspective; rather than wishing for forgiveness and salvation for his enemies, he hoped for retribution and destruction.

We can conclude that in the hermeneutics of the vengeance Psalms there seems to be a mismatch between what exegetical and theological research has presented as results and the practice in communities or, in fact, the non-practice of these prayers today. On the one hand, the exegesis on Psalms has shown the importance and value of the vengeance Psalms. On the other, this importance and value are not recognized in Christian communities, in spirituality or in their relation with the world's injustice.

---

[16] Bonhoeffer, op. cit. (note 3), 40–45.
[17] Cf. His sermon on a vengeance Psalm (Ps 58) of 11 July 1937, Dietrich Bonhoeffer, *Prédicas e Alocuções* (São Leopoldo: Sinodal, 2007), 66–72.
[18] Bonhoeffer, op. cit. (note 3), 43–44.

THE VENGEANCE PSALMS AS A
PHENOMENON OF CRITICAL JUSTICE

In 1983, Fritz Stolz, a theologian and scholar of religion, published a small book entitled, *Psalmen im nachkultischen Raum*.[19] He deserves more attention in research and contemporary discussion relating to understanding the vengeance Psalms.

Stolz is concerned with understanding two phenomena which he identifies in various Psalms and other Old Testament texts: the cultic crisis and the wisdom crisis.[20] These two categories describe and mediate order, make life in the world possible and give it meaning. In worship (cultic activity), the psalmist experiences the presence of God. God hears his prayer, forgives his sins, strengthens his life and helps him to understand his relationship to God and to other people. Wisdom, on the other hand, mediates to the psalmist the existing order between God, human beings and the world. God is in control of this world. One can know God and the world in which one lives and have a relationship with God commencing at the principle of wisdom, known as the fear of God. In wisdom, the human being is instructed about the blessing of the just and the perdition of the unfaithful. Nonetheless, the human being involved in these two categories experiences moments that are contradictory to this order guaranteed by cultic activity and wisdom. Human beings experience misfortune, natural catastrophes, infirmity, harassment, attacks from enemies, slander, powers contrary to life, including death—experiences that reveal the chaos in life. These moments isolate human beings and disintegrate the communion and life itself. But, through rituals, humans have the opportunity of coming back to life inside the order established by cultic activity and by wisdom. Just as the thanksgiving Psalms praise God for blessings received, the sorrow Psalms ask God to reestablish the lost order. In relation to people who are unjustly accused before God, they have the chance of raising their voice in prayer in the temple. Sacrifices and rites accompany their sorrow and requests for God to hear their prayers. Besides this, the accused has the opportunity to protest and to proclaim his/her innocence.[21] The questions Stolz asks in his book include:

---

[19] Fritz Stolz, *Psalmen in nachkultischen Raum*, Theologische Studien 129 (Zürich: Theologischer Verlag, 1983).

[20] Stolz analyzes the following Psalms: 77, 22, 39, 94, 73, 62, 32, 49 and 37. Outside the Book of Psalms, Stolz analyzes the Book of Job, the Confessions of Jeremiah and the worship hymns in Qumran and the Book of Ezra, as examples of the post-cultic and post-wisdom phenomena.

[21] About this, cf. Hans-Joachim Kraus, *Psalm 1*, BKAT Band XV/1 (Neukirchen-Vluyn: Neukirchener, 1961), xlviii–xlix.

What can a psalmist do when,

- In spite of his prayers and his affirmation of innocence, he is not absolved?

- He appeals to God and God seems not to hear him?

- Knowing that he is just, he experiences the punishment destined for the unfaithful?

- He sees the prosperity of the evildoer and the suffering of the just?

- He suffers injustice and is persecuted by his enemies and no longer finds God's justice to avenge him?

In this context, Antonius Gunneweg affirms that two factors explain why wisdom fell into a crisis in Israel. On the one hand, as in the ancient Orient, the wise and just are subjected to suffering. On the other, God and faith in YHWH are no longer understandable and God's actions no longer foreseeable.[22] The same applies to the cultic crisis. Instead, what is experienced here is God's absence and the challenge of continuing to believe in a God who is hidden from the psalmist.[23]

Stolz refers to this experience as the post-cultic and post-wisdom phenomenon. He defines post-cultic and post-wisdom not as chronological terms but as phenomena that exist when the cult and wisdom can no longer fulfill their role and attain their goal of establishing order in the psalmist's life. For Stolz, it is clear that this experience exists as long as cultic activity exists.[24] In the Psalms analyzed by Stolz, this is the posture and reflection of the psalmist, who remains *coram Deo* even when experiencing the *Deus absconditus*. According to Stolz, the psalmist seeks the assurance that is, of a new orientation and certainty of the saving act of God, as well as guidance on how he can live alongside the contradictory experiences of his relationship with God and with people.[25]

In this connection, it could be considered that the judiciary tradition and context of Old Testament law deal with the phenomena described by Fritz Stolz. This dimension was not approached by him however. The existence and discussion of the phenomena that could be called post-judiciary

---

[22] A.H.J. Gunneweg, *Biblische Theologie des Alten Testaments* (Stuttgart: Kohlhammer, 1993), 239.
[23] Stolz, op.cit. (note 19), 74.
[24] Ibid., 19.
[25] Ibid., 27-29.

is something I tried to develop in response to the work of Stolz and Melanie Köhlmoos.[26] I did not, however, focus on the Psalms, but on the Book of Job.[27] Unfortunately, I cannot expose all of the discussion here. I would like, however, to point out that beyond cultic experience and wisdom, the law and the judiciary tradition of the Old Testament likewise underwent a process of critical reflection when faced with its own crisis. Job is described as a just, whole, God-fearing and evil-diverting man (Job 1:1). In his suffering, he appeals to God for justice, but does not experience it. Job even prays vengeance Psalms against his friends, who became his enemies (Job 24, 27). Job, like the psalmist, knows his own innocence and believes in God's justice, but what he experiences is that this justice is far away. This distance is evidenced by accusations (Job 22), annoying consolations (Job 16) and the observation that the just suffer while the impious prosper (Job 21). Not to let go either of his own innocence or of the certainty of God's justice, Job and the psalmist pray vengeance Psalms. This is what they learned and what is left when law and justice, like cultic activity and wisdom, are unable to reestablish the order destroyed by suffering and by enemies.

You may be asking yourself the reason for the term "critical justice." The terminology used by Stolz to describe this phenomenon [*Nachphänomen*] has been questioned by some scholars.[28] Others retain it.[29] The biblical texts that present this phenomenon critically reflect the cultic, wisdom and law crises without renouncing these categories. Cultic activity continues to exist, but in a critical manner, that is, springing from theological reflection elicited by the experience of God's absence. Wisdom continues to mediate the world's order, even when human beings discover that they are unable to understand all of God's mystery and God's *sapientia abscondita*. The same happens to law, which is not abolished even when God's justice is not forthcoming in response to enemy attacks. This is why I use the term critical justice.

The vengeance Psalms as Psalms of a critical justice do not deny God's justice. God continues to be just, but God's justice no longer seems to be accessible to the psalmist. By the experience with the *Deus absconditus*, it becomes a *iustitia abscondita*. Justice, beyond being an attribute of God, is

---

[26] Melanie Köhlmoos, *Das Auge Gottes. Textstrategie im Hiobbuch*. FAT 25 (Tübingen: Mohr Siebeck, 1999).

[27] Roger Marcel Wanke, *Praesentia Dei. Die Vorstellungen von der Gegenwart Gottes im Hiobbuch*, BZAW 421 (Berlin/Boston: De Gruyter, 2013).

[28] Siegfried Kreuzer, op. cit. (note 2), 340–41.

[29] Jürgen van Oorschot, *Nachkultische Psalmen und spätbiblische Rollendichtung*, ZAW 106 (1994), 69-86. Cf. Manfred Oeming. *Die Psalmen in Forschung und Verkündigung. Gerhard Sauter zum 60. Geburtstag. Verkündigung und Forschung*, 40. Jg. Heft 1 (1995), 28–51.

only found in God. Because the vengeance Psalms are examples of critical justice, they teach the psalmist to pray to God, calling for his vengeance over enemies and for the certainty, against all odds, of the actions of God; they even help him to remain *coram Deo*.

LUTHER AND THE VENGEANCE PSALMS

Since Hans-Peter Grosshans has already dealt with Luther's interest in and theology of the Psalms and his contribution to hermeneutics, I shall merely raise some questions that I think are pertinent to an understanding of Luther's interpretation of the vengeance Psalms.

Luther studied the Book of Psalms in diverse forms and at countless moments throughout his life. [30] His academic life started on 16 August 1513, with his Lectures on Psalms. And at the end of his life, "Psalms" was one of his last words (Ps 31:5; 68:20). Luther lived the Psalms. They were part of his whole theological existence, that is, of his theological teaching, preaching in the community and of his pastoral care. But how did Luther read and interpret the vengeance Psalms?

In his *Vorrede auff den Psalter* of 1545,[31] Luther generally affirms that in the Psalms we find the position of the psalmist before God, before his friends and before his enemies. Comparing the life and heart of the psalmist with a boat in high and agitated seas, what for Luther predominates in the Book of Psalms is a capacity of seriously speaking with God amidst all kinds of turmoil.

Already at the end of his *Summarien über die Psalmen und Ursachen des Dolmetschens* of 1530,[32] Luther presents a brief division of the Psalter into five categories according to literary genre. The first refers to the Psalms he calls prophetic, to which belong all those containing promises for the just and threats against the impious. The second covers the didactic Psalms, which aim at teaching and living according to the Torah. The third refers to the consolation Psalms which fortify and console the saints who are

---

[30] Here his sermons on Psalms are highlighted: "Dictata super psalterium" (1513-1515), *WA* 55/I/1 e; *WA* 55/II/1; "Operationes in Psalmos" (1519-1521), *WA* 5:19-654; "Interpretation on the First 25" (1530), *WA* 31/I:263-383; Summary on the Psalms (1531-1533), *WA* 38:18-69; "Sermons on the Gradual Psalms" (1532/33, 1540), *WA* 40/III:9-475; "Interpretation of Psalm 90" (1534/35, 1541), *WA* 40/III:484-594. About Luther's sermons on Psalms, cf. Heinrich Bornkamm, *Luther und das Alte Testament*, (Tübingen: Mohr Siebeck, 1948), 230-33. Not least, Luther used various Psalms in the services through hymns.
[31] "Vorrede auff den Psalter," *WA DB* 10/I:99-105.
[32] *WA* 38:9-18.

afflicted and in suffering and which, on the contrary, curse and terrorize the tyrants. To this genre belong all the Psalms that console, warn, counsel patience and curse the tyrants. A fourth category refers to the prayer Psalms, to which belong all of the Psalms that lament and cry out and complain about enemies. Lastly, Luther mentions thanksgiving Psalms, which praise and glorify God for all the blessings and help received. We should note that in this classification, enemies—the word most often quoted Luther—is mentioned in three different genres: prophetic Psalms, consolation Psalms and prayer Psalms.

On the interpretation of Psalm 6 in "Operationes in Psalmos" Luther defines enemies as "stubborn pursuers," who practice iniquity and who thus deserve to suffer God's judgment. In the words of Psalm 6:11, enemies should be punished and humiliated to enable them to recognize the grace of God. Luther affirms

> The Word of God becomes understandable for fools if they have been tormented by suffering. The cross of Christ is the only instruction of God's words, the most pure theology [...] For this reason, while enduring the wrath of God is impossible, it is absolutely necessary for the incredulous and foolish, for only this is sufficiently powerful to humiliate them [...] We have many similar passages in the Scriptures in which the violent confusion and turmoil in the hearts of the saints are described. These feelings are also expressed by the impious; afflicted, oppressed and thus humbled, they may be comforted and exalted. God works in this way because he wants all men to be saved and no one to perish.[33]

There is also a text in which Luther interprets two vengeance Psalms. I would like briefly to look at Luther's interpretation of one of them, Psalm 94. In 1526, Luther has left behind the Peasant's Revolt, the conflicts with Erasmus, Zwingli, Thomas Münster and Karlstadt. He has been married to Katharina von Bora for less than a year. He is still on his honeymoon and it is a happy period but, at the same time, he is exposed to his enemies' attacks as well as his own reflections and questionings. Suddenly, the news arrives that the Turks have invaded Hungary because King Ludwig has not paid the demanded tribute.[34] The Turkish army then attacks the Hungarian army. On 29 August 1526, the Hungarians are defeated and King Ludwig is killed while attempting to escape. Hungary is devastated and is experiencing internal political quarrels. Queen Mary, Ludwig's wife, was a princess of Spain, Emperor Carl V's sister and sympathetic

---

[33] *WA* 5:19–654.
[34] On the background and political developments, cf. Reinhard Schwarz, *Luther*, 3. Auflage [UTB 1926] (Göttingen: V&R, 2004), 195–98.

to the Reformation. After her husband's death, she tries to manage these internal issues, including manifestations against the Reformation. Luther has no difficulty in consoling the Queen, dedicating his interpretation of four Psalms that he called consolatory [Ps 37, 62, 94 e 109] to her.[35] The work is completed on 1 November 1526; nothing is known of Queen Mary's response to this dedication. Two of these Psalms, 94 and 109, are today considered vengeance Psalms.[36]

Luther interprets Psalm 94 verse by verse. He begins with a brief introduction in which he calls it a "common prayer of all pious children of God and of the spiritual people against all their persecutors." Luther defines these persecutors firstly as tyrants who violently attack the Word of God and, secondly, as false masters, heretics and sectarians who persecute people with lies and falsehoods. He then relates this to his own days, suggesting that the Psalm can be prayed against the Pope, the bishops, the princes and lords who violently oppose the gospel through the false and incorrect interpretation of the Scriptures.

When interpreting verse 1, in which the expression "God of vengeance" appears twice, Luther, like Paul, understands it as one of God's attributes. As God is a God of hope (Rom 15:13), of patience and of consolation (Rom 15:15), God is also a God of vengeance. Here, Luther makes it clear that this conclusion is based on the lamentation of the psalmist. That God is a God of vengeance is part of the Old Testament theological conception. Knowing this motivates the psalmist to appeal to God to exercise God's vengeance. Luther says to God, "If vengeance is Your work and You know it is sorely missed, why do You hide yourself in darkness and refuse to allow Yourself to be seen?"

Luther also asks himself, in light of Matthew 5:44, how pious and spiritual people ask for vengeance. His answer is marked by an interesting distinction between faith and love. For Luther, "faith and love are two distinct things. Faith does not tolerate anything, love suffers everything. Faith curses, love blesses. Faith seeks vengeance and punishment, love treats with respect and forgiveness." What for Luther becomes the criterion and legitimation for praying a vengeance Psalm is not the situation of the psalmist alone, but the fact that his enemies are God's enemies who put faith in danger. Love, in return, does not let the psalmist perpetrate vengeance with his own hands, but delegates it to God. In his interpretation of verse 5, Luther affirms, "This is what tyrants do, for with violence they persecute the Word of God and kill and torment the people. Yes, the

---

[35] *WA* 19:542–615.
[36] *WA* 19:582–94. Cf. The interpretation of Ps 94 by Fritz Stolz, op. cit. (note 19), 42–46.

heretics help and contribute to this also. The psalmist complains before God and calls for vengeance."

Another interesting point in Luther's interpretation of this Psalm is the fact that he calls Psalm 94 a consolation Psalm. It is true that this aspect is contained in the Psalm itself (v. 19). But Luther interprets all instances of praying a vengeance Psalm as a consolation for the psalmist. Luther says:

> But it is God who gives me patience, who instructs me above and beyond my reason, who topples the wicked. He permits me to suffer so terribly at the hands of the wicked to teach me that I would be ruined without His help and that my own power is useless. Thus this verse and the two that follow are nothing but a thanksgiving for the grace that God comforts us in the day of trouble, when the tyrants and the heretics rage, as we have heard. [37]

Luther concludes his interpretation of Psalm 94 by underlining what in my own and probably Fritz Stolz's opinion are the two objectives of a vengeance Psalm: the certainty of faith that believes in God's justice even against all odds, and God's instruction to deal with enemies. Luther says: "Whoever believes in this [God's vengeance] and is instructed by God can be patient and permit the wicked to rage, for he considers their end and waits it out."[38]

What can we conclude after looking briefly at Luther's interpretation of Psalm 94?

Generally speaking, Luther transforms the Psalms of *nāqam* into Psalms of *naḥam*, meaning that Luther understands vengeance Psalms as consolation Psalms. It is interesting to realize that this approach also reflects recent research on the Book of Psalms. There is a certain tendency to question whether the terminology for this kind of Psalms has been right. Erich Zenger, for instance, suggests that the vengeance Psalms (or curse Psalms) might be called zealous Psalms or even justice Psalms.[39] Along the same lines, Bernd Janowski affirms that calling them curse or vengeance Psalms leads to error, for in fact they aim at the restoration of justice by the saving grace of God. According to Janowski,[40] the point of the vengeance Psalms is not in the joy of the psalmist in the light of his sanguinary triumph over the impious (cf. Ps 58:11), but in the fact that the psalmist did not let go of God's justice. Thus the psalmist's lamentation is a cry for God's justice in a world marked by injustice.

---

[37] *LW* 14, 253; *WA* 19:591-92.
[38] *LW* 14, 256; *WA* 19:594.
[39] Zenger, op. cit. (note 2), 370.
[40] Janowski, op. cit. (note 6), 129-33.

Perspectives for further research

Arriving at the end of this approach, I see that three tasks remain before us:

- First of all, there is the question, Is what Dietrich Bonhoeffer, Erich Zenger, Bernd Janowski and other theologians (not forgetting Luther of course) discussed and wrote the final word about the vengeance Psalms? I think that Fritz Stolz's reflections can help us to understand the vengeance Psalms as a "politically incorrect" language (*coram inimico*), but one which comes from a theologically correct *coram Deo*.

- Secondly, the topic of Luther's hermeneutics on the Psalms, especially the vengeance ones, deserve closer attention from specialists on Luther. There are implications and consequences of his hermeneutics, especially for analysis of the dangerous anti-Semitism that might be deduced from Luther's approach to the vengeance Psalms. I do not wish to delve deeper into this topic for lack of space, but Luther's interpretation of Psalm 109 could legitimate such anti-Semitism. The distinction between faith and love in Luther's approach could be deepened and verified in his interpretation of the other vengeance Psalms.

- Lastly, I see that Luther's interpretation of the vengeance Psalms leaves us with a practical task. What are the implications for church service and liturgy today? What challenges do the vengeance Psalms pose us as Psalms of a critical justice that lives in the distinction between faith and love, and the certainty and instruction by God, even against all evidence and faced with local and global injustice?

If for Luther, the Psalms are a "little Bible" and a "mirror," then the vengeance Psalms also have a place in this canon and in the experience of whosoever knows themselves as justified by God. That the just will live by faith is not something that underpins only Luther's theology. It is also the foundation for the psalmist, who is deprived of his rights and of justice. We remain in a dialectical tension between what the beginning of Psalm 94 and the end of Psalm 58 say: "O Lord, you God of vengeance, you God of vengeance, shine forth! Rise up, O Judge of the earth; give to the proud what they deserve!" (Ps 94:1-2); "Surely there is a God who judges on earth" (Ps 58:11). It is precisely in the experience of this tension that we can also feel comforted today. May the Book of Psalms continue to give us the necessary words, when we lack them, as much to praise God as to cry out to God.

IV. Psalms from the Old Testament and Their Reception in the New Testament

Psalms Outside the Biblical Psalms Collection—the Example of Jonah

Karl-Wilhelm Niebuhr

Introduction

The discovery of the Dead Sea Scrolls has shown that the collection of Israel's writings, later to be called Old Testament by Christians, was not yet finished at the time when the texts of what later became the New Testament were written. The Psalms scrolls from Qumran, in particular, differ considerably in content, order and wording from the later Masoretic text that was transmitted completely only in medieval manuscripts. The manuscript called 11Q Ps^a, for instance, consists of many canonical Psalms belonging to the Masoretic Psalter (but in a different order) as well as of the Hebrew versions of other Psalms, known up to then only in their Syriac version, and of so-called "non-canonical Psalms" completely unknown so far.[1]

Of course, even before the Qumran findings, it had been clear that, in early Jewish literature, there had existed other Psalms collections in addition to the collection which only later became "biblical." But the full breadth and diversity of early Jewish Psalms traditions had not been disclosed for biblical scholarship before the Dead Sea Scrolls were published. In addition, we also know of an independent Psalms collection from ancient Christianity consisting of several poetic compositions from the Old Testament and early Jewish hymns as well as of hymns of much later origin, among which are also poetic pieces extracted from New Testament writings. This collection called "Odes" (but not to be confused with the "Odes of Solomon" alleged to be Gnostic!) has been transmitted in fifth-century Greek Bible ("Septuagint") manuscripts.[2] Apparently, it was used also in Christian liturgy.

---

[1] J. A. Sanders, *Discoveries in the Judean Desert*, vol. iv: *The Psalms Scroll of Qumran Cave 11* (Oxford: Oxford University Press, 1965, 1997); Peter W. Flint, "Psalms and Psalters in the Dead Sea Scrolls," in James H. Charlesworth (ed.), *The Bible and the Dead Sea Scrolls*, vol. I, *Scripture and Scrolls* (Waco: Baylor University Press, 2006), 233-72.

[2] Therefore, today "Odes" can be found in all modern editions or translations of the Septuagint, although there remain many open questions about the origins and the

Not only poetic texts from Old Testament writings such as the "Reed Sea Song" (Ex 15:1-19), the Song of Moses (Dt 32:1-43), the Song of Hannah (1 Sam 2:1-10) and other songs from the prophetic writings belong to "Odes," as well as the *Magnificat* and the *Nunc Dimittis* from Luke 1f. The collection ends with the song of the angels from Luke 2:14 ("Glory to God in the highest ...") which flows into a Trinitarian doxology to God (Ode 14).

At the heart of this collection, following the songs from the Books of Habakkuk and Isaiah and followed by songs from Daniel, we also find the Psalm which Jonah sang in the belly of the great fish (cf. Jon 2:3-10). According to its place in the Odes and as part of this collection, Jonah's Psalm was apparently counted here as belonging to the Old Testament. Therefore, like other Old Testament Psalms, it may have been used on weekdays in the liturgy of the Hours. But, as part of the canonical tradition consisting of the Old and the New Testaments, it was evaluated at the same time as part of the Christian Bible. Therefore, the collection of Odes was focused on Jesus' incarnation and its conclusion was marked and highlighted by the Trinitarian glorification of God. Interestingly enough, by this principle of composition even New Testament texts had been incorporated within the Old Testament, as for instance the hymns from Luke 1 and 2. But, at the same time, the Trinitarian doxology had become a constitutive part of the Old Testament, emphasizing that the Triune God, according to a Christian understanding, is no other than the God of Israel. Therefore, the testimony for God, the Father of Jesus Christ and for God, the Holy Spirit, can be found not only in the New Testament, but also in the Old Testament as long as it is read from the perspective of Christian belief.

As a result, we can infer certain principles for a biblical theology based on the testimony of the New Testament from the history of transmission of the Psalm of Jonah in the Christian Bible. In ancient Christianity, this understanding of biblical theology also shaped the Christian Bible, consisting of the Old and New Testaments. This was already reflected hermeneutically by theologians in ancient Christianity.[3] From the perspective of the Christian Bible, the New Testament cannot be adequately understood apart from the Old; in the same manner, the Old Testament cannot be understood without the New. Attempts have been made to break this relationship of

---

history of transmission of the ancient Greek Bible. Cf. J. M. Dines, *The Septuagint* (London/New York: Clark, 2004); Michael Tilly, *Einführung in die Septuaginta* (Darmstadt: Wissenschaftliche Buchgesellschaft, 2005).

[3] Cf. Karl-Wilhelm Niebuhr, "Schriftauslegung in der Begegnung mit dem Evangelium," in Friederike Nüssel (ed.), *Schriftauslegung*, Themen der Theologie 8 (Tübingen: Mohr, 2014), 43-103, here 54-69; Volker Drecoll, "Exegese als Grundlage der Theologie in der Alten Kirche und im Mittelalter," in ibid., 105-40, here 110-27.

understanding between both parts of the Christian Bible, starting with the Christian theologian and bishop Marcion in the second century and reaching as far as our recent past in Germany. In Eisenach, the Christian theologian and New Testament professor Walter Grundmann (1906-1975) and his like-minded friends from the "Deutsche Christen" movement attempted completely to remove the Old Testament from Christian use as well as to cut every link to the Jewish tradition in the Bible, theology and church life. In pursuit of this aim, they founded the Institut für die Erforschung und Beseitigung des jüdischen Einflusses auf das deutsche kirchliche Leben [Institute for Research on and Elimination of Jewish Influence on German Church Life].[4] Mercifully, such attempts were never officially accepted by the mainline churches. Today, the Old Testament is an undisputed part of the Christian Bible and sometimes Old Testament stories or books are better known in Christian or even in secular circles than parts of the New Testament.

The Book of Jonah is pertinent in this respect. It not only contains one of the most familiar and colorful stories of the whole Bible, but it is also quoted or alluded to quite frequently in the New Testament as well as in early Judaism. In this way, it was passed on to readers, each time with a different and updated focus. The Book of Jonah thus played an important role in the transmission and interpretation of the Christian Bible,[5] starting with the collection of "Odes," as we have already seen and with interpretations by ancient theologians.[6] This was continued by the widespread

---

[4] Cf. Oliver Arnhold's extensive monograph *"Entjudung"–Kirche im Abgrund: Die Thuüringer Kirchenbewegung Deutsche Christen 1928-1939 und das „Institut zur Erforschung und Beseitigung des jüdischen Einflusses auf das deutsche kirchliche Leben" 1939-1945* (Berlin: Institut Kirche und Judentum, 2010).

[5] For references see the volume of collected essays edited by Johann Anselm Steiger and Wilhelm Kühlmann, *Der problematische Prophet. Die biblische Jona-Figur in Exegese, Theologie, Literatur und Bildender Kunst*, Arbeiten zur Kirchengeschichte 118 (Berlin/New York: Walter de Gruyter, 2011); Beat Weber, *Jona. Der widerspenstige Prophet und der gnädige Gott*, Biblische Gestalten 27 (Leipzig: EVA, 2012), 125-75; Uwe Steffen, *Die Jona-Geschichte. Ihre Auslegung und Darstellung im Judentum, Christentum und Islam* (Neukirchen-Vluyn: Neukirchener, 1994); Uwe Steffen, *Das Mysterium von Tod und Auferstehung. Formen und Wandlungen des Jona-Motivs* (Göttingen: Vandenhoeck und Ruprecht, 1963); Mishael Caspi and John T. Greene (eds), *How Jonah is Interpreted in Judaism, Christianity, and Islam. Essays on the Authenticity and Influence of the Biblical Prophet* (Lewiston: Mellen, 2011).

[6] See the commentaries by Jerome S. Risse (ed), *Hieronymus Commentarius in Ionam Prophetam / Kommentar zu dem Propheten Jona*, FC 60 (Turnhout: Brepols, 2003), and Theodore of Mopsuestia, Charlotte Köckert, "Der Jona-Kommentar des Theodor von Mopsuestia. Eine christliche Jona-Auslegung an der Wende zum 5. Jahrhundert," in Steiger and Kühlmann, ibid., 1-38 (German translation of the com-

reception of the book in Christian art in Late Antiquity as well as in the Middle Ages, extending into modern art and literature.

Martin Luther also dedicated a small commentary as well as an academic lecture course to the Book of Jonah and he also expressed his understanding of Jonah in his "Table Talks."[7] For Luther, the prophet in the belly of the big fish was "ein Zeichen der Auferstehung der Toten" [a symbol for the resurrection of the dead] but, at the same time, Jonah was also a "dubious saint" who, in spite of his rescue from mortal danger, still wanted the city of Nineveh to be abolished by God. In his exegesis of the Book of Jonah, Luther methodologically followed the rules of medieval exegesis, distinguishing between a *sensus literalis* and a *sensus spiritualis*. Theologically, however, he interpreted the mortal danger of Jonah and his rescue by God according to the model of "Law and Gospel":

> Now the whale, that is, death and hell, appears and devours Jonah. This is the sequence: first the Law, then sin, and finally death. ... Then comes the living Word of God, the Gospel of grace, and addresses the fish, that is, it commands death not to touch man. That is where faith sets in, and man is freed both of sin and of death and lives in grace and righteousness with Christ.[8]

In his "Table Talks," Luther explicitly explains that the Jonah story is not history, but should be understood as a symbol of the resurrection. The story of the survival of Jonah in the belly of the fish is "sehr lügerlich" [mendacious], and he himself would not believe it if it were not part of Holy Scripture.[9]

Thus for Luther, the historical value of the Jonah story is not decisive. Rather, it is its spiritual meaning which can be developed only by taking Christian faith as the starting point for interpretation. Nevertheless, in what follows, I will not deal further with Luther's exegesis of the Book of

---

mentary, 21-38). Other interpreters of the Book of Jonah from the ancient church include Gregory of Nazianz, Ephraem the Syrian, Theodoret of Kyros, Theophylaktos, Origen, Augustin, Ambrose and Gregory the Great. Cf. Steffen, ibid., 75-87.

[7] For Luther's interpretation, see Johan Anselm Steiger, *Jonas Propheta. Zur Auslegungs- und Mediengeschichte des Buches Jona bei Martin Luther und im Luthertum der Barockzeit*, Doctrina Pietatis II/5 (Stuttgart: frommann-holzboog, 2011), 13-54; Johann Anselm Steiger, "Gottes 'Bilderbücher'. Die Auslegung der Jona-Erzählung bei Luther und im Luthertum der Barockzeit," in Steiger and Kühlmann, op. cit. (note 5), 53-87.

[8] Martin Luther, "Jonah—1526," in *LW* 19, 100-101. Cf. also Steffen, op. cit. (note 5), 107-11.

[9] *WA TR* 736 (Aurifaber collection).

Jonah,[10] but concentrate my investigation on the problem of how the Book of Jonah, and Jonah's Psalm in particular, may contribute to our own understanding of the biblical Psalter in the setting of a biblical theology today.

JONAH'S PSALM AS PART OF THE BOOK OF JONAH

The Book of Jonah forms a particular case among the prophets in the Bible as well as in the Book of the Twelve. Indeed, it can almost be classified as a foreign object in the collection of prophetic books. There is only a single prophetic saying in the whole book, consisting of just five words in Hebrew (Jon 3:4), although in the Old Testament canon, the book has always been transmitted as part of the *nebiim* and was considered as belonging to the collection of the Twelve Prophets already in early Jewish writings.[11] The only prophetic saying in Jonah reads: "Forty days more, and Nineveh shall be overthrown!" With the exception of this saying, the Book sounds much more like a sapiental tale with predominantly pedagogical or paraenetical intentions. Therefore, it would better fit the third part of the Hebrew Bible, the Writings, like the Books of Tobit, Judith or Job or other ancient Jewish wisdom tales.[12]

Another particularity of the Book of Jonah in literary terms is the long Psalm which Jonah prays when he is trapped in the belly of the fish, rendered in Jonah 2:2-9.[13] This piece of poetry looks like a biblical Psalm, as was already noted by ancient Christian readers, who extracted it from its literary context and put it together with other hymns from the Old

---

[10] For interpretation of the Book of Jonah by the Reformers, cf. Jens Wolff, "Providenz und Meeresforschung. Auslegungsgeschichtliche Beobachtungen zu Johannes Calvins Jona-Kommentar," in Steiger and Kühlmann, op. cit. (note 5), 139-58.

[11] Cf. *Sir* 49,10; *Vitae Prophetarum* 10.

[12] For a narrative critical analysis of the Book of Jonah, cf. Peter Weimar, *Eine Geschichte voller Überraschungen. Annäherungen an die Jonaerzählung*, SBS 217 (Stuttgart: Katholisches Bibelwerk, 2009); Ehud Ben Zvi, *Signs of Jonah. Reading and Rereading in Ancient Yehud*, The Library of Hebrew Bible and Old Testament Studies (Sheffield: Sheffield Academic Press, 2003); Rüdiger Lux, *Jona. Prophet zwischen "Verweigerung" und "Gehorsam". Eine erzählanalytische Studie*, FRLANT 162 (Göttingen: Vandenhoeck & Ruprecht, 1994); cf. the commentary by Jack M. Sasson, *Jonah. A New Translation with Introduction, Commentary, and Interpretation*, The Anchor Bible 24B (New York: Doubleday, 1990), 328-51.

[13] For recent research on the Psalm of Jonah see Lux, ibid., 165-86; Meik Gerhards, *Studien zum Jonabuch*, BThSt 78 (Neukirchen-Vluyn: Neukirchener, 2006), 11-26; Hermann J. Opgen-Rhein, *Jonapsalm und Jonabuch. Sprachgestalt, Entstehungsgeschichte und Kontextbedeutung von Jona 2*, SBB 38 (Stuttgart: Katholisches Bibelwerk, 1997).

and the New Testaments, and thus formed the collection of "Odes." In Old Testament scholarship, this particularity of the Book of Jonah has been taken as a starting point for analyzing its literary history. Today, it is usually assumed that the Book found its literary shape only in late Persian or early Hellenistic times.[14] All attempts to reconstruct different stages of the literary history of the book, e.g., by assuming that the Psalm in chapter 2 existed independently of its literary context and possibly originated in pre-exilic times and milieus similar to other biblical Psalms, did not prove successful. The narrative links between Jonah's Psalm and its context in the Jonah story are too close to separate both, and in the Psalm itself there are several motives which can be explained only by the story told before and after.[15] Although it is possible to allocate the Psalm of Jonah to the genre of "songs of gratitude" [Danklieder, *todah*], the motifs in the description of distress specifically refer to the situation of the drowning Jonah.[16] Therefore, we can assume that the Psalm and the narrative interpret each other. They belong together and were written by the same author.[17]

Having said this, we should focus our interpretation even more strongly on the links between Jonah's Psalm and other biblical Psalms in relation to their motifs. A close look at the Psalm of Jonah shows that it can be called a mosaic of motifs taken from biblical Psalms. The genre of *todah* Psalms determines its structure.[18] This explains why the description of Jonah's rescue is already mentioned in his prayer when he is still in distress.[19] Even

---

[14] For older research, cf. Hans Walter Wolff, *Studien zum Jonabuch*, BSt 47 (Neukirchen-Vluyn: Neukirchener, 1967); Hans Walter Wolff, *Dodekapropheton 3: Obadja und Jona*, BK 14/3 (Neukirchen-Vluyn: Neukirchener, 1977), 54-56; Wilhelm Rudolph, *Joel – Amos – Obadja – Jona*, KAT 13/2 (Gütersloh: Gerd Mohn, 1971), 328-30. More recent research includes, Gerhards, ibid., 15-26; 55-65; Opgen-Rhein, ibid., 213-30; Sasson, op. cit. (note 12), 20-28; Ben Zvi, op. cit. (note 12), 7-9.

[15] This is the result of the critical analysis by Gerhards, op. cit., (note 13), 53-55; cf. Sasson, op. cit. (note 12), 16-20; Douglas Stuart, *Hosea-Jonah*, Word Biblical Commentary 31 (Waco: Word Books, 1987), 438-40; 471f. See also Lux, op. cit. (note 12), 170, who asserts that "das Gebet notwendig zur narrativen Konzeption des Erzählers gehörte." Slightly more optimistic with regard to the reconstruction of different literary levels in the book are Opgen-Rhein, ibid., 129-46, and Rudolph, ibid., 347-51.

[16] Cf. v. 5: "the waters closed in over me; the deep surrounded me; weeds were wrapped around my head."

[17] For a more detailed analysis see Lux, op. cit. (note 12), 171-81; Opgen-Rhein, op. cit. (note 13), 34-73; Stuart, ibid., 472-74; Sasson, op. cit. (note 12), 160-215; Weber, op. cit. (note 5), 66-69.

[18] Cf. Opgen-Rhein, op. cit. (note 13), 147-54; Weber, op. cit. (note 5), 71-82.

[19] In *todah* Psalms the description of distress and the call for rescue is followed by an intervention of God and a reaction to this by the praying person consisting of

single phrases of Jonah's Psalm borrow their wording from biblical Psalms, as for instance:[20]

> v. 2: I called to the Lord out of my distress, and he answered me; out of the belly of Sheol I cried, and you heard my voice.
> cf. Ps 130:1f: Out of the depths I cry to you, O LORD. Lord, hear my voice!

> v. 3: You cast me into the deep, into the heart of the seas, and the flood surrounded me; all your waves and your billows passed over me.
> v. 5: The waters closed in over me; the deep surrounded me; weeds were wrapped around my head.
> cf. Ps 42:7: all your waves and your billows have gone over me

> v. 4: I am driven away from your sight; how shall I look again upon your holy temple?
> cf. Ps.31:22: I had said in my alarm, "I am driven far from your sight." But you heard my supplications when I cried out to you for help.

> v. 6: I went down to the land whose bars closed upon me forever
> cf. Ps 40:2:He drew me up from the desolate pit, out of the miry bog.

By this composition of biblical Psalm phrases, the prophet himself becomes a paradigm for any pious Israelite. Even though Jonah protested against God's will and was unfaithful to his task and thus fell into the deepest existential distress, he was allowed to return to his God in prayer begging for rescue. Everyone who is in a similar situation should follow his example. For God is a merciful God, a saving God, unlike the miserable idols of the Gentiles (cf. Jon 2:8). God deserves to be praised in God's holy temple (Jon 2:7, 9). Jonah, as portrayed in the biblical Book of Jonah, can praise his God even before he is thrown onto dry ground, for he lives by his faith in a merciful God.

This biblical understanding of God as the savior from distress who forgives the sins of God's people determines the whole Book of Jonah, not only Jonah's Psalm.[21] Within this theological framework, Jonah is an exem-

---

expressions of gratitude as well as of a vow to praise God's name in the congregation. Cf. Erich Zenger, "Das Buch der Psalmen," in Erich Zenger et al, *Einleitung in das Alte Testament* (Stuttgart: Kohlhammer, 2008), 348-70, here 361f.

[20] More parallels are noted by Alfons Deissler, "Jona," in Alfons Deissler, *Zwölf Propheten II* (Würzburg: Echter Verlag, 1984), 26-28; Weber, op. cit. (note 5), 74-80; Rudolph, op. cit. (note 14), 351-54.

[21] Cf. for other important theological questions raised in the Book of Jonah, Gerhards, op. cit. (note 13), 73-135 (esp. 131); Friedhelm Hartenstein, "Die Zumutung des barmherzigen Gottes. Die Theologie des Jonabuches im Licht der Urgeschichte

plary figure who witnesses to God's merciful acts towards God's people of Israel. He is an extraordinary character as part of a narrative theology of the Old Testament. A modern exegete has therefore suggested "The story of YHWH with his Prophet Jonah" as a proper title for the book.[22]

In addition to this theological framework of Jonah's Psalm, several other theological motives are articulated in the book. Among them is the view that the God of Israel at the same time is "the Lord, the God of heaven, who made the sea and the dry land" (Jon 1:9), whom nobody is able to escape (Jon 1:3f). God rules over the powers of nature (Jon 1:4, 15) and is to be feared even by Gentiles (Jon 1:16). Chapter 3 will show that Gentiles in particular (more than Jonah the Israelite!) are ready to return and may even be able to persuade God to change God's mind and turn God's wrath away from them (Jon 3:8f). And in fact, this is exactly what happens in the story: When God saw their repentance he "changed his mind about the calamity he had said he would bring upon them; and he did not do it" (Jon 3:10).[23] Here again, Jonah is portrayed as an exemplary Israelite, but now in a negative sense. He knows God's nature well, but rebels against it.

> O Lord! Is not this what I said while I was still in my own country? That is why I fled to Tarshish at the beginning; for I knew that you are a gracious God and merciful, slow to anger, and abounding in steadfast love, and ready to relent from punishing (4:2).

Obviously, Jonah is quoting one of the fundamental confessions of Israel in the Torah here (cf. Ex 34:6f), according to which God's promise of grace is followed by the announcement of God's judgment.[24] But exactly at this turning point of the biblical confession, Jonah stops the quotation.

This is an indication of the understanding of God in the Book of Jonah. God is the judge whom nobody will ever escape, least of all one who thinks

---

Gen 1-11," in Angelika Berlejung and Raik Heckl (eds), *Ex oriente Lux. Studien zur Theologie des Alten Testaments* (FS R. Lux), ABG 39 (Leipzig: EVA, 2012), 435-55; Jörg Jeremias, "Der Psalm des Jona (Jona 2,3-10)," in Michaela Bauks et al (eds), *Was ist der Mensch, dass du seiner gedenkst? (Psalm 8,5). Aspekte einer theologischen Anthropologie* (FS B. Janowski) (Neukirchen-Vluyn: Neukirchener, 2008), 203-14.

[22] "The story of YHWH with his prophet Jonah," Deissler, op. cit. (note 20), 20

[23] Cf. Weber, op. cit. (note 5), 98-103. For the motif of God's own sorrow and repentance in the Book of Jonah, cf. Jan-Dirk Döhling, *Der bewegliche Gott. Eine Untersuchung des Motivs der Reue Gottes in der Hebräischen Bibel*, HBS 61 (Freiburg i. Br.: Herder, 2009), 429-84.

[24] Cf. Weber, op. cit. (note 5), 104-13; cf. Ruth Scoralick, *Gottes Güte und Gottes Zorn. Die Gottesprädikationen in Exodus 34,6f und ihre intertextuellen Beziehungen zum Zwölfprophetenbuch*, HBS 33 (Freiburg i. Br.: Herder, 2002), 182-85.

of themselves as being a pious Israelite and a proclaimer of God's judgment against Gentiles.[25] But above all, God is a merciful God, even for Gentiles who are willing to return to God and to learn to fear God. Even more, God will also be merciful towards this cross-grained Israelite of little faith who presumes to be incapable of tolerating God's grace!

Jonah is therefore a test case for Israel's trust in God (originating probably in post-exilic or perhaps even early Jewish times), and at the same time he is an involuntary proclaimer of God's grace. Jonah's Psalm articulates a confession to God who rescues human beings out of their deepest distress. The story of Jonah is a narrative representation of God's mercy toward all human beings who will trust God's gracious judgment. If one wishes to apply the Lutheran distinction between Law and gospel to Old Testament writings, the Book of Jonah, even though at the narrative level it is open-ended, obviously belongs to the gospel.

JONAH IN EARLY JEWISH LITERATURE

The story of Jonah was popular in Antiquity, as the writings of the New Testament and the reception history in ancient Christianity demonstrate. Even in early Judaism, Jonah was well known in different contexts. The main criterion for reception of the Book of Jonah in Greek-speaking Judaism was the Septuagint, which also became the textual foundation for the Book's reception in ancient Christianity. This can be inferred from several details such as, for instance, the term used for the plant that God nurtured for one night to offer shadow for Jonah, but that withered during the next night after being attacked by a worm (Jon 4:6f). According to the Hebrew text, this was a castor-oil plant/*ricinus communis* (σιλλικύπριον), but a pumpkin (κολόκυνθα) according to the Septuagint and ivy (κισσός) in the Greek version of Symmachus. Highly educated church fathers such as Jerome or Augustine could argue happily about what kind of plant it actually was. But obviously, Jerome, in his argument in favor of his translation, was not so much interested in botany as in the authority of the true language of the Bible and its proper translation and understanding. He was interested in the *hebraica veritas*, by which the revelation of God was accessible to human beings.[26]

---

[25] See for this Gerhards, op. cit. (note 13), 175-93.
[26] Cf. Risse, op. cit. (note 6), 204-9. On the serious background of this rather funny quarrel about pumpkins see the explanation given by Risse, op. cit. (note 6), 20-37. The focus was on the use of the Bible in the church, preferring either the Septuagint and its Latin translation or a version translated directly from the Hebrew, the so-called *hebraica veritas*

Another detail relates to the animal which rescued Jonah from drowning and kept him alive for three days and three nights in its belly (Jon 2:1). According to the Hebrew text, this was a big fish, but the Septuagint calls it a κῆτος, a mythical oceanic monster.[27] The whole story of Jonah thereby acquires a somewhat mythical tone, which also influenced its reception by Matthew (cf. Mt 12:40). More important is a third alteration of the Hebrew wording by the Greek translators: the period of repentance for Nineveh (Jon 3:4) is forty days according to the Hebrew wording, but shortened to only three days in the Septuagint, making the portrait of Jonah as the prophet of judgment even fiercer

Nevertheless, there was no fixed or unified picture of Jonah in early Jewish literature. Josephus, for instance, retells only part of the story of the Bible.[28] After Jonah's prophecy against Nineveh (Jon 3:4), he suddenly interrupts his retelling with the remark "then he returned home," only to assert afterwards that he had reproduced the story as he had found it in Scripture. Obviously, when writing and interpreting the biblical history of Israel from his theological point of view, Josephus was primarily interested in Jonah's proclamation of salvation for Jerobeam (cf. 2 Kings 14:23-29) rather than in the Jonah story as such. In 3 Maccabees, a legendary and edifying tale of how the Jews of Egypt were saved from a pogrom in third-century Alexandria,[29] Jonah appears in a prayer of intercession pronounced by the aged priest Eleazar (3 Macc 6:1-8). Here, Jonah belongs to a series of biblical personalities or scenes that taken together figure as examples of God's saving acts towards the people of Israel. These began with Abraham and his offspring and continued with the Exodus story, the miracle at the Reed Sea, the rescue of Jerusalem from the Assyrian king Sancherib, the recovery of the three boys from the furnace and of Daniel from the lion's den according to the Book of Daniel and eventually ending with "Jonah who vanished without a trace in the belly of the monster that lives in the depths of the sea," but "was shown alive again to his relatives." Arguing from the context of the prayer and the selection of events, the motif of the protection of Jonah in the body of the fish is the only scene from the whole book cited as an example of how God can rescue from death.

The *Vitae Prophetarum*, another Jewish writing, presumably stemming from the first century CE,[30] addresses other aspects of the biblical Jonah

---

[27] Cf. also Ps-Philo, *De Jona 16*; 3 Macc 6:8; Jos. Ant. IX 213.

[28] Josephus, Ant. IX 205-14.

[29] The Greek text according to the Septuagint; for an English translation see H. Anderson, "3 Maccabees," in James H. Charlesworth (ed.), *The Old Testament Pseudepigrapha*, vol. 2 (Garden City/New York: Doubleday, 1985), 509-29.

[30] For an English translation, see D. R. A. Hare, "The Lives of the Prophets," in ibid., 379-99.

figure and adds several elements to the story that have no biblical basis at all. The paragraph on Jonah briefly mentions the biblical Jonah story which nevertheless is obviously known to the author and his audience.[31] More important for the author is what follows afterwards: Jonah left his home country "he sojourned in Sour, a territory (inhabited by) foreign nations; for he said, 'So shall I remove my reproach, for I spoke falsely in prophesying against the great city of Nineveh'" (10:2f).[32] In the background here is the biblical episode when Jonah had wished to die (cf. Jon 4:1-3) and also, perhaps, his leaving Nineveh (cf. Jon 4:5). Nevertheless, the reason for mentioning this is no longer his reluctance to accept the repentance of Nineveh, but his false prophecy against the city.

The most extensive text known to us from early Jewish literature relying on the biblical Book of Jonah is a synagogue sermon transmitted as part of the work of Philo of Alexandria.[33] Nothing reliable can be said regarding its place and date of origin, apart from that it certainly was not written by Philo.[34] Nevertheless, it stems from the Greek-speaking Jewish Diaspora which existed only up to the first quarter of the second century CE in Egypt/Alexandria, but much longer in other parts of the Mediterranean. In this very long sermon almost every aspect and detail of the Jonah story are explained and interpreted running through the book according to the sequence of the biblical text. The intention of the writing is mostly paraenetical and edifying. If one wants to highlight a guiding theological idea then it is the testimony to God's goodness and philanthropy which can be learned from Jonah as well as from the city of Nineveh.[35] In this sermon the Psalm of Jonah is also rendered (chapters 19-25), but it is now completely changed into a prayer of

---

[31] *VitProph* 10:2f (quotation from Hare, ibid., 392).
[32] According to the biblical text, Jonah, son of Amittai, was from Gath-hepher, a place in Galilee (cf. 2 Kings 14:25). According to VitProph his home city was Aschdod at the sea, a place close to "the city of the Greeks."
[33] The text is preserved only in Armenian translation. For a German translation based on a retranslation from Armenian into Greek, cf. Folker Siegert, *Drei hellenistisch-jüdische Predigten. Ps.-Philon, "Über Jona", "Über Simson" und "Über die Gottesbezeichnung 'wohltätig verzehrendes Feuer'". I: Übersetzung aus dem Armenischen und sprachliche Erläuterungen*, WUNT 20 (Tübingen: Mohr Siebeck, 1980). See also Steffen, op. cit. (note 5), 13-16.
[34] Cf. Folker Siegert, *Philon von Alexandrien. Über die Gottesbezeichnung "wohltätig verzehrendes Feuer" (De Deo). Rückübersetzung des Fragments aus dem Armenischen, deutsche Übersetzung und Kommentar*, WUNT 46 (Tübingen: Mohr Siebeck, 1988), 2.
[35] Cf. Siegert, op. cit. (note 33), 7: "Als Thema oder Roten Faden könnte man für *De Jona* benennen: 'Der gütige Gott' ... Daß in *De Jona* die φιλανθρωπία Gottes ... unter völligem Absehen vom Gesetz des Mose gepriesen wird, ... erklärt sich sowohl aus dem Predigttext als auch aus dem Anlaß, zu dem dieser ... vorgelesen wurde: es war der Nachmittag des Versöhnungstages (Megilla 31 a). Die Geschichte

repentance expressed by an exemplary sinner who asks the philanthropic and merciful God for God's grace. Motifs from the biblical Psalm of Jonah only sporadically occur in this prayer of repentance, as for instance the drowning of Jonah in the depth of the sea (chapter 19). Of far more interest is the oceanic monster which is very colorfully described with teeth like prison bars (chapter 22), the mouth of a beast (chapter 20) and the belly which encloses the prisoner like a tube (chapter 21). Nonetheless, even under this condition, poor Jonah prays in favor of the oceanic monster that God may free it soon (like himself) so that it can live again in freedom. For by Jonah's presence in its belly the monster is detained from taking food (chapter 22). Apparently, God is not only philanthropic but also animal-loving![36] The penitential sermon, which was already part of the biblical image of Jonah, in this edifying and paraenetical speech has become its main intention.

REFERENCES TO JONAH IN THE SYNOPTIC TRADITION

In the Synoptic Gospels the Jonah story is not retold, but it is presupposed to be known to the authors as well as their readers.[37] The state of discussion about the pre-literary history behind the synoptic tradition is rather complex and cannot be presented here.[38] Basically, there have been two independent units in the synoptic tradition, one from the Markan tradition and another from the "double tradition" ("Q"), which have been combined in different ways by Luke and Matthew. In addition, both have made use of additional sayings stemming from their own tradition (*Sondergut*). In any case, it is clear that the synoptic Jesus is arguing with the Pharisees as the representatives of his opponents, and he points them to the "sign of Jonah." Less clear is what exactly this "sign" was showing more precisely.[39]

---

von der Buße der Niniviten, mit denen sich Gott versöhnte, gab diesem Tag eine nichtexklusive, der ganzen Menschheit geltende Deutung ...".

[36] Cf. Ps 36:7.

[37] Cf. Mk 8:11f; Mt 12:38-42; 16:1-2a; 4; Lk 11:16; 29-32.

[38] Cf. Michael Wolter, *Das Lukasevangelium*, HNT 5 (Tübingen: Mohr Siebeck, 2008), 414-26; Ulrich Luz, *Das Evangelium nach Matthäus*, vol. 2, EKK I/2 (Zürich/Neukirchen-Vluyn: Benziger/Neukirchener, 1990), 271-85; Joachim Gnilka, *Das Evangelium nach Markus*, vol. 1, EKK II/1 (Zürich/Neukirchen-Vluyn: Benziger/Neukirchener, 1980), 305-308.

[39] For further discussion, see John S. Kloppenborg, *The Formation of Q. Trajectories in Ancient Wisdom Collections* (Minneapolis: Fortress, 1987), 128-34; Martin Hüneburg, *Jesus als Wundertäter in der Logienquelle. Ein Beitrag zur Christologie von Q*, ABG 4 (Leipzig: EVA, 2001), 214-23; James D. G. Dunn, *Jesus Remembered, Christianity in the Making 1* (Grand Rapids/Cambridge: Wm. B. Eerdmanns, 2003),

According to Mark, Jesus refuses in principle to present any sign, but Mark does not mention Jonah. The parallel texts in Matthew and Luke, in comparison with Mark, expand Jesus' refusal to present a sign, and both announce one exception: the "sign of Jonah." However, according to Luke, Jesus after refusing the Pharisee's request (Lk 11:16) brings forward several other disputation sayings before he mentions the "sign of Jonah" (Lk 11:29). Only thereafter Luke hints at what this sign may show. He refers to Jonah's prophecy of judgment against Nineveh. Just like Jonah formerly became a "sign" to the Ninevites, so "the Son of Man" will stand up and give testimony against "this generation" at the last judgment (Lk 11:30). Furthermore, because the Gentile Ninevites repented at that time (like the "Queen from South"[40] who came from the ends of the earth to listen to the wisdom of Solomon), they will also testify against "this generation;" i.e., against the Israelites who are not willing to believe in Jesus, at the last judgment. For "here is more than Solomon" and "more than Jonah" (Lk 11:31f). In the gospels, Jonah is therefore turned into a paradigmatic prophet of judgment from the first covenant and into a model for Jesus' own proclamation of the eschatological judgment.

According to Matthew, Jesus refuses to present a sign to the Pharisees,[41] referring them, like Luke, to the "sign of Jonah" (Mt 16:2a, 4; 12:39). But then he continues, at least in one of the two places, by adding two explanations for this "sign of Jonah." First, he interprets Jonah's three-day stay in the belly of the "oceanic monster"[42] as a model for the three-day stay of "the Son of Man in the heart of the earth" (Mt 12:40), thus pointing indirectly to Jesus' resurrection from the dead. Second, he invokes the people of Nineveh as witnesses against "this generation" at the last judgment because they had repented in reaction to Jonah's prophecy (Mt 12:41). Like Luke, Matthew also refers to the "Queen from South" (Mt 12:42), but only second to the Ninevites, as a biblical model for Gentiles who have been repentant, unlike to "this generation." In Matthew like in Luke, therefore, Jonah appears predominantly as an eschatological prophet of judgment. Moreover, only in Matthew he is also a biblical model for the resurrection of Jesus, "the Son of Man."

Given this rather complex synoptic tradition it is risky to reconstruct what Jesus himself, the "pre-Easter" Jesus, knew about Jonah. We would

---

658-60 and, most recently, Peter Lampe, "Jona in der Jesustradition des ersten Jahrhunderts auf der Grundlage literarischer und archäologischer Zeugnisse," in Petra von Gemünden/David G. Horrell and Max Küchler (eds), *Jesus - Gestalt und Gestaltungen. Rezeptionen des Galiläers in Wissenschaft, Kirche und Gesellschaft* (FS G. Theißen), NTOA/StUNT 100 (Göttingen: Vandenhoeck & Ruprecht, 2013), 347-72.

[40] Cf. 1 Kings 10:1-13.
[41] And also to the scribes, cf. 12:38, or to the Sadducees, cf. 16:1.
[42] Κῆτος like the Septuagint!

have to start with two disputation sayings which, independently of one another, were incorporated into the Synoptic Gospels. Originally one was part of a disputation talk with the Pharisees when Jesus refused in principle to grant them any sign.[43] The second piece of tradition originated as another disputation saying when Jesus referred to the Ninevites as the audience of Jonah's judgment prophecy as well as to the "Queen from South." This saying was transmitted by the double tradition of Matthew and Luke ("Q"). Both the Ninevites as well as the "Queen from South"' are used here as models for Jesus' own proclamation of the last judgment against "this generation." Matthew as well as Luke combined both traditions, and Matthew even doubled them and incorporated them in two different places in his gospel story. In addition, Matthew used the motif of Jonah in the belly of the oceanic monster as a model for the resurrection of Jesus which apparently presupposes the Easter confession of his community. This fits well with Matthew's dealing with Scripture in other places in his gospel. Therefore, it was probably Matthew who added this saying to the tradition about Jonah which he had found in his sources. Whether he could hereby make use of his *Sondergut* may remain open.

In conclusion, Jesus himself may have known about Jonah as a prophet of judgment and he may also have made use of him as an example of his own teaching about the last judgment. Perhaps, he also referred to the Ninevites already as examples for non-Jews being repentant.[44] In any case, he could use this biblical paradigm polemically against his Jewish contemporaries who were dismissing his preaching. If we can assume this, then the prophetic confrontation of Israelites and Gentiles, which implicitly was part of the Jonah story, may have already been used by Jesus in his disputations with his opponents. This assumption could explain the extension of the Jesus-movement to non-Jews which obviously is picked out later as a central topic in Matthew's Gospel.[45]

---

[43] Mark 8:11f. Probably, the pre-Markan tradition already implied a reference to the "sign of Jonah," which was removed by Mark because of the new context of this piece of tradition in his gospel; without such a hint, the saying would have been completely incomprehensible as a polemic against the Pharisees.

[44] Cf. Florian Wilk, *Jesus und die Völker in der Sicht der Synoptiker*, BZNW 109 (Berlin/New York: de Gruyter, 2002, 270–86). For Jesus' intention to address Gentiles at least in exceptional cases, see Dunn, op. cit. (note 39), 537–39.

[45] Cf. Mt 28:16–20.

JONAH AS A MODEL IN BIBLICAL THEOLOGY (CONCLUSION)

The Psalm of Jonah does not play a role in the Jesus tradition. The belly of the fish is only a model for Jesus' tomb but not a place for singing a Psalm. Even this probably only applies to the time after Easter and perhaps only to Matthew. Step by step, the Book of Jonah became a biblical model for the resurrection of the dead.[46] In fact, the first steps of this history of tradition have left their traces in the Synoptic Gospels. But, only in Matthew, do we find for the first time the motif of Jonah in the belly of the fish as a symbol of the resurrection of Christ. Nevertheless, it was this layer of tradition which took the lead in the interpretation of the Book of Jonah in Christian reception history, not the emphasis which Jesus himself probably had laid on it. It was the post-Easter faith in Jesus' own death and resurrection that determined the Christian understanding of Jonah's fate.

This is decisive for a Christian reading and understanding of the Psalm of Jonah. If, today, we ask what we are to understand by Jonah addressing us out of the mouth of the fish from the perspective of Lutheran hermeneutics, then we have to focus on the message that the Bible, consisting of both testaments, has to say. What comes out of the mouth of the fish for us today? Let me conclude with some brief remarks on Jonah as a model in biblical theology.

The Book of Jonah can be regarded as a test case for a biblical theology in a Christian sense. Decisive for such a theology is not the preaching of the "pre-Easter" Jesus or even of the "historical" Jesus as somehow or other reconstructed, nor the message of the eighth-century BCE "historical Jonah" as reconstructed by means of modern historical scholarship. Decisive for a Christian understanding of the Book of Jonah is the confession to Jesus who died on the cross and was resurrected by God on the third day. This confession controls the interpretation of the texts from the New as well as the Old Testament. This does not mean that any historical analysis of the biblical texts or any interpretation of texts from the Old Testament according to Jewish exegetical traditions is useless or even dangerous. On the contrary, both can be quite helpful better to understand the texts transmitted to us in a more differentiated way. But all this historical investigation is not an end in itself. It can only be a means to achieve an appropriate theological understanding of the Bible consisting of both Old and New Testament as testimony of God's saving work in Jesus Christ, his Son.

---

[46] See the many references in Steffen, op. cit. (note 5), 141–238.

What we see here is the eighteenth-century pulpit in the (former Lutheran) church in Bad Reinerz in Silesia, now part of Poland. You may recognize the animal. It looks more like an oceanic monster than like a friendly fish. The pulpit is carried by the four evangelists. Above the mouth of the fish there are several Old Testament prophets. The risen Christ is at the top, but one may also admire (or be afraid of) the white teeth in the mouth of the fish. In the middle of the mouth there is nothing but an empty space and a blood-red background. But if one looks more carefully one see a microphone and a bookrest, and above of them the Holy Spirit like a dove surrounded by a circle of rays.

What comes out of the mouth of the fish will depend on who enters the pulpit and how they understand and present the story. In their sermon, they will either highlight the fish or the risen Christ or the Holy Spirit or something else that they have read in the gospels or in the whole Bible. It needs a living voice, a believing human being, to preach the gospel so that it can be understood and accepted as the word of life by the people of today. There are many ways of understanding biblical stories and they all have their own contexts. But there is only one gospel to proclaim. From the perspective of Lutheran hermeneutics of today it will be decisive whether we can discover in all these very different and sometimes also disturbing stories and texts of the Bible the *viva vox evangelii*, the message of the living Word which feeds all people who are in need of it.

In terms of the Lutheran tradition, God's Word has to be proclaimed to human beings as Law and gospel. The biblical Jonah—although still without any knowledge of Luther and his distinction of Law and gospel—formed the model of a Lutheran pastor in that he or she, sometimes against their own will and understanding, take over the task of preaching God's message to human beings. By this they turn out to become the mouth of God.

INTERPRETATION OF THE PSALMS IN THE NEW TESTAMENT: WITNESS TO CHRIST AND THE HUMAN CONDITION

CRAIG R. KOESTER

The Psalms had an important role in shaping Luther's understanding of the life of faith. In his "Preface" of 1528, Luther calls the Psalms "a little Bible" and a "handbook" that summarizes all of Scripture.[1] Luther's context was the late medieval world, which he described as one filled with legends and examples drawn from the lives of the saints. Yet, he noted that the Psalms have the unique power to inspire faith, which he hoped to convey by translating them so that people could read the Psalms in their own language. He encouraged the reading of the Psalms for two reasons: First, he said they conveyed the promise of Christ's death and resurrection, thereby emphasizing what Christ has done.[2] Second, they offered more than pious examples. They speak honestly about the human condition with its grief and sadness, its hope and anticipation. The Psalms are like a mirror that shows people what they are, calling each person to "know yourself" in relation to God, the communion of saints and all creatures.[3]

The members of the global Lutheran community read and understand the Psalms in contexts that are different from the one in which Luther composed his "Preface." Moreover, the historically-focused biblical scholarship, common in academic circles, emphasizes the need to relate the Psalms to their earliest contexts in Israel's history. Such contexts range from the time of the monarchy and First Temple to the exile and the period after the exile. That approach demonstrates the significance of the Psalms for people in the

---

[1] Martin Luther, "Preface to the Psalter," in Theodore Bachmann (ed.), *Luther's Works*, vol. 35 (Philadelphia: Fortress Press, 1960), 253–57, esp. 362. The English edition is abbreviated *LW*. German text in *D. Martin Luthers Werke*, Kritische Gesamtausgabe, Die Deutsche Bibel 10/1 (Weimar: Hermann Böhlaus, 2001), 98–105, esp. 98. The German edition is abbreviated *WA.DB*.
[2] Luther said that "here we find not only what one or two saints have done, but what he has done who is the very head of all the saints," for the Psalter "promises Christ's death and resurrection so clearly" (*LW* 35, 254; cf. *WA.DB* 10/1, 98).
[3] *LW* 35, 255, 257; *WA.DB* 10/1, 100, 104.

centuries before Christ, but raises questions about how the Psalms can be related to Jesus. Yet, the Psalms continue to have a place in Lutheran worship, teaching and preaching worldwide. In those contexts they are interpreted theologically and pastorally in ways that address the worshippers. Therefore, it is important to ask what it means to read the Psalms within a community that is bound together by its faith in the crucified and risen Christ.[4]

Consideration of the Psalms in the New Testament has a place in the discussion, since New Testament writers drew on the Psalms when addressing issues facing their communities. Because the Psalms are used throughout the New Testament, the topic is a large one. Here we will focus on the book of Acts and the Gospel of John, where the Psalms are quoted with reference to Christ in various ways.[5] We will turn Luther's observations about the Psalms into interpretive questions, asking how these writers relate the Psalms to the crucified and risen Jesus and to the wider human situation. As we do so, we will explore the implications for the interpretation of the Psalms in our own contexts. Although our focus is on Lutheran hermeneutics, our world is ecumenical. That, too, is a reason to explore the use of Psalms in Acts and John, since Christians throughout the world share a biblical canon that includes both the Psalms and these New Testament writings.

Psalms in the Book of Acts

The Psalms play an important role in the book of Acts, where they bear witness to Jesus' death and resurrection.[6] We begin with Peter's Pentecost

---

[4] Interpreters who relate the Psalms in settings in Israel's history explore their theological significance in later contexts in the church. Among German scholars note the references to Luther and Calvin in Hans-Joachim Kraus, *Psalms*, Continental Commentaries, 2 vols (Minneapolis: Fortress Press, 1993, 2000) and his *Theology of the Psalms* (Minneapolis: Augsburg Fortress, 1992). Among American writers, see J. Clinton McCann Jr., *The Book of Psalms*, New Interpreter's Bible 4 (Nashville: Abingdon, 1996), 641-677. For an African perspective, see Cyril C. Okorocha, "Psalms" in Tokunboh Adeyemo et al (eds), *Africa Bible Commentary* (Nairobi/Grand Rapids: WordAlive and Zondervan, 2006).

[5] Psalms are quoted or paraphrased in most of the books in the New Testament. The Psalms used come from each part of the Psalter. For a list of quotations, see Wayne A. Meeks (ed.), *The HarperCollins Study Bible* (New York: HarperCollins, 1993), 2342-43. A more extensive list of quotations and allusions is given in Erwin Nestle, Barbara Aland, et al, *Novum Testamentum Graece*, 27th edition (Stuttgart: Deutsche Bibelgesellschaft, 1993), 785-90. For an overview of the topic, see Steve Moyise and Maarten J. J. Menken (eds), *The Psalms in the New Testament* (London and New York: T. & T. Clark, 2004).

[6] At the conclusion of the Gospel of Luke, Jesus says, "These are my words that I spoke to you while I was still with you—that everything written about me in the

sermon in Acts 2:14-36, which uses a theological framework that is typical of Acts. The idea is that Jesus' crucifixion reveals the depth of human resistance to God, because Jesus' opponents killed the Messiah, whom God had sent to heal and proclaim the good news. Yet, God responded by raising Jesus from the dead, so that the resurrection shows God's refusal to let human opposition have its way. By raising Jesus, God demonstrates that God's desire is to give life, so that people now have the opportunity to repent and believe the gospel message. This perspective is clear in the conclusion of Peter's sermon, which says that Jesus is the one "you crucified and killed by the hands of those outside the law. But God raised him up," so that "God has made him both Lord and Messiah, this Jesus whom you crucified." When people ask what they should do, Peter replies that they are to repent, be baptized and receive forgiveness (Acts 2:23-24, 36, 38).[7]

The sermon maintains that God was aware that people would resist God's Messiah, so that God made a place for their hostility in God's plans. Peter says that Jesus was handed over "according to the definite plan and foreknowledge of God" (Acts 2:23). The point is that Jesus' opponents did not surprise God by putting Jesus to death. Rather, God expected that to happen and was ready to respond by raising Jesus from the dead, in order to show that God's purposes were ultimately for life and salvation. To support this claim, Peter appeals to the Psalms, which are understood to have revealed God's purposes long before the time of Christ.

The interpretation of the Psalms in this passage has its own internal logic.[8] The basis is God's promise to establish an enduring kingdom through the heir to David's throne (2 Sam 7:12-13). The sermon recalls the promise in the language of Psalm 132:11, which summarizes a major biblical theme: "The Lord swore to David a sure oath from which he will not turn back: 'One of the sons of your body I will set on your throne'" (cf. Acts 2:30). The question is how God would keep that oath. The sermon responds by noting that David was a prophet, an idea drawn from 2 Samuel 23:1-7, where David speaks by God's Spirit, as a prophet would do. And since David was a prophet, Peter infers that he had the ability to "foresee" how God's

---

law of Moses, the prophets, and the Psalms must be fulfilled" (Lk 24:44). The book of Acts continues the story by including the fulfillment of the Psalms in the witness of the early church.

[7] For another example of the pattern, see Paul's sermon in Acts 13:16-41. The sermon recalls how the residents of Jerusalem and their leaders failed to recognize Jesus and had Pilate condemn him to death (Acts 13:26-29). Then it adds, "But God raised him from the dead" (Acts 13:30). Paul's sermon also used Psalm 16 as testimony to Jesus' resurrection, as Peter's sermon does in Acts 2 (see Acts 13:35).

[8] Peter Doble, "The Psalms in Luke-Acts," in Moyise and Menken, op. cit. (note 5), 83-117, esp. 90-97.

promise would be fulfilled through Jesus' death and resurrection (cf. Acts 2:31).[9] The sermon supports this idea by looking for a foreshadowing of the resurrection in the Psalms, which are ascribed to David.

A key passage is Psalm 16: "I keep the Lord always before me; because he is at my right hand, I shall not be moved;" "For you will not abandon my soul to Hades, or let your Holy One experience corruption. You have made known to me the ways of life; you will make me full of gladness with your presence" (Ps 16:8-11; Acts 2:25-28).[10] The Psalm is a prayer for help that expresses firm trust in God's unfailing care. Taken on its own, the psalmist's confidence that he will not be abandoned to Hades can be understood as hope of being saved from death. But Acts gives the Psalm a new dimension, so that it does not mean escaping death altogether—after all, Jesus died. Instead, the Psalm is taken to mean that God will not "abandon" the person by letting him remain in death long enough for the body to undergo "corruption." From that perspective, the Psalm depicts the story of Jesus, who died by crucifixion and was raised to life on the third day, before his body decayed.

The final piece of the argument comes from Psalm 110:1: "The Lord said to my Lord, 'Sit at my right hand, until I make your enemies your footstool'" (Acts 2:34-35). This Psalm celebrates the enthronement of a king. Since the king or "lord" in the Psalm is elevated to God's right hand, Peter's sermon identifies the enthronement with Jesus' ascension to heavenly glory.[11] This point brings the argument full circle. If the Davidic hope begins with God's promise to put one of David's descendants on the throne (Ps 132:11), it is realized by God delivering Jesus from death by means of resurrection (Ps 16:10), and enthroning him through ascension to heaven, where he now rules (Ps 110:1).

From the perspective of modern historical scholarship, it seems problematic to interpret these Psalms as prophetic texts, since they presumably

---

[9] On David's role as prophet and the prophetic character of the Psalms, see Margaret Daly-Denton, *David in the Fourth Gospel: The Johannine Reception of the Psalms* (Leiden: Brill, 2000), 91-94.

[10] The quotation is from the Greek translation of Psalm 16, which follows the Hebrew quite closely. The Greek "Hades" corresponds to the Hebrew "Sheol." Paul's sermon at Antioch in Pisidia uses Psalm 16 in a similar way, as a witness to the resurrection (Acts 13:35-37).

[11] Psalm 110:1 is the passage from the Psalms that is most widely cited in the New Testament (Mt 22:44; Mk 12:36; Lk 20:42; Acts 2:34; 1 Cor 15:25; Heb 1:13; cf. Rom 8:34; Eph 1:20; Heb 1:3; 8:1; 10:12). See David Hay, *Glory at the Right Hand: Psalm 110 in Early Christianity* (Nashville: Abingdon, 1973); Michel Gourgues, *A la droite de Dieu: Resurrection de Jesus et actualisation du psaume 110:1 dans le Nouveau Testament* (Paris: Gabalda, 1978).

did not function that way when first written. The approach taken in Peter's sermon might also suggest that the main task of interpretation is to equate passages from the Psalms with events in Jesus' career, instead of allowing the literary flow of the Psalms to shape the understanding. Finally, many Psalms are general enough to fit multiple situations, so that it would not be appropriate to limit them to the story of Jesus. Yet, with those cautionary remarks in mind, I want to revisit the question and ask what Acts 2 might contribute to contemporary theological interpretation of the Psalms and the discussion of Lutheran hermeneutics.

Psalm 16 is an expression of trust in God's constant care.[12] After telling of his faith in God, the psalmist recounts the many blessings God has provided. He says that people who follow other gods will have reason for grief, but the psalmist firmly trusts in God and lives in "pleasant places" (Ps 16:4–6). God offers good counsel and strengthens the psalmist, so that he will not be moved (Ps 16:7–8). Because of the blessings the psalmist has received, he can be sure that God will not abandon him to Hades, but will continue to provide joy and delight (Ps 16:9–11). Such an expression of faith is eloquent, but the experiences of modern readers will often call it into question. There are contexts in which there is no clear connection between faith in God and enjoying a pleasant life. Suffering comes even to the most faithful people.

Here is where reading the Psalm in light of Jesus' crucifixion and resurrection can be helpful. The interpretation of Psalm 16 in Peter's sermon shows that God's purposes cannot be reduced to helping people avoid difficult circumstances. God did not preserve Jesus from Hades by shielding him from death. Rather, God preserved him by bringing him through death to life. God's faithfulness can take the form of the blessings depicted in Psalm 16, but it also takes the form of meeting people in the contexts where the forces of death and destruction are at work. From that perspective the Psalm offers a word of promise, for as people encounter the forces that threaten their well-being, God's purposes are ultimately directed toward life.

The context in Acts also suggests perspectives on Psalm 110:1 that offer a triumphant picture of the king who reigns at God's right hand. But a significant dimension of the Psalm is that conflict continues even after the king's enthronement. The Psalm speaks of the "enemies," who must be brought under the king's dominion. Paul's interpretation of Psalm 110:1 emphasizes that Christ's reign as the risen Lord is the scene of conflict, in which all the powers that oppose God must be overcome. He adds that the

---

[12] It has been called a confession of faith and a song of confidence by Erhard Gerstenberger, *Psalms*, 2 vols (Grand Rapids: Eerdmans, 1988, 2001), vol. 1, 90.

last enemy to be destroyed is death, which will be fully overcome at the final resurrection (1 Cor 15:24-26).

The book of Acts does not develop the theme of cosmic powers as Paul does, but it depicts a situation in which Christ has been exalted to glory at God's right hand, even as his followers continue to face threats on earth. His followers are to bear witness to him throughout the world, yet at each step their witness is given in the face of hostility, imprisonment and death. The apostles' arrests, Stephen's martyrdom and Paul's imprisonment show that the "enemies" of Christ remain active, and yet their efforts to suppress the gospel message actually lead to it being made more public. In the face of persecution, Jesus' followers take the gospel from Judea to Samaria and finally to Rome, where Paul arrives as a prisoner. The message of Christ's lordship might seem to be contradicted by the ongoing experience of opposition, but Psalm 110 reframes that perspective. Christ's reign is not characterized by the absence of conflict. Rather, it is shown by the Spirit fostering Christian witness and community in the midst of conflict.

This approach to the Psalms is further developed in the prayer that Jesus' followers offer when facing hostility (Acts 4:23-31). The setting is one in which Peter has been arrested because of his preaching and then released. In response, the community joins in a prayer that draws on Psalm 2, which they relate to the situation of Jesus and to their own context. The Psalm refers to God's anointed king, to whom God says, "You are my son; today I have begotten you" (Ps 2:7). That language invited a connection with Jesus, who was identified as God's Son and the "anointed one" or Christ.[13] The opening lines tell of the nations opposing God's anointed one: "Why do the nations conspire, and the peoples plot in vain? The kings of the earth set themselves, and the rulers take counsel together, against the Lord and his anointed" (Ps 2:1-2). After picturing such widespread hostility, the Psalm continues by affirming that God will defeat those adversaries and establish the reign of God's anointed one to the ends of the earth (Ps 2:4-6, 8-11).

At one level, the prayer in Acts 4 relates the Psalm to the opposition against Jesus, which led to his crucifixion. Where the Psalm refers to hostile kings and rulers, Jesus faced Herod the king and Pilate the Roman governor. Where the Psalm tells of angry nations and peoples, Jesus' adversaries included both Gentiles and Jews (Acts 4:27). The interpretive framework is like that of Peter's sermon earlier. The prayer assumes that

---

[13] Psalm 2:7 is quoted with reference to Jesus in Acts 13:33; Heb 1:5. The words "you are my son" and similar expressions are used at Jesus' baptism (Mk 1:11; Lk 3:22; cf. Mt 3:17; Jn 1:34). On the importance of Psalm 2 in the New Testament, see Sam Janse, *"You are my Son": The Reception History of Psalm 2 in Early Judaism and the Early Church* (Leuven: Peeters, 2009).

Jesus' opponents are responsible for the crucifixion, while insisting that God anticipated their actions and included them in God's plans. The crucifixion was not a defeat for God and a victory for his opponents. Rather, those who crucified Jesus did what God expected. Their actions fit what God's "plan had predestined to take place," which was to bring life out of death through Jesus' resurrection (Acts 4:28). God's purposes are ultimately for salvation (Acts 4:12), and through the opposition that led to crucifixion, God's purposes were being carried out.

This Christological interpretation of Psalm 2 leads the community in Jerusalem to apply it to the challenges they face in their own context.[14] In the past, Jesus encountered sharp opposition from those in authority, and the arrest of Peter and John showed that hostility continued to threaten his followers in the time after his resurrection. The literary context uses expressions from the Psalm to describe the apostles' interrogation before the Jewish leaders: the "rulers" of the people "gathered together" against them, as they had previously done against the Lord's anointed (Acts 4:5, 26). What gives confidence to the community is the conviction that God continues to be at work. Since God could carry out God's purposes through the opposition facing Jesus, believers can pray that God will also empower them to speak the word "with all boldness" as they encounter opposition in their own contexts (Acts 4:29).

We can focus our reflections on the interpretation of Psalm 2 in this prayer by asking what it reveals about God's way of working. The Psalm depicts a God whose anointed king reigns in a context of opposition. If God has "decided beforehand" to work in this way, then God's purposes are not accomplished apart from human hostility but through it. The Psalm assumes that hostility to God is the context in which God works and mentions that opposition in its opening verse. But the Psalm also shows that in the face of such hostility, God is accomplishing God's designs, which are ultimately salvific. That understanding of God is what allows the Psalm and the passion story to be taken together, in order to encourage believers who face conflict in the time after Jesus' resurrection and ascension. In Lutheran language, it is a way of reading that reflects a theology of the cross, in which God's power to save is revealed through the reality of conflict and suffering.[15]

---

[14] Beverly Roberts Gaventa, *The Acts of the Apostles* (Nashville: Abingdon, 2003), 98.
[15] See Michael Parsons, "Luther, the Royal Psalms and the Suffering Church," in *Evangelical Review of Theology* 35 (2011), 242–54. On Luther's perspective, see sections 19–20 of the "Heidelberg Disputation," in *LW* 31, 52–53. For the Latin text, see *D. Martin Luthers Werke: Kritische Gesamtausgabe*, vol. 1 (Weimar: Hermann Böhlaus, 1883), 361–62. See also Paul Althaus, *The Theology of Martin Luther*

Psalms in the Gospel of John

John's Gospel is like the book of Acts in that it interprets the Psalms in light of Jesus' death and resurrection. But it differs in that the gospel has its own theological framework. John's emphasis is on the paradoxical quality of divine revelation. In the Fourth Gospel, the crucifixion reveals the world's hostility toward God as well as God's own love for the world. Like the book of Acts, the gospel sees human opposition to God being revealed in the events that culminate in the crucifixion of Jesus, the one whom God has sent. But John also sees Jesus laying down his life willingly, so that his death conveys the highest form of sacrificial love for others (Jn 15:13). Jesus says that he lays down his life out of obedience to his Father (Jn 10:17-18). By going to the cross, Jesus reveals his own love for God and God's love for the world (Jn 3:14-16; 14:31).[16]

John recognizes that those aspects of the crucifixion are not self-evident, so the gospel must disclose them through the narration of Jesus' actions and quotations from Scripture. One of the most important texts is Psalm 69, which is a plea for God's help in a time of deep distress. The Psalm is used as a commentary on the meaning of Jesus' death at several points, beginning with the cleansing of the temple in chapter 2. The action centers on Jesus driving out the merchants and the animals used for sacrifice, and overturning the tables of the moneychangers. The bystanders do not understand what Jesus has done, so they ask him to perform a miraculous sign in order to show his divine authority. Jesus replied, "Destroy this temple, and in three days I will raise it up." (Jn 2:19). The crowd had no idea what Jesus meant, and it was only after Easter that his disciples "remembered" that he said this, and recognized that Jesus spoke of his opponents destroying the "temple" of his body through crucifixion and to his being raised up through resurrection (Jn 2:21-22).

The gospel interprets Psalm 69 from this post-resurrection perspective. It was after Easter that the disciples "remembered" that it was written, "Zeal

---

(Philadelphia: Fortress, 1966), 25-34. A theology of the cross does not negate the importance of the resurrection, but it insists that resurrection be seen in light of the suffering and death that are inextricably connected to it. See Bernard Lohse, *Martin Luther's Theology: Its Historical and Systematic Development* (Minneapolis: Fortress, 1999), 39.

[16] On the meaning of Jesus' death in John's Gospel, see Craig R. Koester, *The Word of Life: A Theology of the Gospel of John* (Grand Rapids: Eerdmans, 2008), 108-23; Jörg Frei, "Die '*theologia crucifixi*' des Johannesevangeliums," in Andreas Dettwiler and Jean Zumstein (eds), *Kreuzestheologie im Neuen Testament* (Tübingen: Mohr Siebeck, 2002), 169-238.

for your house will consume me" (Jn 2:17).[17] The quotation is drawn from Psalm 69:9 and it offers commentary on the story of Jesus at two levels: First, the quotation emphasizes that Jesus' actions in the temple are done out of a zealous commitment to God and God's sanctuary. By driving out the merchants, Jesus was not opposing God. Instead, he was carrying out God's desire that God's house not be turned into a marketplace (Jn 2:16).

Second, the Psalm shows that the cleansing of the temple foreshadows the crucifixion. To make the connection to the cross clear, the gospel changes the verb tense used in the Psalm from the past to the future. Instead of saying that zeal for God's house "has consumed" Jesus, as in the Psalm itself, the gospel says that it "will consume" him, when his opponents try to destroy the temple of his body.[18] From this perspective, the Psalm emphasizes that Jesus' death comes from his zealous commitment to God. The result is that the crucified and risen Jesus is the "temple" or focus of worship for the Christian community. If the temple was where God was uniquely present and where sacrifice was made, it is Jesus who uniquely embodies the presence of God and makes atonement for sin through his sacrifice (Jn 1:29; 10:30).[19]

The next time Psalm 69 is cited is during Jesus' conversation with his disciples at the last supper. Before going to his death, Jesus speaks of the hatred of the world, which is now directed against him and will also be directed against his followers in time to come (Jn 15:18-25). In this context he says that the world's opposition fulfills what was written, "They hated me without a cause" (Jn 15:25). Jesus seems to recall Psalm 69:4, "More in number than the hairs of my head are those who hate me without cause." Yet Psalm 35:19 uses similar language and the theme of senseless hatred

---

[17] Initially, the flow of the narrative could suggest that the disciples "remembered" Psalm 69:9 at the time Jesus was cleansing the temple. But there are important reasons to think it refers to post-resurrection reflection. One is that the word "remember," which is used for remembering Psalm 69 in John 2:17 is also used in John 2:22, where it makes clear that insight into Jesus' words and the Scriptures came later, after he was raised from the dead. In John 12:16 it is clear that the disciples' "remembering" and understanding the Scripture occurs after Jesus' resurrection rather than before it.

[18] Both Hebrew and Greek forms of the Psalm use past tense forms of the verb "consume." On John's adaptation, see Maarten J. J. Menken, *Old Testament Quotations in the Fourth Gospel: Studies in Textual Form* (Kampen: Kok Pharos, 1996), 37-45; Andreas Obermann, *Die christologische Erfüllung der Schrift im Johannesevangelium*, WUNT II/83 (Tübingen: Mohr Siebeck, 1996), 114-128; Daly-Denton, op. cit. (note 9), 118-31.

[19] On the temple imagery and its relationship to Jesus' death, see Craig R. Koester, *Symbolism in the Fourth Gospel*, 2nd ed. (Minneapolis: Fortress, 2003), 86-89.

also appears in other Psalms (Ps 109:3; 119:161).[20] The gospel draws on the theme of hatred, which appears in various Psalms to characterize the situation of Jesus and his followers.

The gospel says that the world's hatred was to "fulfill" (*plēroun*) what was written in Scripture (Jn 15:25).[21] In John, "fulfillment" has to do with revealing of Scripture's fullness of meaning. The idea is not so much that Psalm 69:4 and similar passages predicted a specific event, which must then take place in Jesus' ministry. After all, there was senseless hatred before the time of Jesus, and Jesus warns that his followers will experience it after his resurrection. Instead, Jesus' ministry fulfills the Psalm by disclosing its fullness of meaning. Jesus prefaces his quotation by saying that his works provoked hostility, recalling the negative reactions to his signs (Jn 15:24). After he gave sight to a man born blind, his adversaries showed their blindness to God's purposes by condemning him for healing on the Sabbath (Jn 9:40-41). After he raised Lazarus from the dead, his opponents saw him as a threat and determined to put him to death (Jn 11:47-53). In the Fourth Gospel, the way Jesus' opponents decide to kill the giver of life fulfills the Psalms by showing more fully what senseless hatred means.

This approach to interpretation recognizes that Psalm 69:4 and similar passages can speak of hatred in a way that applies to multiple situations. It does not limit the Psalm to a commentary on the opposition that brought about Jesus' crucifixion. It also invites reflection on how it can be meaningful to read the Psalm in light of its use by Jesus in John's Gospel. Taken on its own, the Psalm calls out for help to a God who may seem distant from the situation. But in John's Gospel, Jesus is sent by God to enter fully into the situation and experiences the hatred of which the Psalm speaks. If God is present in Jesus, as the gospel says he is, then God is present in the situations where those who follow Jesus face the kind of senseless hatred depicted in the Psalm.

The use of Psalm 69 in John's account of the crucifixion fits this pattern of locating Jesus' suffering in the broader context of human experience.

---

[20] Daly-Denton focuses on the use of Psalm 69 in this passage, op. cit. (note 9), 201-208. The sense that the passage recalls multiple Psalms is noted by others. See Menken, op. cit. (note 18), 139-45; Obermann, op. cit. (note 18), 271-82; Bruce G. Schuchard, *Scripture within Scripture: The Interrelationship of Form and Function in the Explicit Old Testament Citations in the Gospel of John*, SBL Dissertation Series 133 (Atlanta: Scholars Press, 1993), 119-23.

[21] In John 15:25, Jesus says that his opponents fulfill what is written in their "law," using "law" in a general sense for the Scriptures, which include the Psalms. On the revelatory dimension of the term "fulfill" in John, see Obermann, op. cit. (note 18), 81-87. He notes the connection with Jesus being "full" of grace and truth and making God known (Jn 1:14-18).

Although all four gospels mention that Jesus was given sour wine to drink, only John explicitly connects that action to the Psalms by stating that it fulfills Scripture, so that readers are made aware of the biblical connection.[22] As the moment of death approaches, the gospel says that "when Jesus knew that all was now finished, he said (in order to fulfill the Scripture), 'I am thirsty.'" And a bystander gave him sour wine. After receiving it, Jesus said, "It is finished" and gave up his spirit (Jn 19:28-30). Although the scriptural passage is not quoted, the gospel recalls Psalm 69:21: "for my thirst they gave me vinegar to drink."

Using the word "finished" or better, "accomplished" (*teleioun*) for the fulfillment of Scripture in this context (Jn 19:28) encourages readers to understand the Psalm in light of what Jesus has "finished" or "accomplished"(*telein*) through his ministry (Jn 19:30). John's Gospel uses the image of "thirst" to describe the human need for the life that God provides. The gospel assumes that "life" has a physical dimension, and that people need ordinary food and water in order to survive. But it also recognizes that "life" in its fullest sense is lived in a trusting relationship with God. People who are physically alive and yet alienated from God do not have "life" in the full theological sense. Human thirst for life with God is met when people are brought to faith through Jesus' words and actions and the ongoing activity of the Spirit. In John's Gospel, true life is called "eternal life," because it begins in the present, in faith, and has a future beyond death through the promise of resurrection.[23]

Jesus spoke of human thirst for God when he met a Samaritan woman beside a well and offered to give her living water. He told her, "Everyone who drinks from this water" in the well "will be thirsty again, but those who drink of the water that I will give them will never be thirsty. The water that I will give will become in them a spring of water gushing up to eternal life" (Jn 4:13-14). Later, he told a crowd of worshippers in Jerusalem, "Let anyone who is thirsty come to me, and let the one who believes in me

---

[22] The words "My God, my God, why have you forsaken me?" from Psalm 22:1 are quoted without introduction in Matthew 27:46 and Mark 15:34; The words "Into your hands I commit my spirit" from Psalm 31:5 are quoted in Luke 23:46. On the use of "finish" or "accomplished" in relation to the Scriptures in John, see Obermann, op. cit. (note 18), 87-89. On the importance of John's explicit citations, see Marianne Meyer Thompson, "'They Bear Witness to Me': The Psalms in the Passion Narrative of the Gospel of John," in J. Ross Wagner, C. Kavin Rowe and A. Katherine Grieb (eds), *The Word Leaps the Gap: Essays on Scripture and Theology in Honor of Richard B. Hays* (Grand Rapids and Cambridge: Eerdmans, 2008), 267-83, esp., 271-75.

[23] On "life" in John's Gospel, see Koester, op. cit. (note 16), 31-32, 44-47, 55-56, 179-82.

drink," for he said that "Out of the believer's heart shall flow rivers of living water," referring to the Spirit, which the crucified and risen Christ would give (Jn 7:37-39). When Jesus says I thirst at the conclusion of his ministry, he puts himself in the position of the thirsty people for whom he has come. He meets the thirst of others by suffering thirst himself, to convey the fullness of divine love. When he dies, water flows from his side as a sign of the life that the crucified Christ provides (Jn 19:34).

The narration of the crucifixion scene and its reference to Psalm 69 relate Jesus' thirst to his drinking sour wine. In the Fourth Gospel, wine plays an important role. Jesus' ministry began at Cana, where he turned water into the highest quality wine. It was a sign of divine favor, reminiscent of various Old Testament passages about God's blessings (Am 9:13; Joel 3:18). In this gracious way, the sign reveals Jesus' "glory," a term for divine power and presence (Jn 2:1-11). At Cana, Jesus told his mother that his "hour" had not yet come, alluding to the coming hour of his death (Jn 2:4). The gift of the best wine, at the beginning of his ministry anticipates the fullness of divine grace that comes through his death at the end. His gift is a costly one, as is shown by his final gesture: He gives others the best wine, while drinking the sour wine himself. That is the way his life-giving purposes are "accomplished," as the Psalm attests (Jn 19:28-30).

John's Gospel uses Psalm 69 to provide perspective on the meaning of Jesus' death. But, with the question of hermeneutics in mind, we might also move in the other direction, by looking back from John's account of the crucifixion to the Psalm itself. What does it mean to read Psalm 69 in light of the cross? Taken on its own, the Psalm is a vivid picture of human suffering and divine deliverance. It begins with anguished cries for God's help (Ps 69:1-29) and it concludes with prayers of thanksgiving for the salvation that has been received (Ps 69:30-36). Using the Psalm in the gospel does not narrow its significance, as if readers are to see the Psalm depicting only the suffering of Jesus and not the suffering of others. Instead, the connection with the story of Jesus encourages readers to ask how God is present and active through the suffering depicted in the first part of the Psalm, as well as in the joy expressed in the second part.[24]

The interpretive perspective I am developing here reflects a Lutheran theology of the cross. That perspective challenges the idea that God's invisible things are clearly seen by the human eye. Instead, it recognizes that God's presence and actions are hidden and revealed in contexts that

---

[24] For theological reflections on reading Psalm 69 in light of Jesus' suffering and wider human suffering, especially in east Africa, see Anastasia Boniface-Malle, "Interpreting the Lament Psalms from the Tanzanian Context: Problems and Prospects" (Ph.D. diss.; Saint Paul: Luther Seminary, 2000), 122-26.

seem to be the opposite of power and glory, namely, in the weakness and shame of Jesus' crucifixion.[25] This perspective works against the idea that God's hand is to be seen primarily in the actions of the strong over against the weak or in the powerful rather than in the powerless. It does not make God the author of suffering, as if suffering is what God desires. But it does affirm that God carried out God's purposes through the entire story of Jesus—not only in his miracles and his resurrection, but in the crucifixion itself. That is where God's love is revealed in its most radical form, as Jesus is "lifted up" on the cross (Jn 3:14-16).[26]

With these dynamics in mind, we turn again to John's crucifixion narrative, where it would appear that the cross is a victory for Jesus' opponents. Jesus' interrogation ends when Pilate hands Jesus over to be crucified (Jn 19:16a). Next, the soldiers carry out Pilate's decision by having Jesus carry the cross to the place of execution, which was a way of humiliating Jesus (Jn 19:16b-17). The soldiers continue by crucifying Jesus in order to carry out Pilate's will. And Pilate seems to get his way when he places a sign above the cross, announcing that he is crucifying the King of the Jews—a sign he refuses to change when asked to do so (Jn 19:19-22). The impression is that Jesus' opponents are in control, and it continues as the soldiers divide Jesus' clothing among themselves. They "take" what they want from Jesus and "make" what they will of it, so that each soldier gets a share (Jn 19:23).

To the human eye, it appears that Jesus' adversaries have the upper hand. Rightly or wrongly, victory seems to belong to them. If God is powerful, then one might think that God is on their side. But if God is with Jesus, then it would seem that God has been defeated, because Jesus is being killed. But the gospel works against that perspective by saying that the soldiers' actions fulfill the Scripture: "They divided my clothes among themselves, and for my clothing they cast lots" (Jn 19:24). The quotation is from Psalms 22:18. Like many passages from biblical poetry, it makes use of parallelism. The Psalm's references to dividing up and casting lots for Jesus' clothing repeat the same basic idea in two different ways. The gospel, however, gives each part of the verse due weight, so that the soldiers' actions fit the Psalm exactly: Dividing up Jesus' clothes fits the first part of the verse, and casting lots for his tunic fits the second part.

---

[25] On the theology of the cross, see note 15 and the international studies in note 31.
[26] The verb "lift up" (*hypsoun*) can include both physical elevation and exaltation in glory. John's Gospel uses the term to bring both ideas together. The sense of physical elevation through crucifixion is clear from the comparison with Moses lifting up the serpent on the pole (Jn 3:14), Jesus' enemies lifting him up (Jn 8:28), and Jesus relating the term to the type of death he would die (Jn 12:32-34). Yet, in John, the cross shows the glory of divine love and is part of his return to God.

The quotation of the Psalm challenges the impression that this scene is determined by human action alone. If the soldiers conform to a pattern attested to in Psalm 22, then it suggests that their actions must be seen in light of God's wider purposes. Interpreters sometimes ascribe more specific meaning to the scene, arguing that Jesus' seamless tunic points to his status as high priest, or that not tearing his tunic means that his kingdom will not be torn away from him as it was torn away from previous kings in Israel.[27] But attempts to find such specific symbolism in the passage seem forced. Here it is enough to note that the quotation of Psalm 22 signals that God's purposes are being carried out, even in a scene where they seem to be hidden.

Earlier in the gospel, Jesus "took off" or literally "laid down" his outer robe in order to assume the role of a slave by washing the disciples' feet (Jn 13:4). That action revealed the depth of his love for them, and by laying down his clothes he anticipated his crucifixion, when he would lay down his life for others in his greatest revelation of divine love.[28] When the soldiers divide up Jesus' clothing at the cross, their actions seem purely self-serving. Each wants to get as much as he can. But the earlier references to Jesus laying down his clothing remind readers that Jesus' purposes are different. His actions reflect how much he is willing to give up for others. And the way the soldiers do what was foreshadowed in the Psalm indicates that their actions ultimately serve God's greater redemptive purpose.

When we ask what it means to read Psalm 22 in light of John's passion narrative, the result is similar to what we noted above. Psalm 22 is another lament, which begins, "My God, my God, why have you forsaken me?" As a lament, it moves from an extended account of suffering (Ps 22:1-21a) to the final section giving thanks for deliverance (Ps 22:21b-31). In the first part of the Psalm, suffering seems to mean that God is distant and that God's actions are to be seen in the second part, when the Psalmist has been brought out of suffering. Yet John's Gospel relates the first part of the Psalm to Jesus, in a way that shows God's purposes being carried out in a context where suffering is real. Suffering does not mean that God is absent. God is present even there, working to carry out God's will, which is directed at life.

---

[27] On possible interpretations, see Margaret Daly-Denton, op. cit. (note 9), 208-219. For more reserve, see Gail R. O'Day, *The Gospel of John*, New Interpreter's Bible 9 (Nashville: Abingdon, 1995), 831.

[28] When John speaks of Jesus taking off and putting on his outer robe, he uses unusual Greek verbs that literally say that Jesus "laid down" and "took up" his robe (Jn 13:4, 12). The verbs recall how Jesus spoke earlier about "laying down" and taking up his life (Jn 10:17-18). See O'Day, ibid. 722. On foot washing as an expression of divine love, which anticipates the crucifixion, see Koester, op. cit. (note 19), 127-34.

The conclusion of John's passion narrative may refer to one more Psalm. The context is that the Roman soldiers break the legs of those who were crucified alongside Jesus in order to hasten their deaths. So when they find that Jesus is already dead, they do not break his legs but pierce his side with a spear (Jn 19:31-34). Then John cites two passages that fulfill Scripture: "None of his bones shall be broken" and "They will look on the one whom they have pierced" (Jn 19:36-37). Here we focus on the first quotation, which probably has multiple levels of significance. At one level, Jesus was put to death on the day of Preparation for Passover, when the Passover lambs were sacrificed. Therefore, it seems likely that the gospel calls attention to the requirement that none of the Passover lamb's bones were to be broken (Ex 12:46; cf. Num 9:12). In the Fourth Gospel, Jesus dies as the Lamb of God who takes away the sins of the world (Jn 1:29, 35).

At another level, the same words about the bones appear in Psalm 34, which tells of God's care for the righteous person. God even looks after the righteous person's bones, so that "not one of them will be broken" (Ps 34:20).[29] If we consider the crucifixion in light of the Psalm, it shows that Jesus died as a righteous person. Although his opponents declared that he was guilty and therefore deserved death, the way his bones were protected is a sign of his innocence in the sight of God, as the Psalm said.

When we reverse the process and read Psalm 34 in light of the crucifixion, we find that it adds an element of depth. On its own, Psalm 34 can give the impression that people who trust God may encounter difficulties, but things always turn out well. They will be "saved from every trouble," they "have no want," and not one of them "will be condemned" (Ps 34:6, 9, 22). But the crucifixion shows that the Psalm cannot be taken to mean that the righteous never suffer. Jesus' bones were not broken, but Jesus did die. God does not always deliver people from suffering but is present in and through suffering. The story of Jesus will show that God's care does not mean an escape from dying. Rather, it will lead to deliverance from death through resurrection.

Conclusion

We began by recalling how Luther related the Psalms to the crucified and risen Christ, as well as to human situations of grief and hope. His perspec-

---

[29] On the combination of the Passover text with that of the Psalm see Menken, op. cit. (note 18), 147-66. The connection with Passover is emphasized by Obermann, op. cit. (note 18), 298-310. The connection with Psalm 34 is emphasized by Daly-Denton, op. cit. (note 9), 229-40; Thompson, op. cit. (note 22), 278-79.

tive was shaped by the use of the Psalms in the New Testament, where similar connections are made. In our study of Acts and John, we looked how those writings saw the Psalms offering perspectives on what God was doing in Jesus, and how that work of God engaged the human situation more broadly. We also asked what it might mean to read the Psalms in a canonical context that includes the New Testament's witness to the death and resurrection of Jesus.

We can summarize the discussion by using categories that scholars have developed for the study of the Psalms. First, some of the Psalms used in the New Testament are prayers for help. Psalms 22 and 69 follow the traditional pattern of initially giving voice to the reality of suffering and then giving thanks for God's help. Significantly, John's Gospel relates Jesus' experience specifically to the parts of those Psalms that deal with suffering, rather than thanksgiving. From that perspective, God does not remain above the context of suffering but enters into it through Jesus, and even there works to accomplish his purposes which are for life and salvation.

Second, Psalm 16 is a prayer for help that expresses trust in the God who continually cares for God's people. It is similar to Psalm 34, which is a prayer of thanksgiving that also speaks of God's care. On their own, these Psalms can give the impression that God's activity is mainly evident in the way in which God protects people from suffering. The problem is that experience often contradicts that view, since even people of faith suffer. When seen in light of Jesus, however, such Psalms can be read as promise. Jesus did not escape suffering and neither do his followers. But, in the face of suffering, people can trust that God's purposes are directed at life and well-being, which culminate in the resurrection from the dead.

Third, the royal Psalms 2 and 110 celebrate the enthronement and reign of God's king. The New Testament writers understand kingship in relation to Jesus, God's anointed one. That connection works against interpreting the Psalms as songs about easy victory. Jesus' crucifixion draws attention to the elements in the Psalms that tell of God's power confronting widespread hostility. In Jesus, the king himself experiences the brunt of opposition, and his victory comes out of death. The early church saw a continuation of Jesus' story in its own experiences of injustice. The reign of God's king does not remove Jesus' followers from the conflict, but calls them to bear witness to the character of his rule in contexts where the destructive forces that oppose God's reign are at work. The royal Psalms celebrate the reign of God that is often hidden from human eyes, but is given as a promise that God's just and life-giving ways will ultimately prevail.

This approach to the Psalms reflects a Lutheran theology of the cross, which finds God's power revealed in contexts were it would seem absent. It is a perspective that has engaged people in many cultural contexts ranging from Africa to South and East Asia, as well as Latin America, North America and Europe.[30] It allows the Psalms to address members of the global Lutheran community, who face challenges ranging from poverty and injustice, to disease and conflict, secularization and indifference. The challenges take different forms in various cultural contexts, though the reality of grief and the need for hope are shared by all. Reading the Psalms in light of the New Testament witness to Jesus' death and resurrection allows them to be heard as vivid expressions of life in relation to God and others, acknowledging the realities of suffering, while affirming that God is present and will be true to God's saving purposes.

---

[30] On the implications for South Asia, see Jhakmak Neeraj Ekka, *Christ as Sacrament and Example: Luther's Theology of the Cross and Its Relevance for South Asia* (Minneapolis: Lutheran University Press, 2007); A. J. V. Chandrakanthan, "Proclaiming Christ Crucified in a Broken World: An Asian Perspective," in *Mission Studies* 17 (2000), 59-67. For Africa see Simon S. Maimela, "The Suffering of Human Divisions and the Cross" in Yacob Tesfai (ed.), *The Scandal of a Crucified World: Perspectives on the Cross and Suffering* (Maryknoll, NY: Orbis, 1994), 36-47; Timothy Palmer, "Luther's Theology of the Cross, and Africa," in *Africa Journal of Evangelical Theology* 24 (2005), 129-37; Claudia Nolte, "A Theology of the Cross for South Africa," in *Dialog* 42 (2003), 50-61. For Latin America, see Paulo Suess, "The Gratuitousness of the Presence of Christ in the Broken World of Latin America," in *Mission Studies* 17 (2000), 68-81. For rural North America, see Paul A. Baglyos, "Lament in the Liturgy of the Rural Church: An Appeal for Recovery," in *Currents in Theology and Mission* 36 (2009), 253-63.

The Christological Reception of Psalms in Hebrews

Anni Hentschel

Martin Luther read and understood the Old Testament from the perspective of the New Testament. For Luther, the two parts of the Bible form one unity. "What drives home Christ" serves as the key for understanding and interpreting both Testaments. The Psalms, especially familiar to Luther because of the monastic liturgy of the Hours, became a central text both for his belief and scholarly Bible studies. Because of the Psalms' form and dialogical character, they have been prayed time and again by Jews and Christians up until the present day. Martin Luther asserts that,

> Hence also it comes to pass that the Psalter is the Book of all the Saints; and every one, whatsoever his case may be, find therein Psalms and words which suit his case so perfectly, that they might seem to have been set down solely for his sake, ...[1]

Since the Psalms transmit experience, one can always find a Psalm to suit one's own case. Believers can see their own lives through the psalmist's eyes and bring their lives to God with their words; Jesus's life, too, can be seen and interpreted with the help of the Psalms. In his Preface to the Psalter (1531), Martin Luther wrote,

> Yea, the Psalter ought to be precious and dear, were it for nothing else but the clear promise it holds forth respecting Christ's death and resurrection, and its prefiguration of His kingdom and of the whole estate and system of Christianity, insomuch that it might well be entitled a Little Bible, wherein everything contained in the entire Bible is beautifully and briefly comprehended, and compacted into an enchiridion or Manual.[2]

---

[1] Martin Luther, "Preface to the Revised Edition of the German Psalter (1931)," at **www.cprf.co.uk/quotes/martinlutherpsalter.htm**.
[2] Martin Luther, "Preface," in *WA* DB 10/1, 98, 20–22, at **www.cprf.co.uk/quotes/martinlutherpsalter.htm**.

However, the question of whether this way of reading the Psalms is legitimate is disputed in publications on the hermeneutics of Hebrews.[3] Two different aspects are discussed with regard to Martin Luther and Hebrews. First comes the question of whether the Christological reception of the Old Testament withdraws their Holy Scripture from the Jews, since they do not understand Jesus as the announced Messiah. Secondly, this Christological interpretation is challenged because it deprives the Psalms of their historical sense. New hermeneutical models can help us to approach these questions. According to reader response criticism, the meaning of a text emerges during the act of reading.[4] Understanding and interpreting a text are always determined by the reader's worldview and interests. The historical sense, often equated with the author's intention, cannot be regarded as the one and only, and therefore normative, meaning of a text. Furthermore, neither the author's intention nor the interpretation of the first readers can be grasped today. Thus, a text does not have only a single meaning, but offers potential meaning for different readers to understand it in different ways in relation to their worldview. In a nutshell, one text can have a multitude of true interpretations.[5]

The author of Hebrews understands the Psalms from the perspective of his Christian belief and he does so in a hermeneutical way.[6] He is famil-

---

[3] For a brief survey, see Angela Rascher, *Schriftauslegung und Christologie im Hebräerbrief*, BZNW 153 (Berlin: Walter de Gruyter, 2007), 35–37.

[4] Cf. Gerhard Haefner, "Rezeptionsästhetik," in Ansgar Nünning (ed.), *Literaturwissenschaftliche Theorien, Modelle und Methoden. Eine Einführung* (Trier: Wissenschaftlicher Verlag, 2004), 107–118; Ralf Schneider, "Methoden rezeptionstheoretischer und kognitionswissenschaftlicher Ansätze," in Vera Nünning/Ansgar Nünning (eds), *Methoden der literatur- und kulturwissenschaftlichen Textanalyse* (Stuttgart: Metzlersche J.B. Verlagsbuchhandlung, 2010), 71–90. Constitutive is the work of Umberto Eco, *Lector in fabula. Die Mitarbeit der Interpretation in erzählenden Texten* (München: Carl Hanser, 1987). Concerning a theological evaluation, cf. Ulrich H. J. Körtner, *Einführung in die theologische Hermeneutik* (Darmstadt: Wissenschaftliche Buchgesellschaft, 2006), 82–84; 102–105.

[5] Nevertheless, this implies that misunderstandings of a text can be identified. Reader response theories do not necessarily imply that "anything goes" in matters of interpretation.

[6] Cf. Harold W. Attridge, *The Epistle to the Hebrews. A Commentary on the Epistle to the Hebrews* (Philadelphia: Fortress Press, 1989), 23–25; Michael Theobald, "Vom Text zum 'lebendigen Wort' (Hebr 4,12). Beobachtungen zur Schrifthermeneutik des Hebräerbriefs," in Christof Landmesser, Hans-Joachim Eckstein and Hermann Lichtenberger (eds), *Jesus Christus als die Mitte der Schrift*, BZNW 86 (Berlin: De Gruyter, 1997), 751–90. In detail, Rascher, op. cit. (note 3); Graham Hughes, *Hebrews and Hermeneutics. The Epistle to the Hebrews as a New Testament Example of Biblical Interpretation* (Cambridge et al: Cambridge University Press, 1979).

iar with the language and the worldview of the Psalms and uses them to understand the story of Jesus Christ. At the same time, his belief in Jesus Christ as the Messiah determines his understanding so that the old words take on new meaning. The hermeneutical approach of Hebrews acknowledges what reader response theories have pointed out: while texts shape our worldview, our worldview shapes the interpretation of texts. Therefore, if one text can have a plurality of meanings, then both the Jewish and the Christological interpretations of the Psalms are possible true interpretations, depending on the interpreter's perspective. The hermeneutical consequence of this insight is that the Christological interpretation of the Psalms does not imply that the Jewish interpretation is obsolete. According to modern reception-oriented hermeneutical theories, the Jewish as well as the Christian readings of the Psalms can be understood as true interpretations of the same text. The author of Hebrews allows the words of God to speak afresh "today" to his Jewish and non-Jewish readers without denying that these words were originally addressed to the Jewish people only.[7]

The Letter to the Hebrews—if the designation as "letter" is appropriate at all[8]—generally hampered a historical interpretation concentrating on the author and his intention. This epistle does not begin with an epistolary preface including a salutation and the naming of author and recipients, although it has an epistolary conclusion (Heb 13:20-25). The author of Hebrews is unknown, as are the circumstances, the precise date and location of its composition.[9] Obviously, the author does not want to focus on himself but on the voice of God. He integrates himself into the group of listeners; he is part of the "we" who listen to God's Word.[10] By presenting the scriptural words as words spoken by God, these words are spoken with ultimate authority. "Today" God's voice itself is to be heard again. For the author of Hebrews, the Psalms function like lenses through which he perceives Jesus Christ. This paper will analyze the interpretative program of Hebrews on the basis of its two opening chapters; they depict the worldview of Hebrews, providing the foundation for the author's further Christological and paraenetical reflections. The interesting question is how the author understands Jesus' life with the help of the Psalms, fully aware that one can see things in different ways.

---

[7] Hebrews does not argue polemically against Israel. Cf. Martin Karrer, *Der Brief an die Hebräer*, vol. I, chapter 1,1-5,10, ÖTBNT 20.1 (Gütersloh/Würzburg: Gütersloher Verlagshaus, 2002), 111-14; Martin Karrer, *Der Brief an die Hebräer*, vol. II, chapter 5,11-13,25, ÖTBNT 20.2 (Gütersloh/Würzburg: Gütersloher Verlagshaus, 2008), 101-105.
[8] Cf. the genre of Hebrews, Attridge, op. cit. (note 6), 13-21.
[9] Note Karrer, op. cit. (note 7), 30-33, who depicts the assets of an interpretation of Hebrews focusing on text pragmatics and the reception by the readers.
[10] Ibid., 43.

One can "see" things in the sense of perception and/or of apprehension or interpretation (Heb 3:9f; see also Mk 4:12). The author differentiates between sensory perception and interpretation and, gradually, wants to enable his listeners to see their reality from a Christological perspective formed by the language and the worldview of the Psalms.

The social and historical situation of the recipients of Hebrews can only be deduced from the text itself and therefore remains hypothetical.[11] Nonetheless, there are good reasons for assuming that the audience—probably Jewish and non-Jewish Christians—is in danger of becoming lax in their commitment to Jesus Christ, possibly because of the delay of the *parousia*.[12] Furthermore, the listeners suffer from social stigmatization and persecution, probably including public ridicule and imprisonment (Heb 10:32-34).[13] The fact that the Christian community worshipped a crucified man as God was a *scandalon* both for Jews and Greeks. God's messenger coming in the name of God and representing God cannot die by means of punishment reserved exclusively for criminals. According to Deuteronomy 21:22f, for Jews a crucified person dies as one cursed and forsaken by God. Jesus' death invalidated his claim to speak in the name of God. A mock crucifix, discovered in 1857 in the ruins of the imperial palaces on the Palatine hill in Rome, illustrates what non-Jews thought about Jesus' death.[14] It shows a crucified man with the head of an ass or a horse and a human figure kneeling before the cross. The Greek inscription explains the scene: "Alexamenos worships his God." The early believers in Christ had to explain how Jesus' human life, including his shameful death, was compatible with his announcing the kingdom of God and their hope that Jesus Christ would eternally reign with God. In Hebrews 2:8-9[15] this problem is addressed:

---

[11] On the presumptions concerning the addressees, see Attridge, op. cit. (note 6), 12f; Karrer, op. cit. (note 7), 98-101. Concerning the feasible social setting of writer and audience, cf. Craig R. Koester, *Hebrews*, AB 36 (New York: Yale University Press, 2001), 64-79.

[12] Karrer even speaks of a liminal theology in Hebrews; Karrer, op. cit. (note 7), 48-53. Contemporary literary criticism points out that the only audience we can actually know are the "implied readers" that the text itself creates. On the concept of "implied reader," see especially Wayne Booth, *The Rhetoric of Fiction* (Chicago: University of Chicago Press, 1961).

[13] Karrer, op. cit. (note 7), 49.

[14] Cf. Fritz Rienecker and Gerhard Maier (eds), *Lexikon zur Bibel* (Wuppertal: Brockhaus, ⁶2006), 943-45.

[15] To a large extent, the translations of Hebrews follow Attridge, op. cit. (note 6). The italic script type shows where Hebrews uses citations or allusions to the Old Testament. Concerning the different forms of reference, cf. Rascher, op. cit. (note 3), 24-26.

> "*subjecting all things under his feet.*" Now in *subjecting all things to him*, God left nothing outside his control. As it is, we do not yet see everything in subjection to him, ⁹ but we do see Jesus, who for a little while *was made lower than the angels, now crowned with glory and honor* because of the suffering of death, so that by the grace of God he might taste death for everyone.

As believers look back at Jesus' life and death, they "see" his humanity, not his already present exaltation and reign, his sitting at God's right hand,[16] which is not perceptible with human senses (cf. Heb 11:26f). The listeners' life situations correspond to this dual perception of Jesus: They do not see themselves as companions of a heavenly calling, a position with honor and glory, but experience humiliation and social stigmatization (Heb 13:13f; cf. Heb 11:9; 12:1-3). How does the author help his listeners to perceive what they cannot see yet with earthly eyes? Where does he tell them to turn their attention?

THE WORLDVIEW IN HEBREWS—THE SPEAKING GOD (HEB 1:1-4)

The first verses of the text describe the worldview that is based on the Holy Scriptures of Judaism, especially the Psalms, as well as contemporary philosophy,[17] and it is within this framework that Hebrews develops its theology. The basic theme of Hebrews 1:1-4 is the speaking God, a leitmotif especially of the following chapters (Heb 1:1-5:10):

> Long ago God spoke to our ancestors in many and various ways by the prophets, but in these last days he has spoken to us by a Son, whom he appointed heir of all things, through whom he also created the worlds. He is the reflection of God's glory and the exact imprint of God's very being, and he sustains all things by his powerful word. When he had made purification for sins, he sat down at the right hand of the Majesty on high, having become as much superior to angels as the name he has inherited is more excellent than theirs (Heb 1:1-4).

---

[16] The importance of this conception for the New Testament writers and early Christianity in general is clearly represented by Martin Hengel, "Sit at My Right Hand!," in Martin Hengel, *Studies in Early Christianity* (New York: Continuum, 1995), 119-225.

[17] Cf. Attridge, op. cit. (note 6), 28-31, referring to the traditions which Hebrews shares, especially the parallels between Hebrews and the Hellenistic Judaism represented by Philo. Concerning spatial and temporal categories in Hebrews, compared with Platonic and apocalyptic conceptions, see Koester, op. cit. (note 11), 96-104.

The central subject of the Greek sentence is the "speaking God." God spoke through the prophets to the fathers;[18] now God speaks through the Son. Both God's speech and the living of the Son comprise time and place. Christ's future possession of all things by God's grace is even mentioned before Christ's role in creation (Heb 1:1-2). The Son is described as the radiance[19] of God's glory[20] and the representation of his essence, creating and sustaining the universe, mediating God's Word and effecting redemption. The syntactical and rhetorical climax of the sentence is the affirmation that the Son himself took a seat at God's right hand, expressed by a finite verb in the midst of a series of participle constructions (Heb 1:3-4).[21] "The focus here, as regularly in Hebrews, is not on the inauguration of Christ's position, but on the fact of its superiority. Christ within the supernal world has a position higher than any other member of the world."[22] In Hebrews 1:4, reference to Christ's position of honor and power is made through the first allusion to Psalm 110:1.[23] Regarding the different aspects characterizing the Son, Hebrews emphasizes the sitting of the Son at God's right hand. This presumption is confirmed by Hebrews 8:1: The author proves that "the main point in what has been said, is that we have such a high priest, who has taken his seat at the right of the throne of the majesty in the heavens."[24] The Son reigns with God eternally and his leadership is powerful. Between heaven and earth, he acts as a mediator, speaking God's Word to human beings and making an approach to God's throne possible.

---

[18] Karrer points out that Jewish and non-Jewish believers are addressed by Hebrews. There is no clear hint that the parallelism in Hebrews 1:1f. is antithetic. God's speech, first through the prophets and secondly through the Son, offers the same message of salvation. At various points in Hebrews, the author suggests that God's message of God spoken through the prophets has direct and special relevance for contemporary hearers of the word. See Karrer, op. cit. (note 7), 111-13.

[19] Cf. Attridge, op. cit. (note 6), 42f., concerning the meaning of the Greek ἀπαύγασμα.

[20] Glory (δόξα) is a common designation of the divine reality. Cf. Attridge, op. cit. (note 6), 43f.

[21] The author of Hebrews displays his Christology without any explicit reference to the resurrection of Christ. Instead, the author emphasizes on the one hand the atoning death and on the other hand his exaltation to God's right hand; cf. Hengel, op. cit. (note 16), 152f.

[22] Attridge, op. cit. (note 6), 47.

[23] Concerning Psalm 110 (Ps 109 LXX), Thiselton speaks of the "key frame of reference" of Hebrews. Antony C. Thiselton, *Hermeneutics: An Introduction* (Grand Rapids: William B Eerdman Co, 2009), 81. It is quoted in Hebrews 1:3; 10:12; 12:2 and alluded to more often. The author of Hebrews probably used a version of the LXX text. For convenience, I cite the Psalms corresponding to the counting of the MT.

[24] The designation of God recalls Hebrews 1:3. The Greek term μεγαλωσύνη is used for God in the New Testament only in Hebrews 1:3; 8:1 und Judas 1:25.

In Hebrews 1:1-4, the author opens up a wide perspective: the readers "see" both the earthly and the heavenly reality; they "see" the past, the present and the future. God is characterized as a speaking God, speaking to us through the medium of human language, through human beings such as the prophets and, finally, through the Son (Heb 1:1-2). Throughout his writing, the author demonstrates how God's voice can still be heard in the presence of the writing and hearing of Hebrews. The Word of God that is written down in the Holy Scriptures is now heard anew in the present situation of the audience. Especially in Hebrews 1-2, the author does not at all interpret, or only scarcely interprets, these words. Obviously, he is convinced that the words of God spoken in the past still have something to say in the present situation. The God who spoke to the fathers through the prophets is the same God who speaks anew through the Son (Heb 1:1-4). This is why the author is not interested in the written word, but in the new meaning that the words of God disclose when they are spoken and heard today. God makes Godself understandable in the present situation and therefore understanding can take place (Heb 1:1f). Like Luther, the author of Hebrews is well aware of the fact that the compliance of the listeners with the Christian worldview cannot be achieved by rational reasoning, but only through the Holy Spirit who brings the Word to the heart of the hearers (Heb 6:3). Through signs and miracles, God shows the effectiveness of God's words even if they are delivered through such human mediums as Christian preachers (Heb 2:3f).

Surprisingly, the author of Hebrews avoids the common introductory formula "it is written" (γέγραπται).[25] While he is not interested in when and by whom something was written (cf. Heb 2:6), this observation does not imply that the author did not know about the origin and the original contexts of his citations (cf. Heb 9:20; 12:21). In fact, it proves how he understands the words of God: God still speaks today by means of the scriptural words. In this new context, these words continue to explicate God's saving will, but they also obtain a new meaning since God now speaks through the Son to listeners in a different situation. Thus, God is faithful to God's promises without being bound to the meaning God's words might have had in the past (cf. Heb 3:7f, 15; 4:7). The Word of God is meaningful because its meaning is not the same once and forever. Because of this insight, the author of Hebrews can quote words from the Scriptures—words written before Jesus' birth, to talk about Jesus and his saving role.

---

[25] Hebrews uses γράφειν only once in Hebrews 10:7. Concerning the OT citations and the special form of quoting in Hebrews, cf. Theobald, op. cit. (note 6), 755-65; Koester, op. cit. (note 11), 116f.

THE SON AS THE VISIBLE REFLECTION OF GOD'S GLORY (HEB 1:5-14)

The medium of God's speaking in the present, "today," is the Son (Heb 1:2.3f), who is more than the angels or such prophets as Moses (Heb 2:2f; 3:5f), who are also God's messengers. Jesus is not only God's agent of revelation; he is the medium of God's glory (Heb 1:3) and the incarnation of the divine reality who has the power to impress others.[26] He atones for our sins and, in the end, leads all believers to glory (cf. Heb 2:10). The Son even reigns with God and thus is far superior to the angels.

Several quotations from the Psalms, presented as God's words to and about his Son (Heb 1:5-14) and reasoning why the Son is superior to the angels, follow the skillfully elaborated introduction. In Hebrews 1:5, God is cited with the words of Psalm 2:7 and 2 Samuel 7:14, providing the validation for the title "Son." In their original context, both verses belong to the concept of kingship in Israel, and the metaphor of the son expresses an intimate relationship between God and the king of Israel.[27] By using further scriptural words (Dt 32:43; Ps 97:7; 104:4; 45:7f; 102:26-28),[28] God reveals the role of God's Son: God predicts an angelic homage of the Son (Heb 1:6), his eternal and righteous lordship and his anointment with the oil of gladness (Heb 1:8f.). Furthermore, God confirms the portrayal of Christ as agent of creation, expressed already in the exordium (Heb 1:10; cf. Heb 1:3), and approves his eternal existence. God addresses his Son with the titles "God" and "Lord" (Heb 1:9f)! The passage ends with a rhetorical question quoting the words of Psalm 110:1 (Heb 1:13f; cf. Heb 1:5) about whether God ever said to an angel, "Sit at my right hand until I make your enemies your footstool." That the Son has accepted God's mandate was already stated in Hebrews 1:3. God's explicit order authorizes the Son and, at the same time, the citation of Psalm 110:1 in Hebrews 1:13 discloses to the audience that the Son is acting in accordance with his Father.[29] The difference between the Son and the angels is grounded in Christ's status as Son (Heb 1:5) and in his exaltation to unique communion with God (1:13f).

The angels are messengers of God's words too, but they only convey messages according to God's commission. The Greek term διακονία/diakonia

---

[26] Cf. in detail Karrer, op. cit. (note 7), 120f.

[27] The proclamation of Christ as Son does not allude to the creation of a new status, but it is the proclamation and revelation of this status to the readers of Hebrews by God. Regarding the discussion of this interpretative problem, see Attridge, op. cit. (note 6), 54f.

[28] Note the block diagram of OT citations in Hebrews, designating original speakers and readers as well as speakers and readers in Hebrews, in Theobald, op. cit. (note 6), 754.

[29] Attridge, op. cit. (note 6), 153.

is to be understood as "fulfilling a mandate, doing something in commission" and can therefore be used as an antonym to ruling (cf. Mk 10:42-45). A sovereign can give orders, a διάκονος has to fulfill orders, he acts on behalf of someone else. Relating to the audience, a διάκονος may appear with authority. In the given context, the commitment is probably that the angels have to convey God's Word to the people in the name of God (cf. Heb 2:2).[30] As God's commissioned agents, they speak in the name of God to the believers. They speak with authority (cf. Heb 2:2), but their authority is a delegated one.[31] The thrust of the passage is not that the angels are at the service of the audience, but that they are God's messengers.[32] Whereas the angels are agents commissioned by God, the Son partakes in God's reign. He is even a sovereign himself, sitting at God's right hand.[33] That the Son is superior to the angels marks his status as Son of God with whom God speaks at eye level, as Hebrews 1 illustrates. Christ, like the angels, is an agent of revelation, but he is far superior to them.

The purpose of Hebrews 1 is to demonstrate the Son's superiority to the angels as a medium of God's revelation. Establishing the Son's authority, the author portrays the intimate relationship between the Father and Son. The exordium (Heb 1:1-4) portrays the speaking God as well as Christ's exalted position and enumerates his different functions as God's medium. The heavenly dialogue (Heb 1:5-14) illustrates Christ's status as the Son to whom God speaks face to face and with whom God reigns eternally.[34] Christ "thus is given *the most immediate form of communion with God,*

---

[30] With the meaning "commissioned to convey the message of God" διακονία is used for example in Rom 11:13; 12:7; 2 Cor 4:1; 5:18; 6:3; 1 Ti 1:12; Acts 1:17, 25; 6:4; 20:24. Cf. Anni Hentschel, *Diakonia im Neuen Testament,* WUNT II/226 (Tübingen: Mohr Siebeck, 2007).

[31] Note Attridge's interpretation concerning Heb 2:2: "The word delivered through angels was 'valid' (βέβαιος), a legal term implying that the word entailed serious obligations. The implications of that validity are now made explicit in the notice that every 'transgression and disobedience' (παράβασις καὶ παρακοή) will be punished"; cf. Attridge, op. cit. (note 6), 65.

[32] Therefore Hebrews 1:14 and Hebrews 2:1-4 are not "superficially linked," Attridge, op. cit. (note 6), 63, but the author is consequently dealing with the status and authority that his—different—messengers have.

[33] Based on this interpretation of διακονία, the comparison between the Son and the angels in Hebrews 1:13f. is not at all out of place; cf. for example Attridge, op. cit. (note 6), 62 concerning the problems with the interpretation of Hebrews 1:13f. The author of Hebrews points out exactly that the Son can act sovereignly—he is the highest king at the right of God—whereas the angels only do what God has told them to do.

[34] Some scholars suppose that Hebrews is trying to correct an angelological Christology, but this thesis remains hypothetical; cf. Attridge, op. cit. (note 6), 51f.

which was comprehensible to a Jew based upon the texts of Old Testament."[35] The worldview that the author of Hebrews has presented in the exordium (Heb 1:1-4) is confirmed and proven by the words of God (Heb 1:5-14). The hearers or readers of Hebrews become witnesses of a heavenly conversation by which Christ is presented as the divine Son of God, as the agent of creation and of redemption, as the eternal sovereign, crowned with honor and praise. He mediates between God and people, delivering God's words and having made purification for sins. Without using the titles, the Son is thus characterized as God's apostle, i.e., God's sent messenger to preach the gospel and as high priest (Heb 3:1).[36]

CONSEQUENCES FOR THE HEARINGS (HEB 2:1-4)

Hebrews 2:1-4 explicates the implications of Hebrews 1 for those who listen to and hear it. It continues the development of the theme of the speaking God, now focusing on the audience. The passage emphasizes the need to pay attention to the word delivered by different agents (cf. Heb 1:1-4), using legal terminology.[37] The message of the angels is "validated" and if the hearers disobey by transgressing God's orders, they will receive a "just recompense" (Heb 2:2). But if the addressees neglect the Son's message, they must fear eschatological judgment. The word delivered by the Son is characterized as a "great salvation" (Heb 2:3). The announcement of the salvific word takes place initially through the Son. After that, there are the first listeners who become witnesses preaching the word. Hebrews is not trying to authorize the message of these first—now called apostolic—figures by appealing to apostolic tradition and their status as eyewitnesses or

---

[35] Hengel, op. cit. (note 16), 148.
[36] Note that Christ is called mediator of a new and better covenant three times in Hebrews (Heb 8:6; 9:15; 12:24). Christ is depicted as holding the two most important offices of Judaism and emerging Christianity: the office of high priest, mediating between God and God's people and the office of an apostle preaching the gospel. Plato, too, enumerates two religious offices, i.e., the priest or priestess and the exegete. The latter is responsible for the ever-new interpretation of holy scriptures; cf. Plato, Leges 759b-759e. In Plato, Politikos 290c, priests are described as mediating between Gods and humans. They are offering sacrifices as gifts in the name of the humans to the Gods and they are praying for help in favor of the humans.
[37] Concerning the legal character of the terminology of Hebrews 2:1-4, cf. Koester, (note 11), 206-209. He points to a Jewish tradition that angels acted as intermediaries at Sinai, conveying the Law in God's name, cf. Koester, (note 11), 205. Given this tradition, Hebrews 2:1-4 would note that disregarding the message of Christ is worse than disobeying the Law.

apostles. It is God who corroborates their testimony (Heb 2:4). God works "signs, wonders and powerful deeds" to confirm the message transmitted by human figures. Only the word of the Son is not in need of a godly authentication, because the glory of the Son's status and reign is the visible radiance of God's glory (cf. Heb 1:3). The Son himself is the incarnated word of God, the visible imprint of God's existence (Heb 1:2-4).

Jesus—for a little while partaker of human existence (Heb 2:5-18)

Quoting Psalm 8:4-6 (8:5-7 LXX) the author now focuses on the earthly life of Jesus (Heb 2:5-18). In its original context, Psalm 8 describes the unconfined dignity of human beings and their mandate to reign.[38] Hebrews uses this Psalm in order to look consciously at the incarnated Jesus and to describe—and interpret—his, for a little while,[39] low status[40] (Heb 2:5-9).

> (5) Now it was not to angels that he subjected the world to come, about which we are speaking. (6) Someone bore testimony (to this) somewhere saying: *What is a man that you should remember him or a son of man that you watch over him?* (7) *You have made him for a little while lower than the angels; with glory and honor you have crowned him*; (8) *you have subjected everything under his feet.* Now in *subjecting all things*, he left nothing unsubjectable to him. At present we do not yet see all things subjected to him; (9) but we do behold the one who *was made for a little while lower than the angels*, Jesus, because of the suffering of death *crowned with glory and honor* so that by God's grace he might taste death for everyone.

Surprisingly this citation—describing Jesus' human existence—also alludes to the glory and power of the Son. The citation ends with the hint that God has placed everything in subjection under God's feet, pointing to Hebrews 1:3.13 and alluding to Psalm 110:1; this Psalm runs like a red thread through the whole text of Hebrews and even through passages describing the human existence of Jesus. That the ruling of the Son is important for

---

[38] Cf. Hans-Joachim Kraus, *Psalmen. 1. Teilband: Psalmen 1-59*, BKAT XV/1, 6. Auflage mit Nachträgen zur Literatur (Neukirchen-Vluyn: Neukirchener Verlag, 1989), 212f. Here Kraus speaks of the miracle of the human existence, of the dignity of all human beings who are crowned with honor and glory by God, their creator.
[39] Concerning the differences between the Hebraic and the Greek version of the Psalm and the interpretation of the Greek βραχύ, cf. Koester, op. cit. (note 11), 214-17.
[40] The author does not speak of humiliation (κενόω κ.τ.λ.), like for example Phil 2:7, but he uses the Greek term ἐλαττόω wich means "to suffer loss"; cf. Karrer, op. cit. (note 7), 171f; Koester, op. cit. (note 11), 216.

the author is especially indicated by the way in which he has embedded the citation. In Hebrews 2:5, the author declares that it was not to the angels that God subordinated the world to come. Without explicitly saying that it is subordinated to the Son, the author presumes that this is the case. In Hebrews 1, the glory and ruling power of the Son were illustrated at length in comparison with the role of the angels, so that the hearers are now well informed about the role of the Son. Furthermore, having finished the citation, the author again points to the reign of the Son (Heb 2:8b): he paraphrases the last proposition of the citation and clarifies it by ascertaining that God really placed everything—without exception—under the Son's dominion. But this reign is not visible for the audience or for himself, he admits. They can only see the low status—in comparison to the angels—of the Son, called for the first time by his name, Jesus.

The lower status of Christ in contrast to the angels probably refers not only to Jesus' death, but to his incarnation in general. In the LXX, the Psalm cited was understood anthropologically as referring to human dignity and honor.[41] It seems likely that the author of Hebrews too interprets the Psalm and, through its lenses, the life of Jesus as well, from this angle. For a little while, God had made him lower than the angels—he became a human being of flesh and blood, i.e., he shared human existence as it is. Nevertheless, God also crowned him with honor and glory as God honors human beings in general (cf. Ps 8). Both in Hebrews 2:6f and in Hebrews 2:14.17, the writer points especially to the fact that Jesus shared the human condition and therefore experienced the weakness and frailty of humankind, including suffering and death.[42] Obviously, the author of Hebrews takes the incarnation of Christ seriously. But based on the anthropology of Psalm 8, he probably has a positive idea of the human being. The only difference between Jesus and the other people is that he is the incarnated Son. Jesus became lower than the angels, but he is still an esteemed human person. The human existence of Jesus that is visible to the listeners explains why they have a congenial and helpful mediator—one who understands human suffering and weaknesses (Heb 2:17; 4:15f). This indicates that the incarnation per se has a positive effect on the relation between Jesus as godly mediator and the humans he will lead to God.

But the author of Hebrews does not stop here. He continues his argumentation. Because of suffering death, Jesus was crowned with honor and glory by God. This means that even the suffering and the death that Jesus

---

[41] Cf. Karrer, op. cit. (note 7), 169, who pursues this understanding.

[42] The term "cross" is used only once in Hebrews 12:2. Hebrews speaks of the incarnation and even of the salvific death of the Son without special reference to the cross or even to the shameful way of dying.

had to experience—in contrast to Greco-Roman conceptions of honor and shame—are not dishonorable: God has crowned him with honor and glory.[43] As a further argument, the author adds that his death is salvific because of God's grace: Jesus experienced (or, put more precisely, "tasted") the bitterness of death vicariously for everyone.[44] Without God, Jesus' shameful death would have been the falsification of his status as Son and agent of God, but with God—because of God's grace—even this death is surrounded by honor and glory (cf. Heb 2:7).[45] The goal of Jesus' incarnation is that the "pioneer to salvation" leads a lot of brothers and sisters to glory (Heb 2:10), i.e., God made him competent for this task by perfecting[46] him through suffering. Jesus fully shared the condition of the brothers and sisters whom he wants to save. And thereby, his status as God's Son can even confer glory upon his followers. The author states that Jesus, the agent of sanctification, and the believers who are sanctified are of one and the same origin (Heb 2:11).[47] As Jesus and the believers are regarded as siblings (Heb 2:10-12), the most likely interpretation of the "one origin" is the idea that Jesus and the believers have the same father. According to this statement, the author points out that Christ was therefore "not ashamed" to call them brothers and sisters and to rank them among his family. In the Greco-Roman world, kinship and friendship were factors influencing the status and prestige of a subject. By calling them brothers and sisters, Jesus places himself on the same level with his believers. This is obviously a question of honor and shame. But the effect here in the text is that the believers obtain higher status because they are seen as children of God.

> Reinforcing the concept of kinship with Christ serves the author's program of reassuring his listeners of their honor as Christians for, in first-century Mediterranean societies, "the advance of one member of an agnatic family would advantage all his kindred."[48]

---

[43] Cf. Karrer, op. cit. (note 7), 172.
[44] Cf. the outcome of this participation according to Hebrews 6:4.
[45] Cf. Karrer, op. cit. (note 7), 172.
[46] Concerning the language of "perfection," see the excursus in Attridge, op. cit. (note 6), 83-87.
[47] In Hebrews 2:17 Jesus is named high priest for the first time. His priestly office that will be illustrated especially in Hebrews 4:14-10:23 is here connected with his human existence. Because he has "tasted" and therefore knows human weaknesses and temptations, he can be an empathetic high priest (Heb 2:17; 4:15).
[48] David Arthur DeSilva, *Despising Shame. Honor Discourse and Community Maintenance in the Epistle to the Hebrews*, SBL Dissertations Series 152 (Georgia: Scholars Press Atlanta, 1995), 291.

Jesus, who wants to lead his believers to the eschatological glory in heaven, makes it possible for them already now to partake of his status as children of God.

This idea is explicated in Hebrews 3:1, where the author calls the listeners "holy brothers and sisters, partakers of a heavenly calling." In Hebrews 3:14, he even states: "We have become partakers of Christ." While Jesus was tasting the bitterness of death as partaker of human existence (Heb 2:9.14), his followers tasted the heavenly gift and also became partakers of the Holy Spirit (Heb 6:4). The incarnation of Jesus—as the author of Hebrews reasons—allows his followers to come closer to God, to become God's children and to partake of God's glory (Heb 2:9-3:1).

Only if Jesus still holds higher status than his followers is it comprehensible when the author of Hebrews points out that Jesus is "not ashamed" to call them his brothers and sisters (Heb 2:11): The verb

> ἐπαισχύνεται does not express an inner feeling, but a public confession, God's testimony on behalf of the ancestors of faith. This confession by God, which gives the believer his or her honor, answers the believer's confession that he or she is a sojourner and foreigner on the earth.[49]

The verb ἐπαισχύνεται is often used in New Testament texts to challenge believers in Christ not to be ashamed of the person and message of Christ. If they will proclaim their belief in Jesus publicly, God will honor them in heaven (e.g., Mk 8:38; Lk 9:26; Rom 1:16; 2 Tim 1:8.12). In Hebrews, this verb is used once more referring to God (Heb 11:16): "God is not ashamed to be called their God." The new status of the hearers who follow Jesus to his and their heavenly home is approved by the Son and by God, who are not ashamed of this kinship. Given that the hearers are God's children, they are Jesus' brothers and sisters and he has no reason to be ashamed to proclaim this kinship. The author of Hebrews lets Jesus speak for himself (Heb 2:12-13), putting scriptural words on his lips (Ps 22:22; Jes 8:17f):

> saying, "I will proclaim your name to my brothers and sisters, in the midst of the congregation I will praise you." And again, "I will put my trust in him." And again, "Here am I and the children whom God has given me."

With the words of Psalm 22:22, Jesus describes himself as a medium of God's Word (cf. Heb 1:2) and— trusting in God like the psalmist, a person in distress who finishes his prayer of supplication with words of praise—Je-

---

[49] Ibid., 293f.

sus publicly praises God in the assembly. Psalm 22[50] has two parts. Psalm 22:1-21a is a prayer of supplication by a believer in deepest distress. He suffers from illness and hardship, from mockery and god-forsakenness. Psalm 22:21b marks a turning point: the psalmist is heard by God: "You have answered me!" (cf. Heb 5:7).[51] The following verse is the citation of Heb 2:12b! The fact that the psalmist was heard by God, that he was saved from hardship and from the threat of death is obviously the reason that he now preaches the name of God in the community and that he sings hymns to God. Thus, the second part of Psalm 22 (Ps 22:22-31) is a hymn of gratitude that praises and preaches the hearing and helping and reigning God to Israel and all nations! It is this Psalm that is extensively quoted in the New Testament passion narratives![52] Jesus is thereby characterized as a believer who trusts in God like the psalmist, even when he is overcome by death (cf. literally Heb 2:9f; 14f). Jesus had to go through suffering and death; he tasted its fear and bitterness, but obviously never ceased to trust in God who saved him (cf. Heb 2:9; 5:7f; Ps 22:19-21.24). God did not save Jesus from death, but preserved him by bringing him through suffering and death. Therefore, Jesus can praise God and he preaches God to his brothers and sisters as the psalmist of Psalm 22 does in the second part of the Psalm and with the same words. As Hebrews 12:3 and especially Hebrews 13:6 presume, Jesus does what the listeners should do. But it is not the believers' endurance and faith that will open the door to heaven for them. Rather, Jesus himself will guide them to heavenly glory (Heb 12:2). The hearers are told to look to him with undivided attention, to see in him "the pioneer and perfecter of faith."

But how does Jesus become the pioneer and perfecter of faith? This is explained in Hebrews 2:14-18 with reference once again to the fact that Jesus and his followers are siblings, similarly partaking of the same flesh and blood. In accordance with Greco-Roman and Jewish conceptions of honor and shame, it is shameful to consider a person who died like a criminal on the cross as a member of your family. But Hebrews does not evoke this—shameful—aspect of Jesus' death.[53] The author has already stated that because of God's will, the death of Jesus was crowned with honor and grace. Jesus even defeated the fear of death and achieved—through his

---

[50] Cf. Kraus, op. cit. (note 38), 320-34.
[51] NET Translation.
[52] Ps 22:1 in Mt 27:46; Mk 15:34; Ps 22:18 in Jn 19:24; cf. Mt 27:35; Mk 15:24; Lk 23:34; cf. Koester, op. cit. (note 11), 230.
[53] Paul's interpretation of the salvific death of the crucifixion with special emphasis on the cross is a different way to construe the redemptive function of Jesus' death. Cf. 1 Corinthians 2, where Paul is emphasizing the shameful manner of Jesus' dying.

death—a victory over the lord of death (Heb 2:9; 14). Thereby, Jesus liberated his followers from slavery, i.e., from the lifelong fear of death.[54] Thus, the listeners metaphorically gain a new and higher status through Jesus' victorious death; they are freed from a slaveholder. In Hebrews, Jesus' high status is not compromised by the manner of his death. The author describes him—in spite of the crucifixion—as "the pioneer and perfecter of our faith, who for the sake of the joy that was set before him endured the cross, disregarding its shame, and has taken his seat at the right hand of the throne of God" (Heb 12:2f).[55] Jesus' death does not challenge either his high status as Son of God or his dominion.

CONSEQUENCES FOR THE UNDERSTANDING OF THE HEARERS (HEB 3:1, 10, 14–16; 12:2)

Through the lenses of Psalm 8:5–7, the author of Hebrews shows his hearers the invisible glory and dominion of the incarnated Jesus on the one hand and, on the other, the visible incarnation due to which Jesus expresses his solidarity with human beings. Both the words of the Psalm and its embedding and interpretation in Hebrews 2:5; 9–18 create a kind of bond between humanity and divinity. Even the most shameful event in Jesus' human life, his death, is characterized as a victory, destroying the power of death and evil and demonstrating the honor and grace that God has given to him.[56] Through the lenses of the Psalms, the first two chapters of Hebrews present a Christology that takes Jesus' human existence, includ-

---

[54] The redemptive effect of Jesus' death here is not explicated as freedom from sin, but Hebrews offers a rather anthropological interpretation that fits well the thrust of the passage.

[55] Accordingly, the reason given for this death by the author is not the plan of God, but the hostility of the sinners (Heb 12:3).

[56] Attridge, op. cit (note 6), 79–83, enumerates different models for explaining Hebrews 2:10–18. Attridge describes similarities to a Hellenistic hero myth. "The application and reinterpretation of the basic mythical scheme may be found already in classical sources. Plato's famous story of the cave may be an early metaphorical application. Cynic and stoic philosophers made out of Heracles a philosophical hero and came to see in his tragic end the true victory over death, which was only symbolized in the myth of his descent to the underworld. A clear example of this development is found in the tragedies of Seneca, where the hero achieves glorification through his suffering and, by example of his stoic acceptance of death, liberates others from the fear of death," Attridge, op. cit. (note 6), 79f. It is not unlikely that the philosophically and rhetorically educated author of Hebrews used these traditions to explain to his Jewish and Greco-Roman hearers the meaning and significance of Jesus' death.

ing his suffering and death, while holding firm to his status as Son and sovereign, seriously. There is no need for the hearers to be ashamed of this agent of God, because even his—from a human point of view shameful—suffering and death is—seen through the lenses of the Psalms—a sign for the glorious mission he fulfills in the name of God.

Based on this demonstration,[57] the author exhorts his listeners to look consciously to Jesus and to perceive in him the apostle and high priest (Heb 3:1). The Greek verb κατανοέω can express an intensive sensory perception as well as discernment. Hearing the words spoken by God and Jesus has qualified the listeners now to see—through the lenses of the Psalms, and of the words spoken by God—not only the human Jesus, but also the apostle and high priest of God mediating God's words and making atonement for sins (Heb 1:3). The community is addressed as "holy brothers and sisters," "partakers of a heavenly calling" (Heb 3:1), they should keep in mind their "boldness" and "boast of the hope" (Heb 3:6). In the house of Christ, the listeners evidently have high status. They can perceive themselves as esteemed people who have the competence to speak publicly. Παρρησία is basically a confident self-assurance expressed in bold speech.[58] In Hebrews 4:14-16, the author summarizes the effects of the mediation of Christ described in Hebrews 1-4, showing that the hearers can confidently approach the throne of God.[59]

> Since, then, we have a great high priest who has passed through the heavens, Jesus, the Son of God, let us hold fast to our confession. For we do not have a high priest who is unable to sympathize with our weaknesses, but we have one who in every respect has been tested as we are, yet without sin. Let us therefore approach the throne of grace with boldness, so that we may receive mercy and find grace to help in time of need (Heb 4:14-16).

Seeing and hearing belong together. By hearing the words of God, the listeners can see the divine reality that surrounds the human Jesus. Through the lenses of the Psalms they see that Jesus is already sitting at God's right hand and they see the glory surrounding even his human existence and his death (Heb 2:8f).

---

[57] Cf. the Greek ὅθεν introducing the new passage.//
[58] Cf. Attridge, op. cit. (note 6), 111f.//
[59] Interestingly, Hebrews balances with these verses the announcement of God's final judgment, to whom the readers must finally render their account; cf. Knut Backhaus, "Zwei harte Knoten. Todes- und Gerichtsangst im Hebräerbrief," in Knut Backhaus, *Der sprechende Gott*, WUNT 240 (Tübingen: Mohr Siebeck, 2009), 131-51. Backhaus focuses on the rhetorical strategies and the pragmatic effect of announcements of judgment.

JESUS—THE PRAYING AND INTERCEDING HIGH PRIEST

In this essay, I have read and understood Hebrews 1-2 from the point of view that the author presented in Hebrews 1:1-4, seen through the lenses of the Psalms quoted in these chapters. The result is a Christology that sees Jesus primarily as the Son of God crowned with glory, sitting at the right hand of God and partaking in the everlasting reign of God. Nevertheless, the author of Hebrews takes seriously Jesus' human existence—including his suffering and death. Yet, he does not interpret the incarnation as complete abandonment of glory or as shameful humiliation. Only for a little while, Jesus was made lower than the angels (Heb 2:7), and his incarnation and even his suffering death are not without glory.

But there is a second passage describing Jesus' human existence in Hebrews 5:7-8. This passage seems to contradict the proposed interpretation in the sense of a Christology that focuses on the high status of Jesus as Son of God. Hebrews 4:14-16 summarizes the ideas developed in Hebrews 1-4 and prepares the subject of Jesus as the high priest (Heb 5:1-10:18). Hebrews 5:1-10 compares the earthly office of high priest (Heb 5:1-4) with the office of Jesus as a priest "according to the order of Melchizedek" (Heb 5:5-10). The motif of Christ as the high priest was already mentioned in Hebrews 2:17. Comparable to the method of argumentation in Hebrews 1-2, the author shows in Hebrews 5:1-10 the priestly role of Christ through the lenses of the Psalms. The author writes (Heb 5:5-10):

> So also Christ did not glorify himself in becoming a high priest, but was appointed by the one who said to him, "You are my Son, today I have begotten you"; as he says also in another place, "You are a priest forever, according to the order of Melchizedek." In the days of his flesh, Jesus offered up prayers and supplications, with loud cries and tears, to the one who was able to save him from death, and he was heard because of his reverent submission. Although he was a Son, he learned obedience through what he suffered; and having been made perfect, he became the source of eternal salvation for all who obey him, having been designated by God a high priest according to the order of Melchizedek.

Both earthly high priests and the heavenly priest are appointed for their office (Heb 5:4-5). While the earthly high priest obtains honor (τιμή)[60] because of his honorable office, the Son gets glory from his father (δοξάζω): he is glorified through the words of Psalms spoken by God (Ps 2:7; 110:4). The passage clearly alludes to Hebrews 1: whereas Christ was installed by the

---

[60] This Greek term is commonly used as a designation for an office; cf. Attridge, op. cit. (note 6), 145.

"speaking God" as Son and king (Ps 2:7; Ps 110:1), now he is installed as Son and priest. Comparable to Hebrews 1, the listeners hear and "see" through the lenses of the Psalms a heavenly scene illustrating the high status of Christ as Son and high priest. But, abruptly, the perspective changes to focus on the humanity of Christ. He is portrayed as praying with deeply felt emotions; "Jesus offered up[61] prayers and supplications, with loud cries and tears" (Heb 5:7-9). The content of his prayers is not indicated and obviously not relevant for the author.[62] What is this scene, showing Jesus sharing the most painful conditions of human life, all about? The lenses of the Psalms can perhaps be helpful here. The language used to describe the praying Jesus points to "a traditional Jewish ideal of a righteous person's prayer," a concept often found in Hellenistic Jewish sources, but based on language used in the Psalms.[63] Roughly speaking, Jesus is portrayed here as a prayer of Psalms.[64]

According to the Psalms, God has the power to save from death (cf. Heb 2:9; Ps 22). Death can be understood in a narrower sense as being threatened by (impending) death or in a wider sense as living in the realm of death—which would be a description of the human condition compatible with Hebrews 2:14f. Two aspects are of special interest concerning Jesus' status as high priest and Son, who in the days of his flesh (cf. Heb 5:7; 2:14f) endures suffering and fear of death. First of all, Hebrews 5:5-10 again illustrates that suffering and death are not incompatible with Jesus' high status. He endures suffering and death that in general belong to human existence, thereby proving his confidence to God. Like the psalmist of Psalm 22, he brings his deepest supplications to God and he is heard. The Son's human life included real suffering and death, but he firmly trusted in God. Suffering and death are not incompatible with his status as high priest, but this is the way that he is led to perfection and made a competent high priest who sympathizes with his followers (Heb 2:17f; 4,15). Secondly,

---

[61] The used verb προσφέρω is in general used in a cultic sense for offering sacrifices; cf. Heb 5:1.3. Using this verb for the Jesus' prayers alludes to the idea that the prayers are the sacrifices he offers to God, but the parallels should not be overly emphasized. See in detail Attridge, op. cit. (note 6), 149.

[62] Different assumptions on what Jesus prayed for and in what way he was heard by God are proposed by scholars. The main problem with a supposed reference to the Gethsemane accounts is that Jesus was not saved from death. Cf. Karrer, op. cit. (note 7), 274f.

[63] Attridge, op. cit. (note 6), 148f. Attridge quotes different documents in support, amongst others Philo referring to Moses as ideal intercessor; Attridge, op. cit. (note 6), 149-51. Cf. also Backhaus, "Gott als Psalmist," in Backhaus, op. cit. (note 59), 101-29, here 22f.

[64] Cf. Backhaus, op. cit. (note 59), 139.

although "Hebrews does not use hortatory language at this point, a concern for the audience is transparent,"[65] Jesus is here presented as a model of how to come to terms with suffering and with fear of death.

Conclusion

Through the lenses of the Psalms, the audience of Hebrews can see both the invisible glory of the Son and his visible human existence. The author particularly focuses on the Son's high status that is not visible to the human eye: The Son is the eternal king who is sitting at God's right hand and he is the compassionate high priest who enables the hearers to approach the godly throne (Heb 2:17f; 4:16). The Psalms spoken as words of God afresh today help the listeners to see not only Jesus' human existence but also his everlasting glory, his dominion and his intercessory activity as high priest. Even suffering and death cannot affect his status. This also has consequences for the believers' self-perception. Moses was terrified to approach the Zion (Heb 12:20f), but the listeners can be self-confident and full of boldness, being invited to a festival gathering in the city of the living God (Heb 12:22f; cf. Heb 4:12-16). "The believers' honor is grounded in God's declaration of association with them, by which he commits to them a share in the divine honor and commits to preserve their honor as an extension of God's own dignity" (Heb 4:9; 11:16).[66]

Furthermore, Jesus presents a model of how to come to terms with suffering. Even if the believers are socially stigmatized because they worship a crucified man, they now see Jesus with spiritual eyes: they recognize that his humanity and death are meaningful and compatible with his status; this is the way Jesus mediates high status and salvation to his followers. They furthermore know that they are siblings of Jesus and children of God. They notice that Jesus was not preserved from death, but God preserved him by bringing him through suffering and death to glory. Even if they have to suffer, they can firmly trust that God will bring them through suffering to his glory. By hearing God's words and by seeing the glory of the Son who confidently trusted in God even during his days of flesh (Heb 2:5-18; 5:5-10), the hearers finally become psalmists themselves. They now see that God's power to save is at work even in the reality of suffering and death. Confidently, even defiantly, they can pray with the words of Psalm 118:6, "With the Lord on my side I do not fear. What can mortals do to me?"

---

[65] Attridge, op. cit. (note 6), 153.
[66] Cf. DeSilva, op. cit. (note 48), 293.

or Hebrews 13:6, "So we can say with confidence, 'The Lord is my helper; I will not be afraid. What can anyone do to me?'"

The author of Hebrews is convinced that God speaks to present-day believers by using the same words once spoken to the fathers. He is well aware of the fact that the ancient words of God get a new meaning when spoken and heard in a new situation. Hebrews relates the Psalms to Jesus, interpreting his life and his significance in the light of their words. But the author is not interested in limiting Scripture to the witness of Jesus Christ and he does not argue polemically against Israel. The Christological interpretation of Hebrews does not outdate the traditional Jewish understanding of the Psalms. Thus, the author of Hebrews assumes and is pleased that the words of God can have different meanings depending on the particular situation of the readers and hearers. To appreciate that all texts, including the words of God, can have different meanings in different situations can free interpreters of biblical texts from the fruitless effort to find the one and only appropriate interpretation. Relating this important hermeneutical insight to Martin Luther's understanding of the Psalms enables us to hold on to a Christological interpretation of the Psalms without denying their earlier contexts in Israel's history and their continuing validity for Jewish believers. The hermeneutical insight that one text can have a multitude of true interpretations can relieve us from searching and defending the one and only true interpretation. In fact, the contemporary global Lutheran community may read the Psalms in different contexts and the resulting plurality of interpretations can be appreciated in confidence that God is speaking to present-day believers in different ways, using the same words once written in the Holy Scriptures.

V. Luther's Interpretation of the Psalms from a Contemporary Perspective

Luther and the Psalms: How Stories Shape the Story

Vítor Westhelle

Introduction

Odd but intriguing assignments have been part and parcel of my work with the Lutheran World Federation (LWF), at least as far as my area of expertise is concerned. And this is no different. The topic assigned to me was "Luther and the Psalms: How Stories Shape Stories." However, in order to present something that is contextual and pertinent I need to change the subtitle to either "how the story shapes stories" or (what is even more interesting) "how stories shape the story." This issue has been discussed in the Lutheran communion for quite some time. Jens Erik Skydsgaard has worked with this problem since the early 1960s in connection with ecumenical challenges that the LWF was facing.[1] Since then the problem has become much more complex as stories have significantly multiplied. Lutheranism is migrating en masse from its bedrock to more fluid places around the planet. Needless to add, stories keep accumulating in reports and consultations about Lutheranism where its future is now presaged. So, how the stories tell the story has been the pressing issue for a communion that, by a stroke of fortune, never settled down and set in stone what its identity finally is, notwithstanding many endless attempts to mine a rock big enough to inscribe it. My reflections in what follows may be at times technical as far as dogmatic issues are concerned, yet it aims at just showing how the story and the stories are related.

---

[1] See Jens Holger Schjørring, Prasanna Kumari and Normal Hjelm (eds), *From Federation to Communion: The History of the Lutheran World Federation* (Minneapolis: Fortress, 1997), 248–83.

The Psalter

On 24 April 1530, the day after Luther arrived at the Coburg castle to be in closer proximity to Augsburg where, at the imperial diet, Melanchthon was presenting the confession of the Reformation, Luther wrote to his friend and co-reformer: "We have come to this Sinai of ours, my dear Philip, but once out of this Sinai we will make a Zion and we will build three tabernacles: one for the Psalter, one for the prophets, and one for Aesop."[2]

That Luther regarded the ancient fabulist Aesop the author of the best literature after the Bible, and even edited and translated him into German, is no secret.[3] But still one wonders about the religious imagery (Sinai, Zion, tabernacle, Psalter, prophets) being associated to this ancient gentile storyteller thus calling for a careful examination, particularly regarding the reason for these three tabernacles. A tabernacle is the dwelling place of that which is most dear and divine, the innermost space in which the heart inhabits and the soul rests. A tabernacle is an enclosure for presence, i.e., a representation of that which cannot be represented. As such a tabernacle for the Psalter is there where the soul and heart of the psalmist are enshrined; the same goes for the prophet, and for Aesop! We know that Luther had the highest regard for the Psalter calling it "a little Bible."[4] So he regarded the prophets' harsh words necessary for curbing idolatry and entailing the promises pointing to Christ. But, why Aesop? Yes, and that too not for who he was or what he did, but for what he said and how he said it. This seems to me the point of this reference to Aesop, whose words were truthful to the human condition, and we are not distracted by the works he did or failed to do.

In his preface to the Psalter (of 1524 and the reworked final edition of 1545), Luther develops an interesting polemic against the popular legends of saints and their deeds. "Other books make much ado about the works of the saints, but they say very little about their words." The Psalter, to the contrary, is about the saints'

> words, how they spoke with God and prayed, and still speak and pray. ... It presents not the ordinary speech of the saints, but the best of their language, that which they used when they talked with God himself in great earnestness and on the most

---

[2] *Pervenimus tandem in nostrum Sinai, carissime Philippe, sed faciamos Sion ex ista Sinai edificabumusque tria tabernacula, Psalterium unum, Prophetis unum, et Aesop unum. WA Br* 5:285, 3-6.

[3] Carl P. E. Springer, *Luther's Aesop* (Kirksville, Mo.: Truman State University Press, 2011).

[4] *LW* 35, 254.

important matters. Thus the Psalter lays before us not only their words instead of their deeds, but their very hearts and the inmost treasure of their souls.[5]

And Luther's praise for the Psalter goes to show that the depth of joy and the profound cry of lamentations, "as into death, yes, as into hell itself."[6]

By this measure Aesop's tabernacle can be explained as stories, fables from a person who has not been acclaimed for sanctity, but who spoke about the human condition from the depth of his heart. And that for Luther would count as earnest prayer! And this is not in spite of the fact that he was not a saint (neither was he a Jew or a Christian for that matter), but more likely because he was not (!) a "saint." Yet, for Luther, he spoke from the depth of his heart, as the psalmists and the prophets did. But there is no illusion in this endeavor. For Luther the translation of a Psalm was not to convey the original meaning, or the possibility of giving meaning, but to express what is in the heart. In other words, a translation allowed for the heart to speak to or communicate with the head!

ON TRANSLATION

Georg Wilhelm Friedrich Hegel recognized only too well the magnitude of this effort when he said, "for the Christians in Germany to have the book of their faith translated into their mother tongue is the greatest revolution that could happen. Only when uttered in the mother tongue is something my property."[7] Even if Luther did not know the Italian play on words—*traduttore/tradittore*—that makes a translator a traitor, he certainly knew the Greek verb *paradidomi* which can mean both "handing over" as in an act of treason or of passing on the tradition (cf. Mk 14:10 and 1 Cor 11:23 in which the same verb is used for Judas' treason and Paul's conveyance of the words that Jesus spoke at the last supper). And it goes unavoidably in both ways: the translator becomes a traitor and the traitor becomes a translator. Luther claimed the latter in his defense of translating Romans 3:28 to include the word "alone," after "justified by faith," while it is not in Paul's original.[8]

Translation does say what that is when it expresses the longings of the heart, and this was above all what Luther found in the Psalter. Walter Benjamin, for whom Luther was an eminent translator, made a difference

---

[5] Ibid., 254f.
[6] Ibid., 256.
[7] Georg Wilhelm Friedrich Hegel, *Werke* 20 (Frankfurt: Suhrkamp, 1971), 16-17.
[8] Ibid., 182-202.

worth considering between translation "as a mode," and translatability as "an essential feature of certain works." And he continues a point that Luther would endorse:

> One might speak of an unforgettable life ... even if all men had forgotten it. If the nature of such a life or moment required that it be unforgotten, that predicate would not imply a falsehood, but merely a claim not fulfilled by men, and probably also a reference to a realm in which it is fulfilled: God's remembrance.[9]

Benjamin makes us ponder how much translatability is not encumbered on us, a task to be fulfilled, as much as it is an unavoidable longing to give the heart a venue to express itself.

Language is the "mirror of the heart," said Luther quoting a popular expression.[10] But it is more and less than that. It is more because it opens a possibility for an encounter with otherness in the transference of semantic realms so that the translated text in a new semantic context says more than a literal translation would convey. However, it is also less, because language is the heart's "prison," drawing the limits of one's world. This is what Luther writes in defending his translations of the Psalms: "... words are to serve and follow the meaning, and not the meaning the words."[11] This is indeed a very debatable statement that evokes irreproducible circumstances. For example, how am I going to establish a meaning that evokes words in my context that was not the context of the original author? How and when to favor a literal translation and when does meaning call for words that are semantically different than the original? Centuries before this became a central question in hermeneutical theory, from Schleiermacher through Dilthey to Gadamer and Ricoeur, the Reformer was struggling with this question.[12]

In his defense of the translation of the Psalter Luther in fact goes both ways, at times he ventures into a freer translation for the sake of vernacular intelligibility,[13] on other occasions he favors a literal translation even if meaning becomes obtuse.[14] Is this arbitrary as it seems *prima facie*? He

---

[9] Walter Benjamin, *Illuminations*, ed. Hannah Arendt (New York: Schocken, 1968), 70.
[10] *LW* 29, 305.
[11] *LW* 35, 213.
[12] See Hans-Peter Grosshans, "Lutheran Hermeneutics: An Outline," in Kenneth Mtata (ed.) *"You have the Words of Eternal Life." Transformative Readings of the Gospel of John from a Lutheran Perspective*, LWF Documentation 57/2012 (Minneapolis: Lutheran University Press, 2012), 23–46.
[13] See, e.g., *LW* 35, 193 ("I must let the literal words go and try to learn how the German says that which the Hebrew expresses ...").
[14] See, e.g., *LW* 35, 194 ("I prefer to do violence to the German language rather than to depart from the word.").

offers a hint of what would be the operational criterion for deciding between the two: "I have been very careful to see that where everything turns on a single passage, I have kept the original quite literally and have not lightly departed from it."[15] Obviously it begs the question, How does one decide what a passage on which "everything turns" is? Arguably the best answer to this question should be found at the very core of Luther's theology, namely, his Christology within the doctrine of the Trinity. In translating and commenting on Genesis 1 he states: "Here I have considered it necessary to repeat the principle I mentioned several times above, namely, that one must accustom oneself to the Holy Spirit's way of expression."[16] And after defending the technical language of different academic disciplines, he does not surrender to them the right of an autonomous theological hermeneutic: "... the Holy Spirit also has His own language and way of expression, namely, that God, by speaking, created all things and worked through the Word, and all his works are some words of God, created by the uncreated Word."[17] This is in fact the key to explain the choices he makes, particularly in translating the notoriously difficult poetic language of the Psalter even for someone proficient in biblical Hebrew.

THE COMMUNICATION OF LANGUAGES

Luther offered his groundwork for translation in his basic Christological principle, especially in his magnificent defense of the *communicatio idiomatum*, the communication of attributes, in the Council of Chalcedon (451) as we have it "On the Councils and the Church of 1539."[18] The communication of attributes or, even more literally, the communication of "idioms," i.e., the communication of language becomes the question of the translatability of the Word into words. If it is the Word of and with God it needs to be made intelligible and visible in one's proper language. And for Luther, nothing was more proper than one's language; or phrasing it differently, nothing is closer to the heart than the vernacular. But can one's heart be in communion with that to which it is external, the words as uttered or written?

In the Genesis lectures that Luther began in 1535 he starts by pointing to the difference between the Hebrew word *dabar* and *amar*.[19] For Luther, the former (*dabar*) denotes the immanent co-eternal distinct person of the

---

[15] Ibid.
[16] *LW* 1, 47.
[17] Ibid.
[18] *LW* 41, 100.
[19] *LW* 1,16.

Triune God, the Word, while the latter (*amar*) describes a speech act that is created in utterance and creates reality in its pronouncement. His point is a Trinitarian one, and indeed Christological. He lifted up this distinction to fend off the attacks of the "Neo-Arians" (enthusiasts, Schwenkfeld?) who were supposedly arguing that because the speech act is a creation of a subject who pronounces it and through which it is posited externally as a creation, this word cannot be co-eternal. Luther's argument is that the Word as a distinct person in the Trinity is ineffable, that only through the work or breath of the Spirit comes into expression as an external word, as flesh, as matter, as a visible, audible and sensuous fact.[20] And this is what we can behold, the word as an external reality, which however ensues from the Father by the Word through the Spirit, and becomes the visible reality we can observe. And this externality, this sensuous reality we call world, matter, flesh is in its frail and corruptible expression nothing less than the veil, wrapping, or mask of the divine reality itself. And this and only this can we behold. The naked God (*deus nudus*) no one can bear to behold and live (Ex 33:20), but the one in the flesh who comes from the heart of God becomes language for us, becomes text woven in the stuff of this world–texture.

This, indeed, is the crux of the matter. Luther's reading of Chalcedon (451) late in 1539, is an attempt to name all that he meant by his Christological principle: the Word of God became flesh and thus was translated into human words. And these words are all there is regarding the frail human condition that God decided to join in, or in the words of Paul that Luther so loved, God became sin. God became the language of human inability to say an authentic word, a word from the heart, and restore that which God revealed.

In introducing the Psalter, the Reformer makes a revealing comparison between the Psalms and the legends of the saints. It was necessary to know where Luther was coming from in his understanding of language, of *idioma* in order to figure out what he meant with the criticism of the "lives of the saints" with all the marvelous accounts of the works and miracles that they did. The works and miracles attributed to the saints had a beautiful and undeniable quality. But they were counterfeit in the following sense: The work, the objective reality produced through a miracle, for example, is indeed an expression of the word, but the produce, the work done, was an external reality that severed its connection to the heart. For the Reformer,

---

[20] It is not spurious to argue that Wittgenstein of the *Tractatus* was giving a modern philosophical frame to the same problem Luther was struggling with, namely, the conditions of possibility for the world to be named. And the conclusion of both, Wittgenstein and Luther, is surprisingly similar.

the works are mute and only as idols do they reproduce themselves. Luther long precedes the historical critical method and the demythologizing program, but he reached similar conclusions as to what really counts in the biblical narrative as Lessing did in his words that became the mantra of the exegetes that followed him: "accidental truths of history can never become the proof of necessary truths of reason."[21]

THE CHRISTOLOGICAL CORE

Luther owes his interpretation of the Psalms to the Christological principle with which he was working. For someone who championed the literal sense of the text and explicitly rejected the allegorical (along with the tropological and the anagogical) interpretation it is surprising to see how much Christ he finds in the Psalter. On the Psalter Luther is allegorical through and through, although it would be better to say that his exegesis is highly metonymical; he uses a literal reference as in referring to Christ by association of ideas common to the described event and Christ. His defense is precisely dependent on the Christological principle applied and what it metonymically evokes in reading the Hebrew Scriptures. When the Reformer claimed to be doing a "literal" reading of the Scripture, instead of a spiritual one, he was thinking in the Latin sense in which *littera*, the letter, is the outer expression of *verbum*, the Word. It was Luther's Christology, his understanding of the second person of the Trinity that controlled his translation.

Yet different from the likes of "Origen, Jerome and many other distinguished people,"[22] Luther read the Hebrew Scriptures not only as pointing to Christ, but indeed prefiguring Christ's presence and praising already what Christ accomplished and accomplishes![23] This can only be explained and justified by the way the *communicatio* works as true interchange between the divine and the human, not only in the historical Jesus, not even in the sacrament, but anywhere and at any time, before, during and after the first decades of the Common Era. For this is what Luther says in his

---

[21] Gotthold Ephraim Lessing, "On the Proof of the Spirit and of Power," in Henry Chadwick (ed.), *Lessing's Theological Writings* (Stanford: Stanford UP, 1956), 53.
[22] *LW* 35, 235.
[23] See for example his reading of Psalm 68:7 "O God when Thou didst go forth before Thy people, when didst Thou march through the wilderness." Luther paraphrases it: "O Christ, at the time when Thou didst go before the Israelites in their exodus from Egypt, Thou didst presage and symbolize Thy resurrection, by means of which Thou didst really precede Thy people out of the Egypt of this world to Thy Father." And so forth, *LW* 13, 8.

Confession of 1528, a text that the Reformer regarded to be the irreversible statement of his faith[24] concerning the three modes of Christ's presence. The first is the historical Jesus, the second is where he promises to be, as in the sacrament, but the third is crucial to understand how Luther reads the Psalms as the story of Christ and of Christendom. According to this "third mode" Christ is

> present in all created things. ... You must place this existence of Christ, which constitutes him as one person with God, far, far beyond created things, as far as God transcends them; and, on the other hand, place it as deep in and as near to all created things as God is in them.[25]

This same point is stressed by Luther in different parts of his confession (and quoted at length in the Formula of Concord).[26] To phrase it in traditional language, for the Reformer the economic Trinity tramples the immanent, at least since the creation of the world by the Word.

This is what Luther's rejection of the spiritual senses in reading the Psalter amounts to: It is not that the Psalms may hint at something not yet realized, but they are already a testimony of that which is always being actualized in any place and at any time, which is made manifest in its plenitude in Jesus the Christ. The story of the earthly life of the Messiah does not change anything about God and the world in their relationship; it provides, however, a hermeneutical key to read the whole of Holy Writ and to read in all that is written, as it reveals in the depth of the heart that which is holy. This is the reason to build a tabernacle for Aesop.

There is no justification through language alone, however. Language only spans the space that the heart inhabits and in which it gains a profile and a mask that joyfully or miserably reveals and answers its secrets and longings and simultaneously conceals and hides mystery. Language is the earthly stuff with which the faithful convey and veil the presence of the Word. Luther said it well: "The Holy Spirit has its own grammar; people who grammatically speak falsely, may, regarding the sense of it, speak the truth."[27] That means: new meanings and realities are not only given shape, but also brought about through language in its heteroglossic dynamic movement, that is, even when grammatically deviant.

---

[24] *LW* 37, 360–72.
[25] *WA* 37:224.
[26] See *Book of Concord*, Formula of Concord, Solid Declaration VII, 101-103; VIII, 82-84.
[27] *WA* 39/II:104.

ON BEING HOLY AND BLESSED

Luther's praises for the Psalter were of such magnanimous dimension exactly because it did not speak about deeds, but it was only about "empty" words, empty as the heart is to be to host the Word. That is the condition and the requirement for God to empty Godself and dwell in it. This is the *kenosis* motif of Philippians 2 seen from the human side in which pure receptivity, *vita passiva*, is the condition for divine evacuation so that the Word can inhabit that bare place, the place of the heart, the depth of the soul and become words. And this is what he reads in this other Psalm that is not in the Psalter, the Magnificat, where he compares the human being to entailing the three compartments of Moses' tabernacle (using here a trichotomist anthropology: body, soul and spirit) in which the spirit designates the holy of holies. In it "God dwells in the darkness of faith, where there is no light."[28]

At the end of his "Confession Concerning Christ's Supper, 1528" Luther makes a remarkable distinction between being holy (*heilig*) and being saved or blessed (*selig*). The context is his discussion of the different orders instituted by God (*ecclesia*, *oeconomia* and *politia*):

> For to be holy and to be saved are two entirely different things. We are saved through Christ alone; but we become holy both through this faith and through these divine foundations and orders. Even the godless may have much about them that is holy without being saved thereby.[29]

The crucial point in this passage is that one can attain holiness in the external orders of the world without realizing the depth of the heart (a metaphor Luther often used in reference to the spiritual dimension in which faith is kindled). One can be holy as one conforms to the God-intended "orders of creation." However blessed is the one who knows by faith that whatever these spheres of promise can become they are the outer expression, the incarnation, the materialization of the Word in words through which matter comes into existence. For Luther matter matters. His apocalyptic proclivities never led him to despise the world. It is holy because the holy of holies has been hosted by it. This is the holy, as mundane as it can and must be. Blessed is the one who knows and believes that it is made effective by the eternal Word through the Spirit.

---

[28] *LW* 21, 304.
[29] *LW* 37, 365.

In the lectures on Genesis, Luther builds an amazing defense for a sect that was condemned for anthropomorphism.[30] His argument for the sake of showing that "a wrong was done to good men ... because they said that God has eyes, with which he beholds the poor; that He has ears, with which he hears those who pray," comes precisely out of his materialism. Only because God has become matter through the Word in the Spirit God says: "Look! Under this wrapper you will be sure to take hold of me."[31] Those who do not apprehend these material and visible signs "will never apprehend God."[32]

To use "postmodern" verbiage, there is no meta-narrative because "The Story" is ineffable, but there are always stories coming from the indwelling of the Word that is hosted in the world. If this ineffable Story can be received in faith and "known" there is definitely a gnostic element in Luther. But if the Word has become creation, matter that decays and dies, this Luther owes to the biblical apocalyptic and the resurrection hope that matter will be restored. And both strands, the gnostic element and the apocalyptic, Luther inherited above all from Paul. This is what allowed him to read the Psalter as stories that came from the heart but did not need external historical evidences to speak on what life in its materiality is about. And that is what he also found in the fables of Aesop who we do not know if he was a holy man, but blessed we can know he was.

> The Astronomer used to go out at night to observe the stars. One evening, as he wandered through the suburbs with his whole attention fixed on the sky, he fell accidentally into a deep well. While he lamented and bewailed his sores and bruises, and cried loudly for help, a neighbor ran to the well, and learning what had happened said: "Hark ye, old fellow, why, in striving to pry into what is in heaven, do you not manage to see what is on earth?" – Aesop, *Aesop's Fables*

---

[30] *LW* 1,14-15.
[31] *LW* 1,15.
[32] Ibid.

The Psalms and Luther's Praise Inversion: Cultural Criticism as Doxology Detection

Brian Brock

As citizens of the modern age, the ways in which we live are deeply shaped by the labor saving conveniences and medical care which saturate our daily practice. We also think like moderns, meaning that we partake of the age of criticism, theologians included. If we are to recover a living relation to the Psalms, I will suggest, we will need to reflect on what it means to say that we are "modern theologians." This will mean asking how the rationality of the modern project relates to the rationality of faith. To ask this question is to ask about the place and function of criticism, which lies at the core of modern rationality. We must ask, What is criticism, theologically conceived? Unfolding this question will allow us to return to the Psalter with fresh eyes, as a forum in which we can learn to respond to our world anew and in a critical and ethically generative way, but without falling into the habit of modern rational criticism to dissolve Scripture and the Christian tradition of reading.

Put briefly, modernity (*Neuzeit*) is the period of Western history in which the old Christian apocalyptic understanding of human events and history as the movement of the two cities that God judges and rules was displaced with an idea of history as progress; progress out of superstition and irrationality and so into a world justified and oriented in the forum of naked, unbiased reason. "Our age," writes Kant in the manifesto of modern rationality, the *Critique of Pure Reason*,

> is the genuine age of **criticism**, to which everything must submit. **Religion** through its **holiness**, and **legislation** through its **majesty** commonly seek to exempt themselves from it. But in this way they excite a just suspicion against themselves, and cannot lay claim to that unfeigned respect that reason grants only to that which has been able to withstand its free and public examination.[1]

---

[1] Immanuel Kant, *Critique of Pure Reason*, trans. and ed. Paul Guyer and Allen W. Wood (Cambridge: Cambridge University Press, 1997), A xi, 100-101.

Critical reason must "doubt everything" (Descartes) in order to free itself from the fetters of the past, sifting and discarding what it takes to be rubbish from what it takes to be valuable. History and tradition are in this new critical world not approached as something one expects to be changed by, but as an obstacle to be cleared away or a resource to be mined for usable building stones.

The effects of this modern criticism reshaping Christian thought were most obvious in the much debated rise of biblical criticism in the nineteenth century, which set out to discern in the Bible what is of enduring value. This critical relation was most influentially applied to Christian ethics in the twentieth century by Ernst Troeltsch in his *The Social Teaching of the Christian Churches*, which sought to discern which moral truths could be distilled from a Christian tradition taken to be ripe for decontamination. In this paper I will work with the assumption that such attempts to rise high enough for reason to get an objective "God's eye view"[2] is not only suspiciously like the self-exalting quest of the builders of the tower of Babel, but renders the Psalms irrelevant today as a collection of texts marked in so many ways as historically particular and ethically ambiguous documents which pose very high hurdles to any project to locate or distill the "rationally verified" nuggets of truth it might contain.[3]

So much for the brief sketch of what I will not be doing. What I will attempt may well be similarly counterintuitive, in that I will assume that the modern account of critical rationality also had an effect on how we understand language in our everyday life. The distilling processes of Enlightenment rationality,[4] which reached their pinnacle in Anglophone

---

[2] "The free intellect will see as God might see, without a *here* and *now*, without hopes and fears, without the trammels of customary beliefs and traditional prejudices, calmly, dispassionately, in the sole and exclusive desire of knowledge—knowledge as impersonal, as purely contemplative, as it is possible for man to attain. Hence also the free intellect will value more the abstract and universal knowledge into which the accidents of private history do not enter, than the knowledge brought by the senses, and dependent, as such knowledge must be, upon an exclusive and personal point of view and a body whose sense-organs distort as much as they reveal." Bertrand Russell, *Prisons* (1911), uncompleted manuscript, in Andrew Brink, Margaret Moran and Richard A. Rempel (eds), *Contemplation and Action*, The Collected Papers of Bertrand Russell, vol. 12 (London: Routledge, 1993), 106.

[3] My account of the role of criticism in defining modern rationality draws on Oswald Bayer, *A Contemporary in Dissent: Johann Georg Hamann as a Radical Enlightener*, trans. Roy Harrisville and Mark Mattes (Grand Rapids: Eerdmans, 2012), chs. 7–8. Originally published as *Zeitgenosse im Widerspruch: Johann Georg Hamann als Radikaler Aufklärer*, 1988.

[4] While affirming the problems inherent in the Enlightenment settlement, I would also want to affirm that there is a much deeper historical problematic to be explored

analytic philosophy, approach language as primarily a medium for communicating information and only secondarily affective states. It thus bequeathed modern Westerners a reified understanding of language. Here the observations of a contemporary anthropologist put us on the way to discovering a much more exiting understanding of the Psalter.

> Could we not...suggest that music and language, as separate symbolic registers, are the products of a movement of analytic *decomposition* of what was once an indivisible expressive totality, namely song?[5]

Based on his observations about the ways human communities use language, Tim Ingold is questioning the modern tendency to understand language as essentially concerned with "information" and "text" abstracted from their actual usage in human communities. Every word, he protests, is in reality "a compressed and compacted history"[6] of peoples' interactions with the material world and each other. Because the way in which we inflect words as we speak impacts how they are heard, we should consider the affective and tonal aspects of communication to be more intrinsic to communication than our modern accounts of language admit. "In short," concludes Ingold,

> whether I speak, swear, shout, cry or sing, I do so with feeling, but feeling—as the tactile metaphor implies—is a mode of active and responsive engagement in the world, it is not a passive, interior reaction of the organism to external disturbance.[7]

Because modern rationality presumes writing to be the paradigmatic form of communication, we speak as if tone of voice were essentially an irrelevant part of communication, if music was something we have the option to add if we want to embellish words, and that it has fallen to a special branch of writing to carry the expressive and aesthetic losses that come with this bargain—poetry.

This bargain obscures the ineradicably affective aspect of our relation to the world, the kaleidoscope of attractions and repulsions and ambivalences we feel to the things which cross into our sensory horizon. The

---

that points to the changes of Christian theology that occurred during the colonial period, as Willie Jennings suggests, in which Christian theology had to learn to position itself as if human bodies were interchangeable units that were not deeply shaped by their embedding in place and social fabric. Willie James Jennings, *The Christian Imagination: Theology and the Origins of Race* (New Haven: Yale, 2010).
[5] Tim Ingold, *The Perception of the Environment* (London: Routledge, 2000), 408.
[6] Ibid., 409.
[7] Ibid., 411.

reality that we constantly respond to the things and persons before us with attraction or repulsion, resistance or embrace, suggests that hope and fear are also woven into the most basic fabric of our everyday existence and moral deliberation. As Friedrich Nietzsche so influentially noted, this affective relationship to the world, our basic embedding in fear, faith and hope, drastically shapes the way our moral thinking proceeds (recovering, we could also say, an insight of Augustine, for whom love was the basic motor of perception). If we face a reality we fear, our moral deliberations will be strongly steered into the quest for moral reasons for justifying our interest in self-protective measures, whereas if we face the same situation in faith and hope, what we will rationally explain as a good act will take on remarkably different contours. In consigning the affective life of the human to the "private" or "anecdotal" realm rather than the realm of the universal and true, modern thought obscures these decisive considerations.

All this suggests that living out faith in the midst of our world cannot but conflict with many ways of living in the world without any hope to hear the Trinitarian God in and through it; responses to the world which experience it as uttering threats that must be controlled or proffering prizes that go to those who grab them will have a very different tenor from lives lived as a response to a creator God who uttered a world out of love and in which Godself has been deeply invested.[8] For theology in modernity, I will suggest, we need to learn once again to hear God as one whose speech, the speech that created this world, is saturated with affective engagement. This is to learn about God the poet, who through the very fabric of the world and human history speaks in a way that can be heard by humans and responded to with affectively engaged love.[9] In what follows I will explain why if we take these starting points seriously, a new critical relation to the world is opened up by the Psalter. Notice that I have used the term "Psalter," by which I indicate a performed text, reserving the term "Psalms" for the canonical collection of 150 Psalms. I will not be looking to see how the "information" conveyed in the "text" of the Psalms is relevant to Christians today, but to understand how "performing the Psalter" as part of worship in lived life can inform our understanding of what it means to live in the world today.[10] By following this line of reasoning I hope it will

---

[8] "How has God the Holy Spirit humbled himself, when he became a historian of the smallest, most despised, most insignificant events on earth, to reveal to humans in their own language, their own history, their own paths, the counsels, the mysteries and the ways of divinity?" Hamann, quoted in Bayer, op. cit. (note 3), 55.
[9] Bayer, op. cit. (note 3), 97-102.
[10] Though I will not be engaging it in this paper, Luther also develops an account of anti-doxology that more straightforwardly interprets the content of the Psalms.

become clear why I believe that theologians today can still be moderns, seeing the value of intellectual criticism in discovering truth. But I will also be indicating the value for modern theology of finding a way to let God's criticism shape and remake our processes of self-criticism, and the central role the Psalter can play in that mode of criticism.

Theologizing the Tradition

My main interlocutor in this paper will be Martin Luther and, more specifically, his readings of the Psalms. I want to suggest that because Luther's ethics is not one of prescription but of perception and affection, the way he reads the Psalms is especially revealing of his understanding of moral transformation. His approach, I will suggest, allows him to deepen and theologically enrich an inversion of perception that played an important role in the ethical thinking of the earlier theological tradition. Before outlining his own view, a few snapshots of how this theme worked in the tradition that preceded him will make his own contribution more evident.

Consider this passage from Gregory of Nazianzus's *Oration 14* in which he tries to show his believing audience why they should learn to see lepers differently. The inversion of perception depicted in this oration was historically important in overcoming the ancient sensibility that health care was only due those whose healing could be considered beneficial to the *polis*, and was integral to his building the institutions of care that were the direct precursors of our modern hospitals.

> There have been instances when people have allowed a murderer to live with them, have shared not only their roof but their table with an adulterer, have chosen a person guilty of sacrilege as their life's companion, have made solemn covenants with those who have wished them harm; but in this person's case [that of the leper] suffering, rather than any injury, is handed down as a criminal charge. So crime has become more profitable than sickness, and we accept inhumanity as

---

For instance, he reads Psalm 2:3 as a literal description of the "song of the godless" (30): "The devil will never cease to sing this verse through the mouths of rulers and kings, though impious doctors, yes even through your own conscience: 'Let us burst Their bonds asunder and cast Their cords from us.'" Martin Luther, "Psalm 2 (1532)," in *LW* 12, 18, [*WA* 40:139–312]. I will be citing the Luther in English from *Luther's Works*, American Edition, 55 vols, edited by Jaroslav Pelikan and Helmut T. Lehman (St. Louis: Concordia Publishing House and Philadelphia: Fortress Press, 1955-1986), hereafter referred to as *LW*. In some cases I will also give the reference from the original source in the *Weimarer Ausgabe*, which will hereafter be referred to as *WA*.

fit behavior for a free society, while we look down on compassion as something to be ashamed of.[11]

Later Augustine was to offer a phenomenologically richer and more theologically developed account of this inversion of perception that exhorts his hearers to seek an eschatological vision that sees not surfaces, but the heart.[12] It is relevant for our inquiry that it is the insight of a Psalm that suggests this theme to him:

> ...now we believe, we do not see; to see what we believe will be recompense for this faith... in the psalm a certain lover says with a sigh, "One thing have I asked of the Lord; this I shall seek after" (Ps 27:4). ...What is it that he seeks after? He says, "That I may dwell in the house of the Lord all the days of my life." And suppose that you dwell in the house of the Lord; whence will be your joy there? "That I may gaze," he says, "on the delight of the Lord." My brothers... What do you desire, I ask you? Can it be seen with the eyes? Can it be touched? Is there some beauty which delights the eyes? Have not the martyrs been loved ardently? And when we commemorate them, do we not catch fire with love? What do we love in them, brothers? Their limbs mangled by wild beasts? What sight is fouler, if you should consult the eyes of the flesh? What is more beautiful if you should consult the eyes of the heart? How does a very handsome young man, but a thief, appear to you? How your eyes do stare in terror! Are the eyes of the flesh terrified? If you should consult them, there is nothing better structured than that body, nothing better arranged. The symmetry of the limbs and the loveliness of his complexion entice the eyes. And yet when you hear that he is a thief, you flee from the man because of your mind. On the other side you see a bent-over old man, leaning on a cane, scarcely able to move, ploughed all over with wrinkles. What do you see that delights the eyes? You hear that he is just; you love him, you embrace him.[13]

Elsewhere Augustine explains that because humans are made in the image of God, they are not only capable of this transposition of perception, which

---

[11] Gregory of Nazianzus, *Oration 14*, trans. Brian E. Daley S.J., in Brian E. Daley, *Gregory of Nazianzus*, The Early Church Fathers (London/New York: Routledge, 2006), 81.

[12] Ingold finds what Augustine is describing to be a crucial aspect of many types of human perception, the distinction, "between two kinds—or levels—of vision: on the one hand, the ordinary sight of pre-existing things that comes from moving around in the environment and detecting patterns in the ambient light reflected off its outer surfaces; on the other hand, the revelatory sight experience at those moments when the world opens up to the perceiver...," op. cit. (note 5), 278.

[13] Augustine, *Tractates on the Gospel of John*, 1-10, trans. John Rettig (Washington D.C.: The Catholic University of America Press, 1988), 91-92.

he calls the "illuminated mind," but this transposition is a constitutive of the process of sanctification.[14] Notice, however, that he follows Nazianzus in framing the inverting power of perception as proceeding by way of a mode of moral perception. He plays our attraction and repulsion to physical beauty against the sometimes very differently configured repulsion we might feel at moral ugliness or our attraction to developed virtues. Though Augustine generally presumes that human loves shape our perceptions of all things,[15] he does not fully articulate how the moral perception that can see beyond surface beauty or ugliness of individual humans relates to human perception of all aspects of creation. This wider theology of the inversion of perception we do find in Luther. His treatment of the gospel pericope of the man born blind is a classic text on this theme, and in it he takes care to position his understanding of human perception biblically and by reference to previous theological authorities.

> ...the reason why all this is said and what causes it, says Augustine, is the transgression of Adam, to whom the devil said, "Your eyes will be opened, and you will be like God, knowing good and evil" [Gen. 3:5]... he is trying to lead them to the form of God, so he says, "Your eyes will be opened," that is, they will become blind. Before their eyes were closed, but after the Fall they were opened. The consequence of this, as Origen, the wise and acute schoolmaster teaches, is that man has two kinds of eyes, his own eyes and God's eyes. But the fact is that both kinds of eyes, our inward eyes and outward eyes, are God's. Indeed, all our members and everything that is in us are instruments of God and nothing is ours if they are ruled by God. But they are ours when God forsakes us. This means that, as Christ says, we must pluck out the eye that scandalizes and offends us and throw it away [Matt. 5:29]. That's why it is that we would rather see what is fine and pretty and well formed rather than what is gold or silver, rather a young Jill or a young Jack than an old woman or an old Jack. And this is the mousetrap that dupes our minds, as

---

[14] Augustine, "The Literal Meaning of Genesis," in John Rotelle (ed.), *On Genesis: A Refutation of the Manichees, Unfinished Literal Commentary on Genesis, the Literal Meaning of Genesis*, trans. Edmund Hill (New York: New City Press, 2002), III.20, 30.

[15] The *locus classicus* statement of this position comes from the *City of God* 19:24. "A people, we may say, is a gathered multitude of rational beings united by agreeing to share the things they love. There can be as many different kinds of people as there are different things for them to love. Whatever those things may be, there is no absurdity in calling it a people if it is a gathered multitude, not of beasts but of rational creatures, united by agreeing to share what they love. The better the things, the better the people, the worse the things, the worse their agreement to share them." Translation in Oliver O'Donovan and Joan Lockwood O'Donovan (eds), *From Irenaeus to Grotius: A Sourcebook in Christian Political Thought* (Grand Rapids: Eerdmans 1999), 162. See also op. cit. (note 13), 20–21.

is written of Adam in the book of Genesis. So our eyes have been opened, which really means that we have become totally blind, so that, as was said a moment ago, we consider the sham to be good and what is poor and misshapen to be evil. This the devil taught us, and it is his eyes that do it. But Christ came to teach these eyes to see and to take away the blindness, in order that we should not make this distinction between young and old, beautiful and ugly, and so on. Rather all are equal, wise man or simpleton, sage or fool, man or woman; it is enough that he is a man with our flesh and blood, a body common to all. For such perception one must have a fine, acute, and well-trained mind.[16]

Luther is serious when he says that such perception requires training, because we do not perceive what appears to God's eyes, that creation is more whole than broken, more "good" than "evil."

But [God] rules in such a way that even physically we always see more of His grace and blessing of His wrath and punishment. For we find a hundred thousand healthy people for every ailing, blind, deaf, paralytic, or leprous person. And even if one member of the body has a defect, the entire person, still endowed with body and soul, shows forth nothing but God's goodness.[17]

The condition of our perceiving the world thus demands the reversal of the "opened eyes" that come with original sin, and here the Enlightenment philosophers were only continuing ancient and late-medieval quests for true perception. But unlike the modern approach to reaching this true perception, with its attempt to disembody communication to find its essence, for Luther the renewal of perception comes via a practice. This practice does not offer us God's "view" in the sense of allowing us to see all things from "above" but does allow us access to God's perception of the world while sensitizing us to an experience of divine activity that is accessible to everyone. For Luther the Lord's Supper is the primal liturgical form in which the goodness of all God's works can be learned, the point at which Jesus Christ's power to open eyes and ears (Mk 7:34–35) is promised to us. This claim is developed by way of a reference to the logic of Passover. As Israel was commanded to recall their divine liberation from temporal death, and to do so by giving the first of the fruit of their labor back to God, so in the Lord's Supper Christians

---

[16] Martin Luther, "Sermon on the Man Born Blind, John 9:1–38 (17 March 1518)," in *LW* 51, 38–39 (*WA* 1:267–273).

[17] Martin Luther, "Sermons on the Gospel of St. John (1537)," in *LW* 24, 73–74 [*WA* 45:527].

should contemplate, diligently regard, and consider what a glorious and beautiful work it is that Christ has delivered us from sin, death, and the devil. Here one should consider what our condition would be if these wonderful works had not been performed for us.[18]

The rescue of Israel and the church from the sinful blindness of human rebellion includes their being schooled to appreciate the magnitude of the divine involvement in ordering the church, society and all creation. The very accessibility and proximity of this divine care, however, tempts humans to complacency. Just as we tend to become jaded about God's grace in creation and political preservation, we also become blasé about the Lord's Supper:

In short, we cannot sufficiently marvel at it and contemplate it in eternity. And yet, when we hear about it, we clods... yawn about it and say: "Oh, is this the first time you have ever seen a rotten apple drop from a tree?"[19]

It is not accidental that Luther illustrates his point using the metaphor of fruitfulness.[20] Doxological perception sees and praises God's provision and care for fertility and new life in all its forms, especially in the worship service. Its opposite, what I am calling anti-doxology, cannot see how worship has taken shape as people have joined a trans-temporal community of praise[21] for God's fecundity and material, experienced care and instead

---

[18] Martin Luther, "Psalm 111," in *LW* 13, 373.
[19] Ibid., 373.
[20] "He [God] wills to speak, then, namely, when we, almost despairing, decide that He will keep silence forever. But what or in what manner will He speak? Here we must observe the Hebrew way of expression. For when Scripture says that God speaks, it understands a word related to a real thing or action [*verbum reale*], not just a sound, as ours is. For God does not have a mouth or a tongue, since He is a Spirit, though scripture speaks of the mouth and tongue of God: "He spoke, and it came to be" (Ps. 33:9). And when He speaks, the mountains tremble, kingdoms are scattered, then indeed the whole earth is moved. This is a language different from ours. When the sun rises, when the sun sets, God speaks. When the fruit is grown in size, when human beings are born, God speaks. Accordingly the words of God are not empty air, but things very great and wonderful, which we see with our eyes and feel with our hands. For when, according to Moses (Genesis 1), the Lord said "Let there be a sun, let there be a moon, let the earth bring forth trees," etc., as soon as He said it, it was done. No one heard this voice, but we see the works and the things themselves before our eyes, and we touch them with our hands." Martin Luther, "Psalm 2," in *LW* 12, 32.
[21] "David calls his psalms the psalms of Israel. He does not want to ascribe them to himself alone and claim the sole glory for them. Israel is to confirm them and judge and acclaim them as its own. For it is essential that the congregation of God,

can only see in the icon of that fecundity, fruit, blemishes and the banality of the "fact" which does not convey any "meaning."

It is not too farfetched to assume that this basic move recurs in the Christian tradition because it is present in Scripture, and the apostle Paul (who so influenced Luther) seems especially attracted to it. Take for instance Paul's response and rebuke to the "strong" ones' who are seeking personal advantage, and who he patiently teaches to be more solicitous toward the conscience of the other in 1 Corinthians 10:31: "So, whether you eat or drink, or whatever you do, do everything for the glory of God." This recommendation contradicts the Corinthian slogan recounted in the previous verse, "If I partake with thankfulness, why should I be denounced because of that for which I give thanks?" In 1 Corinthians 10:30 the emphasis is on my thanks, and by implication its efficacy in justifying behavior, while the focus of 1 Corinthians 10:31 is on the glory of God. It may well be possible to give thanks while giving offense to others, but it is impossible to glorify God while doing so. Giving glory to God is therefore presented as the antithesis to idol worship, which the apostle makes explicit in 1 Corinthians 12:3: "Therefore I want you to understand that no one speaking by the Spirit of God ever says 'Let Jesus be cursed!' and no one can say 'Jesus is Lord' except by the Holy Spirit."[22]

---

or God's people, accept and ratify a word or a song; for the Spirit of God is to dwell in this people, and He wants to be honoured and must be honoured in His people. In that light we Christians speak of *our* psalmists. St. Ambrose composed many hymns of the church. They are called church hymns because the church accepted them and sings them just as though the church had written them and as though they were the church's songs. Therefore it is not customary to say, "Thus sings Ambrose, Gregory, Prudentius, Sedulius," but "Thus sings the Christian church." For these are now the songs of the church which Ambrose, Sedulius, etc., sing with the church and the church with them. When they die, the church survives them and keeps on singing their songs. In that sense David wishes to call his psalms the psalms of Israel, that is, the psalms of the church, which has the same Spirit who inspired them in David and which will continue to sing them also after David's death. He sensed in his spirit that his psalms would endure on and on, as long as Israel or God's people would endure, that is, until the end of time. And that is what has happened hitherto and will happen. Therefore they are to be called the psalms of Israel." Martin Luther, "Treatise on the Last Words of David, (1543)," in *LW* 15, 274-75. For a more fully developed theological account of the place of the Psalms in the communion of saints, see Bernd Wannenwetsch, "Conversing with the Saints as they Converse with Scripture: In Conversation with Brian Brock's Singing the Ethos of God," in *European Journal of Theology*, 18:2 (2009), 125-36.

[22] In Romans the parameters of the 1 Corinthians antithesis is clarified by reference to another set of theological terms. Whereas here Paul speaks of "craving evil" in its connection with idolatry and its opposite of giving God glory, in Romans 14:23

Giving glory to God or worshipping idols are not modes of action immediately perceptible from their surface but are types that can assume a wide variety of forms. This logic explains why, for Paul, both eating and not eating can be instances of either glorifying God or idol worship. This looks like an endlessly perplexing hall of moral mirrors, but in it Paul offers the Corinthians a very clear criterion for judgment: while they need to understand the importance of resisting evil desires they must distinguish this willed, active resistance from the exit provided by God's faithfulness as coalescing in the eucharistic encounter. Paul's interest is to turn the Corinthians' attention away from the quest to protect their freedom and reputation to the quite different quest to hope and love in such a way that the world is known differently.

It is this Pauline move which Luther is apparently picking up and joining with his own doxological hermeneutic. Consider how he turns the prose passage in 1 Corinthians 15:55 ("Where, O death, is your victory? Where, O death, is your sting?") into a hymn of praise. When we read this verse as a promise that we not only believe but can live within,

> Then we will really begin to glory joyfully and defiantly and say and sing "O death, where is thy sting? O Hell, where is thy victory?". ... [Christ] sings this song of defiance against death and hell uninterruptedly: "Dear death, once upon a time you crucified and buried me too... But where are you now? I defy you to pursue me further"...Now we who believe in Him share in this when the hour comes in which we see and feel how death and hell are entirely swallowed up and exterminated. At present, however, we await the hour, assured that this will surely come to pass and that we can already defiantly rely on Christ by Faith over against sin, death, and hell.[23]

Characteristically, Luther ends his lecture/sermon series on 1 Corinthians 15 with a reading of Paul as breaking into song, and as he does so breaks into song himself.[24]

---

he uses the terms "doubt" and "sin" in contrast to their opposite "faith": "But those who have doubts are condemned if they eat, because they do not act from faith; for whatever does not proceed from faith is sin." Both formulations of this antithesis are enriched if we note the ways Paul is deploying what are usually considered quite distinct conceptual packages to explicate his enduring theological and pastoral point, that glorifying God is the opposite of idol worship.

[23] Martin Luther, "Commentary on 1 Corinthians 15 (1533)," in *LW* 28, 207.

[24] See also, Martin Luther, "Exposition of Psalm 127, for the Christians at Riga in Livonia," in *LW* 45, 317.

> St. Paul appropriately concludes with a song which he sings: "Thanks and praise be to God, who gave us such a victory!" We can join in that song and in that way always celebrate Easter... but we must keep this in our heart in firm faith and confirm ourselves in this and always be engrossed in such a message of thanks and sing of this victory in Christ.[25]

Our core question is now squarely in view: Why does Luther keep returning to this picture of sung praise as an essential constituent of the divine inversion of human perception?

Hamartiology reconsidered: Nothingness, chthonic forces and anti-doxology

It is one of the little ironies of the *Church Dogmatics* that in his doctrine of creation Karl Barth emphasized the spectral non-existence of evil,[26] while in his unfinished ethics of reconciliation he returned to the theme to call evil an alienation of created powers.[27] Having gone out of his way to affirm evil as nothingness, in continuity with the Western tradition, Barth later felt the need to deploy the biblical concept of the "chthonic forces" (Gal 4:3) to describe the processes of humans coming to be dominated by the powers of creation, via their own alienation, rather than having dominion over them (Gen 1:28). Ensuing debates about the apparent conceptual tensions in his treatment suggest that his account of the matter would benefit from further elaboration.

This is where Luther's competing account of anti-doxology is conceptually illuminating. In his writings on the Psalms, Luther often describes wickedness as non-conforming Psalm performance, a departure from the Augustinian hamartiology of deprivation. For Luther, sin is made up of concrete but aberrant responses to God's gifts, consisting in filled-out and

---

[25] *LW* 28, 213, cf. 110–11.
[26] Karl Barth, "God and Nothingness," in *Church and Dogmatics*, vol. III, 3, §50 at **www.foundationrt.org/outlines/Barth_Dogmatics_Volume_III.pdf**
[27] "In the sudden or gradual movement with which man breaks free from God, he revolutionizes the natural forces that are coordinated with him and subordinated to him, first those that slumber and then awaken in himself, then the spirits of the earth that are first concealed in the surrounding cosmos but are then discovered and unleashed by his keen-sightedness and skill...Nevertheless...He finds that he himself is subject to their law, which he has foreseen, and to their power, which he has released." Karl Barth, *The Christian Life: Church Dogmatics IV,4 Lecture Fragments*, eds G. W. Bromiley and T. F. Torrance, trans. Geoffrey Bromiley (Edinburgh: T&T Clark, 1981), 228.

personified anti-doxology. He draws on the words of his favorite Psalm to argue that the action and speech of the saints genuinely magnify the Lord: "The right hand of the Lord does valiantly; 16 the right hand of the Lord is exalted; the right hand of the Lord does valiantly" (Ps. 118:15-16). "Singing" thus names the cast of all speaking that properly marks the Christian ethos. "Under 'singing'," says Luther,

> I include not only making melody or shouting but also every sermon or public confession by which God's work, counsel, grace, help, comfort, victory, and salvation are glorified before the world. ... As verse fourteen [of Psalm 118] puts it: "The Lord is my Strength and my Song; He has become my Salvation." God wants to be praised, glorified, honored, and confessed by us in His works and wonders. Faith does this, for faith cannot be silent but must say and teach what it believes and knows about God, to the glory of God and the instruction of man, as Ps. 116:10 says: "I believed, therefore have I spoken."[28]

Those caught up in God's work are being taught to praise God's working in all things, while faith in human works is always detectable as anti-doxology. By using the term "anti-doxology" I mean to grasp Luther's core point that because all action springs from some hope and faith, all speech and action are always expressions of praise and expectation of what can be counted on from some power. Luther sees the Psalter as a primer in which Christian faith is taught to praise, in so doing exposing anti-doxologies and the ways they obscure the living presence of God's tangible and accessible saving activity.

Because every doxology expresses faith in some specific salvation, a doxological social critique directs our attention to the places where humans set up and praise self-protective, self-reliant and self-imposed limits. The task of the moral theologian includes the task of describing the false lords to which praise is given and which so deeply shape the parameters of our moral deliberation. Praise analysis, here paralleling the approach of the Frankfurt philosophical school, comes into its own in the face of emergent social rifts which expose the shape of the loves and fears that motivate our current societies. It meets these upheavals not in faith in Kant's account of the power of self-criticism to overcome the illusions that cause our problems, but by reflecting on the false and denuding hopes and fears which govern our lives and which are exposed by the in-breaking of the God of overflowing bounty.

---

[28] Martin Luther, "Psalm 118," in *LW* 14, 81.

Learning to Praise: Psalm 118

A closer look at Luther's treatment of Psalm 118 will display how he understands Christian performance of the Psalter to break into and reveal sinful and blinding anti-doxologies.[29]

> 15. Shouts of joy and victory resound[30] in the tents of the righteous:
> "The right hand of the LORD does valiantly;
> 16. the right hand of the LORD is exalted;
> the right hand of the LORD does valiantly."
> 17. I shall not die, but I shall live,
> and recount the deeds of the LORD.
> 18. The LORD has punished me severely,
> but he did not give me over to death.

These verses, suggests Luther, put us in the position of praising either ourselves or God: there is no middle position between the two. The claim rests on what we might call a proto-Wittgensteinian idea of the "happy performance," in which our understanding of the function of words begins not with metaphysical realities (such as atoms, ideal forms, or transcendentals), nor subjective states of consciousness (hunches, sensation, mental representations), but with beings in relationship, beings who share basic forms of life (*Lebensformen*).[31] In congruence with Wittgenstein and Ingold, I am reading Luther as deploying an account of language and its relation to what exists that is much more imbedded in human living (as a social and affective activity) and human naming (as activity that takes place in a material creation). By allowing such relationships to inform what we expect words to do, we move beyond the modern assumption that words can be distilled for their (one) "meaning"; they "mean" and "refer" in the context of communicative relationships. The meanings of words are thus defined in their

---

[29] This section develops my treatment in *Singing the Ethos of God: On the Place of Christian Ethics in Scripture* (Grand Rapids: Eerdmans, 2007), 172-79.

[30] I take this phrase from the NIV translation, as it captures the ring of Luther's German better than the more literal NRSV. Luther translates: 15 Man singt mit Freuden vom Sieg in den Hütten der Gerechten: "Die Rechte des HERRN behält den Sieg; 16 die Rechte des HERRN ist erhöht; die Rechte des HERRN behält den Sieg!"17 Ich werde nicht sterben, sondern leben und des HERRN Werke verkündigen.18 Der HERR züchtigt mich wohl; aber er gibt mich dem Tode nicht.

[31] Ludwig Wittgenstein, *Philosophical Investigations*, trans. G. E. M. Anscombe (Oxford: Basil Blackwell, 1968), 225-26. For an excellent discussion of this idea and its implications, see Fergus Kerr, *Theology After Wittgenstein* (Oxford: Basil Blackwell, 1986), especially 69-76, and Oswald Bayer, *Promissio: Geschichte der reformatorischen Wende in Luthers Theologie* (Göttingen: Vandenhoeck, 1971).

usage by communities. When I speak, it is to take up words as packets of this communal meaning in order to reformulate my various relationships with some end in mind. So understood, the Psalms' meaning is not reducible to conceptual "content," though they do refer to reality. Their main role is in calling forth performances which cohere with them, and so function as condensed versions of the relationships out of which they were composed. As such they are language constellations oriented by a formed dialogue and, if taken up, lead back into that same dialogue.[32] The Psalm verses under discussion can thus be understood as conveying to us the relationship with God, out of which they were born, as they guide us into a similar relationship.

These verses, says Luther, train us to rely on God. Those who rely on human power perform them "unhappily"; that is, in ways which do not seek to discover the form of communal life which they demand, instead, cosmetically pasting them onto lives driven by the fear of loss or the desire to possess. When such people take up the words "the right hand of the LORD is exalted," the connotative force of their words and works yields the meaning, "The right hand of man does valiantly; the right hand of princes is exalted."[33] Elsewhere Luther is explicit that two types of false singing are possible. One is a singing which is built on the exchange mentality. These singers "will not praise him unless he does good to them." The more dangerous mis-singing, however, is the anti-song just paraphrased, the praise of self masquerading as divine praise.[34]

By defining wickedness as non-conforming Psalm performance Luther has set up an important critical principle. Because he understands sin as concrete but aberrant responses to God's gifts it is not merely a deprivation of the good, but an enacted and so personified anti-doxology. A theological judgment that a Psalm has been inverted in any specific performance rests on a complex semantic judgment on Luther's account. This insight was deeply to mark modern philosophy. "Luther said that theology is the grammar of the word 'God'," Wittgenstein famously wrote, continuing,

> I interpret this to mean that an investigation of the word would be a grammatical one. For example, people might dispute about how many arms God had, and someone might enter the dispute by denying that one could talk about arms of God. This would throw light on the use of the word. What is ridiculous or blasphemous also shows the grammar of the word."[35]

---

[32] Wittgenstein, ibid., 503-04.
[33] Martin Luther, "Psalm 118," in *LW* 14, 81.
[34] Martin Luther, "The Magnificat," in *LW* 21, 307-308.
[35] Ludwig Wittgenstein, *Wittgenstein's Lectures, Cambridge 1930-1932*, ed. Desmond Lee (Oxford: Basil Blackwell, 1980), 32. Elsewhere: "Grammar tells what kind of object anything is (Theology as grammar)," Wittgenstein, op. cit. (note 31), 373.

Wittgenstein has picked up Luther's suggestion that Scripture reveals the grammar of the divine life, making theology a communal discussion about the proper interpretation of Scripture. Thus understood, the words of the Psalms do not force communal agreement automatically, by recitation, but offer access to and sustain a communal life of faith that is shaped by them.[36] Asking what it means to perform the Psalter well will bring into view the interrelation of a certain mode of articulateness and the formation of the Christian ethos. Faith in human works produces and is produced by anti-doxology: those caught up in God's work are made into those who are being taught to praise God in all things.

For praise to be congruent with the words sung we must define the content that is praised with the phrase "right hand of the Lord," Luther continues. Christ Himself is supremely this "right hand" because, "The stone which the builders rejected has become the chief cornerstone" (Ps 118:22).[37] This rejection by the world of God's mighty work of redemption is most visible at the point when God's conflict with death is at its final extreme: on the cross.

> When the world hears, then, that its highest gifts are disapproved by the Gospel and that only this King is commended, it is not only offended, but even prepares

---

[36] Meaning is not in our internal state, but in our communal interactions, explains Wittgenstein. "Does it make sense to ask 'How do you know that you believe?' — and is the answer; 'I know it by introspection'?" "In *some* cases it will be possible to say some such thing, in most not. "It makes sense to ask: 'Do I really love her, or am I only pretending to myself?' and the process of introspection is the calling up of memories; of imagined possible situations, and of the feeling that one would have if..." Wittgenstein, op. cit. (note 31), 587. The influence of this train of reasoning has continued to circulate both ways, as this highly influential passage from George Lindbeck's *The Nature of Christian Doctrine: Religion and Theology in a Postliberal Age* (Philadelphia: Westminster Press, 1984), 64, illustrates: "For a Christian, "God is Three and One," or "Christ is Lord" are true only as parts of a total pattern of speaking, thinking, feeling, and acting. They are false when their use in any given instance is inconsistent with what the pattern as a whole affirms of God's being and will. The crusader's battle cry *"Christus est Dominus"* for example, is false when used to authorize cleaving the skull of the infidel (even though the same words in other contexts may be a true utterance). When thus employed, it contradicts the Christian understanding of Lordship as embodying, for example, suffering servanthood."

[37] Martin Luther, "Psalm 118," in *LW* 14, 83. Some New Testament scholars concur in showing how various textual clues indicate that the writers of the New Testament understood this passage to speak of Jesus (cf. Acts 4:11). One of the most obvious is that the idiomatic Greek construction of verse 51 of the Magnificat (Lk 1: "He has shown strength with his arm; he has scattered the proud in the thoughts of their hearts") is clearly indebted to the Hebrew formulation of Ps 118:15. See John Nolland, *Word Biblical Commentary, Luke 1:9-20*, vol. 35a (Dallas: Word Books, 1989), 71.

weapons and strives with all its might to vindicate its own gifts against this affront. This is the occasion for the bitterest conflicts; thus the world and this King attack each other with hostile hearts.[38]

The good and bad performance of these Psalm verses is ultimately defined by reference to the conflict of the cross, where the deep grammar of God's redemption of humans is exposed. When Christians say that the right hand of the Lord is exalted, concludes Luther, they can only mean that Christ is exalted, in whom their own merits and eternal reward are found. The linkage of praise and perception inversion begins to emerge as Luther interprets the psalmist's use of the language of "the Lord's right hand" Christologically. Drawing on 1 Corinthians. 15:55–57 and Isaiah 9:4 he concludes that God's power is first Christ, and it is from the bounty of Christ's merits and rewards that benefit flows to those who participate in His life.[39]

Reading Luther with Wittgenstein suggests that in Christian theology and practice the meaning of verses 15–18 of Psalm 118 falls to pieces if severed from their glad performance as songs of Christ's victory. At the same time, the inter-human referent of the happy performance is firmly set within the vertically oriented experience of the divine deliverance they describe. Luther correctly observes that the psalmists explain the genesis of their praise as the experience of rescue.[40] The basis of their hope in what

---

[38] Martin Luther, "Sermons on the Gospel of St. John, Chapters 1-4," in *LW* 22, 62.
[39] "Whoever will, let him apply these three points to the threefold work of Christ, in that He redeems us from the Law, from sin, and from death. This threefold redemption is enumerated in Is. 9:4 and in 1 Cor. 15:55. ...the important thing is to realize that these words are wholly spiritual and must be heard, sun, and understood by faith. He who gapes at these words open-mouthed and uses his reason and natural eyes will take offense and will consider only the opposite in the righteous and holy." Martin Luther, "Psalm 118," in *LW* 14, 83, cf. 81–84 [*WA* 31:140-149]. This was a remarkably stable hermeneutic key to the Psalms for Luther, which he articulated in his earliest lectures on the Psalms in 1513–1515. "The right hand is Christ, the Son of God, as Ps. 118:16 says: 'The right hand of the Lord has made strength,' for the Son of God is the strength, power, and wisdom of God, 1 Cor. 1:24, 30. Second, the right hand of God is the grace of faithfulness or work of God. Thus blessed Augustine correctly says by way of explanation that the right hand means God's propitiation and favor, according to Ps. 45:4: 'Thy right hand shall conduct Thee wonderfully.' The left hand, however, is God's rule or freely given grace, which is common to all. Third, the right hand is the awarding of glory in the future, as Matt. 25:33-34 says, 'He will place these on His right hand and those on His left, and then He will say, etc.' Therefore the right hand is, first, Christ; second, it is the merit of Christians, and third, it is their reward." Martin Luther, "Psalm Seventeen," in *LW* 10, 111.
[40] Luther writes, "Ps. 51:13, 14, 15: 'I will teach transgressors Thy ways...My tongue will sing aloud of Thy righteousness...And my mouth will show forth Thy praise.'

will happen in the future is therefore the experiences of rescue that lie behind them and their perception of events that are already in view, and is not, as in modern rationality, an extrapolation from what has happened in the past to predict what will happen in the future.[41] This is why Luther reads 1 Peter 2:9 neither as prescription nor command, but a description of conversion as the experience of rescue from death: "That you may declare the wonderful deeds of Him who has called you out of darkness into His marvelous light." This description of the experience of God is also an invitation, "For God does these wonders which are prefigured in the Red Sea to anyone."[42]

It is thus not accidental that the form of the Psalms, poetry, is related to their content, praise. The poetic form (with its inherent linkage with music) expresses an immediacy before God via the text which is at root not critical and so is destroyed by critical distance. This is similar to the understanding of poetry for which Paul Ricoeur is well known. "My deepest conviction is that poetic language alone restores to us that participation-in or belonging-to an order of things which precedes our capacity to oppose ourselves to things taken as objects opposed to a subject."[43] The point may also be illustrated by asking why at the end of his life Bonhoeffer wrote poetry. It is only in the last stages of his imprisonment, when death was immanent, that Bonhoeffer took up the form. Eberhard Bethge, rightly I think, suggests that only poetry could achieve the combination of intimacy and decorum demanded by this relationship and the terrible demands being placed on it.[44] Luther's suggestion is that God, who created in love and spoke the beautiful order that is the material creation, has provided humans with poems which make intimate speaking with him possible in the dark and confined places as well as the green pastures of this life.

In Ps. 40, 'He brought me out of the pit, etc.' (v.2), is followed by 'I have proclaimed Thy righteousness' (v.9), and again, 'Thou hast made Thy wonderful works many, O Lord, my God.' Ps. 66:16: 'Come and see, all you who fear God, and I will tell you what great things He has done for my soul.' Ps. 46:8: 'Come and behold the works of the Lord, what wonders He has done.' Ps. 118:17: 'I shall not die but live and tell all His wonderful works.' Ps. 107:2: 'Let the redeemed of the Lord now say, etc.' Ps. 9:1, 4: 'I will tell of all Thy wonderful works...For Thou hast maintained my judgment and my cause.'" Martin Luther, "Psalm Seventeen," in *LW* 10, 36-37.
[41] Tim Ingold, "Dreaming of Dragons: On the Imagination of Real Life," in *Journal of the Royal Anthropological Institute*, vol. 19 (2013), 734-52.
[42] Martin Luther, "Psalm Seventeen," in *LW* 10, 37.
[43] Paul Ricoeur, "Toward a Hermeneutic of the Idea of Revelation," in Lewis S. Mudge (ed.), *Essays on Biblical Interpretation* (Philadelphia: Fortress Press, 1980), 101.
[44] Dietrich Bonhoeffer, *Letters and Papers from Prison*, enlarged edition, ed. Eberhard Bethge (London: SCM Press, 1971), 386.

The architectonic role Luther gives to the metaphor of "singing" thus complexifies and resituates the believer's critical relation to Scripture in establishing a theologically construed critical relation to language itself. If God is a speaking God, then we are always in the midst of learning from God what our grammar is about. Language is not simply "there," but we are learning what it means and thus what it is by listening in the form of prayer. Language is the place that the God who created by speaking has given in order to use it to claim us. In prayer and praise we take up God's words to expose our language and lives to divine remaking. Thus prayer is the dialogical relation with God in which the regeneration of human life originates and is sustained.[45]

Because the theological location of prayer and praise is before God with the community of prayer, a togetherness is created through a multifaceted practice which we can describe (as Luther himself does not explicitly do) as the redemptive process. In Luther's final analysis, these verses' main function is to give access to an eschatologically open and therefore dynamic state of walking with God. Luther calls this state of openness the "art of forgetting the self." "We must keep learning this lesson as long as we live, even as all the saints before us, with us, and after us must do." To such a song of faith, "What can the devil do when he finds a soul so naked that it can respond neither to sin nor to holiness?"[46] Using one of Luther's other metaphorical constructions, we might say that in praise the "devil's eye" in us is displaced by the eyes of Christ, effecting the conversion of perception.

Luther understands this art of forgetting the self through an active and verbal relation to Scripture, God and other humans to be the way that we embrace Christ's victory, won by God's right hand. Luther says of Psalm 118:17,

> We should recognize this verse as a masterpiece. How mightily the psalmist banishes death out of sight! He will know nothing of dying and sin. At the same time he visualizes life most vividly and will hear of nothing but life. But whoever will not see death, lives forever, as Christ says: "If anyone keeps My Word, he will never see death" (John 8:51). He so immerses himself in life that death is swallowed up by life (1 Cor. 15:55) and disappears completely, because he clings with a firm faith to the right hand of God. Thus all the saints have sung this verse and will continue to sing it to the end.[47]

---

[45] Gerhard Sauter, "Reden von Gott im Gebet," in Gerhard Caspar (ed.), *Gott nennen: Phänomenologische Zugänge* (Freiburg im Breisgau: Alber Verlag, 1981), 219-42.
[46] Martin Luther, "Psalm 118," in *LW* 14, 85.
[47] Ibid., 87.

Singing about God's power is thus the proper creaturely response to the experience of God's salvation and so the salvation itself—the earthly form of eternal life. This means that in order to perform the Psalter at all we must begin with the acknowledgement that we are unprepared to pray. Faith must flee to Christ's prayer and allow Christ to pray through it as it clings to God as God has given Godself in the content of the church's prayers. We can and must prepare to pray by learning how to begin, but this beginning is not with method, but with this particular performative clinging.[48] We learn the grammar of life with God by taking these poems on our lips before God; we learn this language by using it.[49]

Attending to Luther's exegesis of the Psalms reveals that for him, faith is the central category of the Christian life, the famous *sola fide*, which orients hope, love and all human action. Because faith is trust in God's Word and promise, its constituent component is the acknowledgement of Christ as Lord, the axiomatic statement of Christian praise, and the one which alone allows non-Jews access to the Psalms. Summarizing the tight set of conceptual connections just outlined Luther offers an equation: "Faith in [God's] promise is nothing other than prayer."[50] The conversation that is prayer envelops the whole of the Christian's living (including their moral deliberation), rendering it a response of appreciation for God's action. Faith is the effect of God's Word and promise entering the heart, making it firm and certain and directing it by remaking human perception. This certainty and perception is understood in highly active terms;

> it bursts into action... impels him to compose beautiful and sweet psalms and to sing lovely and joyous songs, both to praise and to thank God in his happiness and to serve his fellowmen by stimulating and teaching them.[51]

---

[48] "We use the psalms of David and the writings of the prophets in this way as examples, even though we are not David or the prophets, but because we have the same blessings in common with them – the same Word, Spirit, faith, and blessedness – and because we sustain the same dangers and afflictions on account of God's Word. So we rightly take over their voices and their language for ourselves, praising and singing just as they praised and sang." Martin Luther, "Lectures on the Song of Solomon (1530-1531)," in *LW* 15, 192.

[49] This point is wonderfully and simply put in Luther's explanation to his barber about how to pray. Martin Luther, "A Simple Way to Pray," in *LW* 43, 193-211.

[50] Oswald Bayer, "Luther as an Interpreter of Holy Scripture," in Donald K. McKim (ed.), *The Cambridge Companion to Martin Luther* (Cambridge: Cambridge University Press, 2003), 77.

[51] Martin Luther, "Treatise on the Last Words of David," in *LW* 15, 272-73.

The behavior that springs from this confession cannot be a fixed aptitude or *habitus*, but because it is grounded in a conversation will always be a "spirit that falls and rises."[52] We might say, in summary, that the much maligned *sola fide* means "let all your thinking and action be infiltrated by the truth that the crucified and resurrected Christ is still at work and still the Lord of all creation."

Conclusion

Without suggesting that the Psalter is somehow superior to the rest of Scripture, we do well to notice its centrality in the faith and performed worship for Christians through the ages,[53] and that it was explicitly written in a form designed to be performed in the believing community.[54] I have suggested that learning to understand it as the "Psalter" rather than simply "the Book of Psalms" gives us fresh insight into a biblical tradition that is unique within the biblical canon in being wholly devoted to teaching us what it means for faith to be conversational. I have further suggested that by asking what it means for moderns to perform the Psalms the methodological location of (modern) Christian ethics is decisively shifted. Rather than being another discipline under the master discipline of hermeneutics or fundamental theology, it is redefined as reflection on the activity of praise and our life's coherence with it by way of an interrogation of the phenomenon of human perception. Performing the Psalter with the community of saints channels faith into a life of exploration of the divine bounty, so critically exposing our concrete enmeshments in a world praising its own glory and fighting for what it sees as scarce resources to be secured by human efforts.

If we take praise as the condition of all human action that responds to the world as coming from the hand of a good Creator and Redeemer, hope and trust analysis offers Christian theology an analytical tool with broad reach in both revealing the affective layers of experience that drive the way we put our ethical questions, and helping us critically to engage with

---

[52] Martin Luther, "Lectures on Isaiah Chapters 1–39," in *LW* 16, 321. Luther makes this comment as he examines Hezekiah's prayer to discover what it reveals about prayer in all times and places.

[53] See William Holladay, *The Psalms Through Three Thousand Years: Prayerbook of a Cloud of Witnesses* (Minneapolis: Fortress Press, 1996), and Rowland Prothero, *The Psalms in Human Life* (London: John Murray, 1909).

[54] Günter Bader, *Psalterium affectum palestra: Prolegomena zu einer Theologie des Psalters* (Tübingen: J. C. B. Mohr, Paul Siebeck, 1996).

the question of how they might be more appropriately formulated. To end with a few examples, rather than asking in medicine about how to serve consumers of healthcare or protect ourselves from being bankrupted by healthcare costs (whether individually or collectively), we might ask what might be entailed in creating the conditions for healing. Instead of discussions in agricultural ethics and policy aimed at "ensuring our food supply," we might ask what it means, concretely, to receive our daily bread. In business ethics the question about how to manage "human resources" or "risk" or to protect ourselves against financial shocks might be resituated by investigating what it could mean to understand our work out of a desire to receive and hand on God's care for people and creation. These few examples indicate the power of the critical reformulation of the very questions we ask in ethical discourse that praise analysis offers to modern theology.

THEOLOGY OF THE WORD IN "OPERATIONES IN PSALMOS" (1519-1521)

Ľubomír Batka

Luther's theology in "Operationes in Psalmos" (1519-1521) presents a communicative process of God's actions through the Word based on a Trinitarian structure: as an activity of God the Father, Son and Holy Spirit on behalf of human beings realized by the power of the Word.

Luther's second Lecture on Psalms[1] contains an elaborate exegesis of the first twenty-two Psalms. His original plan was to explain all the Psalms, but due to the tumultuous developments around the Diet of Worms (1521)[2] as well as the extent to which these lectures gradually grew in number and volume, the work remained unfinished. Despite this, it is a monumental masterpiece; the length these lectures would have attained had Luther finished commenting all 150 Psalms is astonishing. The work should be considered as one of Luther's central reforming works. He himself described his exegesis as something new; he criticized scholastic theology and confessed that he had moved beyond it.[3] This is confirmed in the autobiographical explanation that appears in the first volume of the Wittenberg edition of his Latin works in 1545:

> Meanwhile, I had already during that year returned to interpret the Psalter anew. I had confidence in the fact that I was more skilful, after I had lectured in the university on St. Paul's epistles to the Romans, to the Galatians, and the one to the Hebrews. I had indeed been captivated with an extraordinary ardor for understanding Paul in the Epistle to the Romans. But up till then it was not the cold blood about the heart, but a single word in Chapter 1[:17], "In it the righteousness of God is revealed," that had stood in my way. For I hated that word "righteousness of God," which, according to the use and custom of all the teachers, I had been taught to understand philosophically regarding the formal or active righteousness, as they called it, with which God is righteous and punishes the unrighteous sinner.[4]

---

[1] Dating of Luther's progress in "Operationes," in *WA* 5:3-5 and more recent dating from *AWA* 1, 108-113.
[2] *WA* 54:186, 21-24.
[3] *WA* 5:22, 18-21.
[4] *LW* 34, 336; *WA* 54:185, 12-20.

Luther described how his understanding of justice had been confirmed by reading different biblical passages. During the years 1519 through 1521, he dealt intensively with questions of authority, clarity and sufficiency of the Scriptures. The search for the proper meaning of Psalms within that of the whole Bible is intertwined with his theological thinking during this period. This search is linked to the growing clarity of the relationship between Scripture and the Word of God.

This article offers an analysis of Luther's hermeneutics of Psalms as based on the Trinitarian doctrine.[5] Although he did not speculate on the Trinity and Trinitarian terms in "Operationes," he did differentiate between God's working as God the Father, as the Son and as the Holy Spirit. This Trinitarian scheme[6] can be seen in Luther's note to Psalm 9:7: "In Scripture one must pay more attention to verbs than to nouns if one wants to understand the spirit."[7] Luther not only grasped the principal characteristics of the Hebrew language,[8] but also demonstrated his progressive theological thinking about God. Theology speaks first and foremost about God's actions, not about his qualities.[9]

Luther's theology of the Word in "Operationes" can contribute to contemporary Lutheran hermeneutics because it offers a substantially theological

---

[5] Luther's Trinitarian theology became a topic in several treatises. For an overview of the most important ones, see Hans-Martin Barth, *Die Theologie Martin Luthers* (Gütersloh: Gütersloher Verlagshaus, 2009), 217, fn. 81. Pekka Kärkkäinen offers an analysis of Luther's Trinitarian Theology in "Operationes," in Pekka Kärkkäinen, *Luthers trinitarische Theologie des Heiligen Geistes* (Mainz: Philipp von Zabern, 2005), 115–18. Cf. Dennis Bielfeldt, "Luther's Late Trinitarian Disputations," in Denis Bielfeldt, Mickey Mattox and Paul Hinlicky, *The Substance of the Faith. Luther´s Doctrinal Theology for Today* (Minneapolis: Fortress Press, 2008), 59–130.

[6] Most studies on Operationes are either interested in Luther's Theology of the Cross with a wide range of Christological considerations. Hubert Blaumeiser, *Martin Luthers Kreuzestheologie* (Paderborn: Bonifatius, 1995); Florian Schneider, *Christus praedicatus et creditus: die reformatorische Christologie Luthers in den "Operationes in Psalmos" (1519-1521), dargestellt mit beständigem Bezug zu seiner Frühzeitchristologie* (Neukirchener: Neukirchen-Vluyn, 2004); Horst Beintker, *Die Überwindung der Anfechtung bei Luther* (Berlin: Evangelische Verlagsanstalt, 1954); or in Luther's hermeneutics, Siegfried Raeder, *Grammatica Theologica. Studien zu Luthers Operationes in Psalmos* (Tübingen: Mohr Siebeck, 1977); Johannes Hilburg, *Luther und das Wort Gottes in seiner Exegese und Theologie* (Marburg-Lahn, 1948). Methodologically, the Trinitarian aspect did not play a big role here.

[7] *WA* 5:298, 11–13.

[8] Raeder, op. cit. (note 6), 30.

[9] This notion is strengthened by H. Blaumeiser, who raised a critical objection to an otherwise impressive work of W. v. Loewenich *Luthers theologia crucis* (1929). He argued that under the influence of dialectical theology, Loewenich became most interested in the question of God's transcendence. Blaumeiser, op. cit. (note 6), 29.

approach and represents a central characteristic of Lutheran theology. It suggests how the Book of Psalms can be approached in a unifying way despite the wide spectrum of theological and spiritual ideas that they contain.

The Father speaks to creation

When God speaks, things happen! The lively, poetic language of Psalms expresses the Creator's activity in a broad spectrum of areas (see e.g., Ps 9:7). God's speaking and God's creating are not two different modes of divine activity, but they are one and the same. The Word does not need a material base with which to create things; therefore, the creation (and also the recreation) of everything happens *ex nihilo*.[10]

In "Operationes," the whole creation (not only human beings) is able to hear the Word of God and to react to it. In his dedication of the first edition of "Operationes" to Elector John Frederick, Luther developed this starting point on hamartiological grounds: "For it is correct to believe that everything reveres the Word of God, through which it was created, except for man and the devil, who became deaf through their ingratitude."[11] Luther focuses on the transgression of the First Commandment. From 1517 on, he taught that the sin of unbelief, originating from a corrupted heart,[12] consists in a turning away from God (*aversio a deo*) and making the self the only center of attention (*conversio ad seipsum*). During this period, the notion of unbelief connects with the critique of human self-righteousness and confidence in good deeds as a depraved form of "unreligious religion."[13]

Unbelief, as original sin, in its universal, total and radical aspect, is most vividly explained with the biblical picture of "root sin" (*peccatum radicale*). In "Operationes," in conjunction with lecturing on Psalm 1:3, in a passage about the antipelagian teaching of Augustine, Luther said: "But I believe it is just as well, or even much better to speak of the whole man

---

[10] WA 5:544, 8-11. Johannes Schwanke shows the fundamental importance of the term ex nihilo in Luther's theology: "Creatio ex nihilo [...] is for Luther a permanent happening: ... The formula is not a footnote of divine action, but a fundamental matrix of God's handlings with man and world." Johannes Schwanke, *Creatio ex nihilo* (Tübingen: Mohr Siebeck, 2004), 5 and 74-75.

[11] LW 14, 281; WA 5:20, 7-8.

[12] LW 14, 289; WA 5:28, 9-14. Also see WA 5:103, 16-20; WA 5:218, 33-36; WA 5:398, 29-30.

[13] WA 5:135, 31-37. Cf. WA 5:139, 15-19. Idolatry is a vivid example of *aversio a deo*, loss of trust, whole desire (*frui*) and love (*delectio*) of God and *conversio* to created things, leading not only to unbelief and distrust of God, but to hate and disregard of God. WA 5:103, 34-37.

as a tree, making the roots the will and the branches the members and strength."[14] Reflecting on Matthew 7:17 and Matthew 12:33, Luther's discussion of sin rooted in the human heart suggests that original sin remains hidden under the surface of external deeds—like a root (*radix*) of a tree.[15]

A true fulfillment of life is love which does not solely serve itself. Creation hears the Word of God and serves the commandment of love. In contrast, since human beings and the devil do not listen to the Word of God, they turn everything toward themselves[16] and become liars. There is no other passage from the Book of Psalms in "Operationes" that Luther quoted more often than Psalm 116:11 (*omnis homo mendax*, cf. Rom 3:4), making an irremediable connection between sin and lies. On the other hand, when lecturing on Psalm 4:3, Luther talked about truth in connection with faith and the Word of God. "The human heart is full of vanity. All of their advice and efforts are lies, because they are without faith in God. But if they are without faith, then they are also without the Word of God, and therefore also without truth."[17] Luther's logic could be put this way: The Word of God stands between the faith and the truth. The Word is truthful, because it comes from God. Those who do not believe in God do not have God's Word and thus ignore the divine truth. Truth cannot be owned; the human being can participate in it through faith in God, since faith unites the human being with the truthful Word of God. It could be argued that the Word of God comes first: everyone without the Word of God is without faith and thus without God and truth. In "Operationes," however, Luther thinks about faith as *affectum* toward God from which arises a proper relation to the Word of God: the Word is not the instrument of God to create faith which unites with God. Obviously, the order is reversed: faith unites with God and with the Word of God. Only if human beings believe in God can they gain truth, and in this way escape their evil predicament.

In other words, a person becomes a good tree only if God, the heavenly gardener, transplants the person from Adam into Christ.[18] The visual image of a tree and a garden unites the Garden of Eden with the Garden of

---

[14] *WA* 5:37, 19–21.

[15] *WA* 5:422, 34–36. If unbelief is the original sin, and original sin is the root of all other sins, then original sin can be called *peccatum radicale*. This terminology is common in Luther's theological vocabulary even if it does not appear in "Operationes." For terminology, see Gerhard Ebeling, *Lutherstudien III* (Tübingen: Mohr Siebeck, 1985), 77–80. Cf. Ľubomír Batka, *Peccatum radicale: Eine Studie zu Luthers Erbsündenverständnis in Psalm 51* (Frankfurt am Main: Peter Lang, 2007).

[16] *WA* 5:190, 35–37. Cf. *WA* 5:38, 14–15; *WA* 5:139, 33–34; *WA* 5:370, 24–25; *WA* 5:411, 37–40; *WA* 5:437, 12–15.

[17] *WA* 5:107, 18–21. See Blaumeiser op. cit. (note 6), 138, fn. 23.

[18] *WA* 5:37, 25–27. Adam-Christus typology in *WA* 5:314, 19–22.

Gethsemane and the garden of Christ)s grave. In the person of Christ, God unites heaven and earth forever.

The Son reveals God the Father as a father

Luther's discussion of God the Son follows his hamartiological presuppositions. Jesus Christ does not reveal the otherwise hidden God. Since humans are deaf to the Word of God, they do not hear God's Word and therefore do not know "what God is doing, what God wants, what God thinks."[19] In the Son, people receive new and understandable words about God. The second person of the Trinity (*logos tou theou*) became flesh, so that people could hear God's speech anew and know God the Father as father.

Luther's Christocentrical exegesis of Psalms is united with his Christological teaching about the two natures within the single person of Jesus Christ. The aspect of unity can be analogically transposed to the debate on how the Word of God reveals its divinity in union with spoken human words. The power of God's Word in the person of Christ is united with the weakness of the bodily word, and this unity is undivided, indivisible, unchangeable and not mixed, as are the natures in the person of Christ. The fact that Christ's words do have a power that human words do not stems from the Christological doctrine of the person of Christ.

Luther's explanation of Psalms 2; 8; 9; 14; 16; 19; 21; 22 in "Operationes" (as in *Dictata*) starts with the presupposition that these Psalms contain prophecies about Christ.[20] Especially here, Luther developed his Christological teaching on all aspects of Christ's life: incarnation, suffering, death, resurrection, descent into hell, ascension and rule; all this, according to Luther, is encompassed in the first twenty-two Psalms.[21]

Again, it is apparent that the entire Christological doctrine is placed in a Trinitarian framework of divine communication, in which the Father with God's authority declares to the Son his divine son-ship first of all. On the other hand, the Son reveals the Father's will, so that people hear the Father's Word through the Son rather than the Son speaking about himself.[22]

---

[19] WA 5:107, 35–39.
[20] Carl Axel Aurelius, *Verborgene Kirche* (Hannover: Lutherisches Verlagshaus, 1983), 62. A Christological approach to these Psalms is given by their use by New Testament writers. Luther's approach is summarized in Hilburg, op. cit. (note 6), 89: "Fast jeder Psalm wird christologisch gedeutet, und zwar ist dies dann der Literalsinn."
[21] *WA* 5:54, 1–3; *WA* 5:75, 14–38; *WA* 5:90, 3–4; Ps 16:10–11; Ps 21:10 and Ps 18:9; *WA* 5:58, 36–42.
[22] *WA* 5:60, 8–10.

Christ does not serve himself—he serves the Father and people who are in need of salvation. This is the way the Father receives honor and glory.[23]

In regard to Christ's humanity, Christ is a real and pure person. Therefore, he suffered all human temptations and anguish.[24] In a rhetorically impressive passage related to Psalm 5:3, Luther highlighted the tragic predicament of the human, who did not want to be human and wanted to become God. But human beings cannot find this in themselves, only in Christ:

> Because Christ with his twofold nature achieved both: through the realm of his humanity ... that is active in faith, He makes us similar to Him by crucifying us. In this way, He turns wretched and proud gods to true people, that is, to poor people and sinners. Because whereas in Adam we ascended to the likeness of God, He descended and became similar to us, and brought us down to an understanding of ourselves. This happens in the sacrament of incarnation. This is the kingdom of faith, where Christ's cross reigns, overthrowing divinity which people desired in a perverse way, and which brings humanity and the scorned weakness of the body back to its proper place, which was deserted in a perverse way. But in the kingdom of divinity and glory, He will make us similar to His glorified body, so that we may be similar to Him. No longer sinners, weaklings or those who are in need of being led or ruled over, only kings and sons of God as angels. ... Whoever has got Christ as man, to him Christ Himself will bring God.[25]

This text expresses the essence of the "theology of the cross,"[26] which first of all represents the cross of Jesus Christ, secondly the word about the cross in the function of the Law and thirdly the suffering of Christians bearing their own cross. It is based on classical Christology and does not make sense without it. It is a process of returning a diverted-from-God and toward-her/himself-converted person back to God, which is not a simple act of conversion. It happens through the paradox of the cross. Because dying on the cross was a true man and a true God. A true God became a true human, even though to the observers he appeared to be neither a God nor a worthy man. Incarnation was hiding what is true, so that the natural man, a "false god" and a "bent

---

[23] *WA* 5:60, 35–37.

[24] *WA* 5:387, 24–29.

[25] *WA* 5:28, 36–129, 6.

[26] *WA* 5:176, 32–33: "*Crux sola est nostra theologia.*" This shall be seen in the context of the Heidelberg Disputations (1518), where Luther introduced the difference between *theologia gloriae* and *theologia crucis,* or more accurately, between a theologian of glory and a theologian of the cross: "*Theologus gloriae dicit malum bonum et bonum malum, Theologus crucis dicit id quod res est.*" [Thesis 21], *WA* 1:354, 21–22. The term *theologia crucis* appears for the first time in *Lecture on Hebrews* (1517-1518). See also *WA* 5:300, 1, and an analysis by Blaumeiser, op. cit. (note 6), 91–109.

human," does not recognize the work of salvation on the cross. To reach the right interpretation of what happens, one needs to listen to the Word of God. The "humbled God" on the cross does not appear to "proud humanity" as a true "instrument of lifting up and blessing," but rather as an "instrument of true deprivation and of death." On the other hand, a believer does not rely on what is apparent to the eyes, but trusts in the preached Word of God. In this way, "Christ becomes exemplar, not exemplum, because He showed how God works on humanity."[27] Christ as the true Word of God speaks most clearly to people and in doing so creates the realm of salvation. And vice versa: His doing speaks to human beings, so that the person becomes a believer.

Luther's most revered Psalm, Psalm 22, speaks primarily about the suffering of the man Jesus, not of the Son of God.[28] His suffering is threefold: physical and spiritual, but foremost the suffering of total abandonment on the cross. Paradoxically, despite all the horrible suffering, the cross became a place of the "renewal of all things."[29] It is the way to light, wisdom, truth, justice, goodness, power, joy, honor, blessedness and all that is good. All this happens *sub contraria*: in death, darkness, foolishness, falsehood, sin, weakness, despair, shame, unrest, condemnation and in all evil.[30] A person without faith is unable to understand the deeper meaning of these events and remains on the level of foolish appearances and false conclusions.[31] The real meaning of the happening on the cross cannot be seen by the natural person. People saw only a "decaying worm" without any hope.[32] Faith appears to be the "hermeneutical tool" to reach the proper meaning.

Luther does not stress the amount of pain, but the intensity of experiencing it. Paul Althaus stated that "Luther's theology surpasses all preceding theologies with the burden that God lets Christ suffer total loneliness and hell. ... He who wants to be our Savior must suffer our own hell."[33] Therefore, Christ suffers more in Gethsemane than on the cross under the weight of

---

[27] Lewis Spitz, "Luther and Humanism," in Marilyn Harran, *Luther and Learning* (Selingsgrove: Susquehanna University, 1995), 69-94, here 75.

[28] WA 5:607, 11-12. Marc Lienhard, "Martin Luthers christologisches Zeugnis," in Helmar Junghans, *Leben und Werk Martin Luthers* (Göttingen: Vandenhoeck Ruprecht, 1983), 77-92, here 89.

[29] WA 5:600, 25.

[30] WA 5:602, 16-19.

[31] WA 5:108, 11-13.

[32] WA 5:614, 16-24.

[33] Paul Althaus, *Die Theologie Martin Luthers* (Gütersloh: Gerd Mohn, 1962), 183. According to Erich Vogelsang, such a strong emphasis on Christ's spiritual suffering cannot be found amongst the church fathers and scholastics, not even by the mystics. Erich Vogelsang, *Der Angefochtene Glaube bei Luther* (Berlin: De Gruyter, 1932), 52-74.

God›s judgment. He experienced the weight of the judgment—and suffered not by the simple death of a man, but by the death of a true spiritual man.[34] In the person of Jesus Christ, the true knowledge of God's Son and pure perception of pure and true man come together.

The only thing that Jesus retained on the cross was his faith. Faith, as a category on its own in the meaning of trust in God the Father, is the real foundation of Christ's sinlessness. Therefore, it is generally true that in the gospel, Christ only expects faith.[35] Only faith leads to divine glory. "To know Christ means to accept the cross and accept God hidden under the crucified body."[36]

Just as Christ in his body appears futile, so at the first glance his words seem weak. But under human words is hidden the Son of God. In faith, one experiences that the "Word of Christ is the word of salvation and peace, the word of life and grace."[37] At the end of Psalm 22, Luther described what Christ reveals to the believer in an impressive way:

> For the way the suffering Christ appeared in the eyes of people, so you appear in the eyes of God. And what people are doing to Christ, devils and your sins are causing for you, only with the difference that when you are doing these things, you are not aware of them. You, like a fool laughing in self-pity, are fond of them. The wise Christ is bearing pain here. ... so then you are the wretched, lonely man, a worm, not even a human being, ridiculed by people, a source of contempt for beggars, mocked by all who see you, brought to desperation, spurned, condemned, surrounded by oxen and bulls, handed into the mouth of a roaring and devouring lion, poured out like water, like someone whose every limb has been severed, whose heart has been melted, smashed like shards, whose tongue is glued to the roof of the mouth, placed in the dust of death, surrounded by hounds and a pack of evildoers, with hands and feet pierced all the way through, all of whose ribs can be counted, all of whose clothes have been taken away and divided up by lottery, so that you will be forgotten for eternity and erased from the memory of all. All of this ... which sin does to the soul, Christ in His person shows to you, who are unaware.[38]

These strong words show the importance of what happened to the person of Christ on the cross and also what happens in the heart of every believer.

---

[34] *WA* 5:603, 34.

[35] *WA* 5:32, 15-16.

[36] *WA* 5:108, 9.

[37] *WA* 5:63, 29-30.

[38] *WA* 5:638, 19-34. According to Luther, everything has two sides: "external" as can be seen by people and "internal," that is "created by God in relation to the future" and can be perceived only "in spirit." Blaumeiser, op. cit. (note 6), 466.

The depth of Christ's descent into hell corresponds to the depth of the fall of sinful humanity.

With Psalm 8:5, Luther thought about the etymology of the words *adam* and *enosh*. Relying on Eusebius, he chose the meaning "the one who forgets." This means that in their souls, human beings forgot about God and therefore also about themselves: "God is no longer God, not Father, not love, but only a judge, an enemy, one who terrifies, as God appeared to Adam when God bore him away from Godself."[39] In a Christological interpretation of Psalm 8:5, Luther argued that the humiliation of Jesus means that he really became *enosh*—a poor and desperate man *coram deo et seipso*—because he became like sinners in sorrow and great trouble, as he had called the anger of the Father upon himself.

The soteriological implication in verse 5 suggests that God does not forget about *enosh* and takes care of human beings. This means that a person first becomes *enosh* and a son or daughter of humankind, thus doing justice to their true nature. In this way, one can become "similar to Christ," who first became similar to human beings.[40] As a "true man" Chrirst became "true sinner," so that in the depth of his human sinfulness and in the breadth of divine righteousness, he can accept the sins of the whole world and save all people. In his exegesis of Psalm 22, Luther is less interested in the question of "why" Jesus suffered than in the fact that he did indeed suffer all this. Toward the end of the passage related to Psalm 22:1-2, Luther touched on the soteriological concept of happy exchange stemming from the miracle of God's rich grace. "Our sins are no longer ours, but Christ's and Christ's righteousness is no more His, but ours."[41] This unification is similar to the unity of "bride and groom in becoming one flesh."[42]

By explaining Psalm 22 in "Operationes," Luther did not try to formulate teaching about justification; this does not even appear as his most important theological problem at this time. It would be more accurate to comment on the "doctrine of salvation"[43] in "Operationes." Luther's perception could be described as a real change in self-perception and acceptance of a new identity through a new perspective on the fellowship with the

---

[39] *WA* 5:269, 32-35.

[40] *WA* 5:272, 12-16.

[41] *WA* 5:608, 7-8; *WA* 5:543, 28-29.

[42] *WA* 5:608, 62-22.

[43] Carl Axel Aurelius, thinking about Luther's exegesis of Psalm 5:9, agrees with Siegfried Raeder that "justice" in the Old Testament means the concept of relations lived in community. Therefore, "justification can hardly be understood as the basic idea on a theoretical system. It has a much larger context and is concerned with the total existence of the human being, notably also with the question of suffering and abandonment." Carl Axel Aurelius, "Luther on the Psalter," in *LQ* (2/2000), 193-205, here 197.

person of Christ. This is possible through the active power of the promise of the gospel and is based on the communicative foundation of the relationship of God to human and human to God.[44] The doctrine of the "happy exchange" is, like the theology of the cross, based on Christology. And as in the proclamation of Christ, his words unite with God the Father, but this word is not the Father. Christ is one with the Father, but he remains the Son. His gospel contains both the speaking Son of God, but simultaneously also the Son of God speaking out of a human mouth. However, this reality changed with Christ's ascension. Nowadays, we encounter only words about God spoken by other people. We do not directly encounter the Son of God. Therefore, the work of the Holy Spirit becomes necessary so that the proclaimed gospel may have the power of touching the human heart.

The Holy Spirit inspires

It is not surprising that the "speaking" of the Holy Spirit appears to be similar to the speaking of the Father and Son, both in relation to authority on the one hand and in to the hiddenness of this authority on the other.

In the explanation of Psalm 5, which seems to be theologically the most valuable one, Luther turns his attention to the community of the Son, the Spirit and the human being arising around the Word. Any speaking at all is possible only from this starting point: "Therefore Christ gave to the apostles and the church his Holy Spirit so that He alone speaks in us, and not we alone."[45] It belongs to the essence of the Spirit's speaking that the Spirit does not talk about himself, but about Christ. The Holy Spirit is the Spirit of Christ (1 Cor 12:3); nobody can talk about Jesus without the Holy Spirit. On the other hand, it is not possible to talk about the Spirit without Christ. If the Father is revealed in the Son, so the Son becomes known in the Holy Spirit. And the Spirit cannot be found more clearly than in the words that he wrote and Jesus spoke. Today, Jesus Christ comes to human beings through the human word which, empowered by the Holy Spirit, becomes a powerful word and an active one.

In "Operationes" Luther taught with full conviction that the Holy Spirit is the author of the Bible. Luther's main interest was to understand the meaning of Scripture and not to theorize about it. In the Bible, the Spirit speaks in a language that people can hear. As divine Spirit, he has the power to open human hearts: "Psalms were written by the Spirit to com-

---

[44] Notger Slenczka, "Allein durch Glaube?," in Christoph Bultmann, *Luther und das monastische Erbe* (Tübingen: Mohr Siebeck, 2007), 291–315, here 311-12.
[45] *WA* 5:132, 9–10.

fort in despair."[46] Therefore, according to Luther, Psalms were not written by human beings to evoke the Spirit. This does not mean that by writing about the Psalms Luther intended to disregard the work of human beings. But he wanted to show the power of the Psalter to comfort, to enable a response and reference to God, the ability to change attitudes and behavior according to the Word of God in the power of the Spirit.

Proper understanding of the Scriptures can be achieved from a unifying point of view, which Luther called the "Spirit of Scripture." However, this does not mean that every part of the Bible is equally understandable. But it does mean that the Scriptures have one, simple and constant meaning.[47] The inspiration of the Scriptures—and of the Psalms—means that the texts contain everything that human beings need for salvation. However, not only the word of the writer, but also the understanding of the reader need to be inspired. The understanding of the text is just as precious as this inspiration. Thus, the fact that these two poles—word and understanding—could be separated by centuries is not a negative but rather a positive factor, enabling the Psalms to become relevant to readers in all periods of time.

The simple meaning of Scripture as a distinct hermeneutical decision leads to discussion about the unity of Scripture and enables the use of the classical hermeneutical approach to the Bible, that is, to interpret the Scripture by the Scriptures. This emphasis was clearly formulated in Luther's debates with Emser and Eck about the clarity versus the obscurity of the Bible. A fundamental question was about who has the authority to interpret the text, i.e., whether or not there is a need for a single authoritative explanation of the meaning of Psalms by the church.[48] Luther knew that he was suspected of putting himself above the authority of the whole church. Needless to say, the hermeneutical figure *scriptura sui interpres* supports only the authority of Scripture and not Luther's own authority.[49] While he was working on "Operationes" in 1520, Luther stated:

---

[46] *WA* 5:102, 21–22.

[47] *WA* 5:280, 35–36.

[48] An outstanding study related to the development of Luther's attitude toward the highest authority in the church, especially during the years 1518-1521, is offered by Christopher Spehr. Regarding the doctrine of authority of the Scripture, based on Luther's *Resolutiones* 1519, Spehr stated: "Weil sich für Luther jetzt die Heilige Schrift als höchste Autorität und Wahrheit gegenüber allen anderen kirchlichen Institutionen herauskristalisierte, konnten die auf dem Konstanzer Konzil verdammten Artikel von Hus, da sie von Luther als schriftgemäß und somit als "wahr" erkannt waren, nicht mehr ketzerisch sein." Christopher Spehr, *Luther und das Konzil* (Tübingen: Mohr Siebeck, 2010), 173-74.

[49] Friedrich Beisser, *Claritas Scripturae bei Martin Luther* (Göttingen: Vandenhoeck Ruprecht, 1966), 169.

> I do not want them to think that I am more learned than others. But I want only Scripture to rule (*solam scripturam*). I do not want the Scriptures to be interpreted by my own or somebody else's understanding (*spiritum*). I want them to be explained in the spirit of Scripture and in its own spirit.[50]

In the same way, just as looking at Christ does not necessarily lead to an understanding of Christ, so the mere reading of biblical text does not automatically lead to the understanding of the meaning of the Bible. Activity of the Spirit and faith are necessary preconditions for understanding.[51] The meaning of Scriptures is revealed through the Holy Spirit. And the Spirit wrote the text through writers and created faith in readers. A person gifted with the Spirit has faith, and faith leads to an understanding of Scripture. Nowhere else in "Operationes" did Luther speak about a deeper spiritual reading that would surpass faith.

The meaning of Scripture, according to Luther in "Operationes," is the witness for Christ (*was Christum treibet*). This does not mean that all biblical passages address Christ equally. It is a statement of faith about the content, a principle for "interpretation, not for selection."[52] The allegorical, tropological and anagogical meanings in the medieval exegetical method were therefore no longer necessary for Luther. To exegete Psalms Christologically means that such an approach is possible, but not obligatory. Friedrich Beisser called such an attitude a "pious naivety"[53] that leaves Scripture as the final authority in the spiritual realm.

Very interesting in this respect is Luther's exegesis of Psalm 9:4. When explaining the text about the "victory over enemies," Luther turned his attention to the office (*officium*) of the word, "revealing God's will, mercy, judgment etc."[54] Revelation does not simply mean formal information, but an event (*Wortgeschehen*); God wins *solo verbo*, not through violence. The efficacy of the Word[55] is twofold: it is able to save, and it is the only protection the church has to survive in the world. For Luther, it is more important to speak about God's activity than to speak about the characteristics of God's divine essence. Similarly, more important and relevant for Luther than debating the essence of Scripture, is its practical use.

---

[50] *WA* 7:98, 40-99, 2 *Assertio omnium articulorum M. Lutheri per bullam Leonis X. novissimam damnatorum* (1520).
[51] *WA* 5:108, 30.
[52] Hans Kramm, *The Theology of Martin Luther* (London: James Clarke, 1947), 115.
[53] Beisser, op. cit. (note 49), 181.
[54] *WA* 5:290, 21-22.
[55] *WA* 5:290, 25-27.

Specifically, Luther held this view in relation to sermons, prayer and meditation. All three are manifestations of a "living voice" (*viva vox*). Luther was firmly convinced that the "the voice is the soul of the Word" (*vox sit anima verbi*) and of Scripture. "The office of the New Testament is not conveyed in stones or dead tables, but it is heard in living voices."[56] The efforts of the church should be oriented toward having more good preachers in the church than good writers.[57]

The preachers must first receive the Word, and only then can these "servants of the Word" lend their mouths to the Lord. A preacher is only an "instrument, not an author" of the Word[58] using grammar and linguistic tools, comparing one passage to another to find the correct meaning of the text. There are many possibilities for experimenting, but only the right one shall be retained.[59] As it was stated above, if one looks at Christ on the cross with human eyes, only a cursed and weak human being will appear. Similarly, looking at a sermon in this manner, one will only see weak human voices speaking weak words. But in and through those words, the Holy Spirit is performing the work of salvation in the world. The cross of Christ and the preaching of men are God's tools operating in the world. Putting the cross of Christ in the center of the office of the Word (*officium verbi*, Rom 1:1-3) is important, because it is the Lord's commandment. Simultaneously, it is a sermon about Christ, God and human beings[60] and therefore, in such a sermon, the power of the Holy Spirit can become effective.

Faith is fully dependent on divine power and a person receives it as a beneficial gift from God.[61] Believers are a new creation (*novae creaturae*) and creatures of divine hands (*opera manuum dei*).[62] An image of a tree that Luther used in reference to Psalm 1 can be used in this context as well; to come to faith is like when the "divine farmer and gardener, God the Father" replants a person "from Adam into Christ." In this way, a human being gains the love of the Word of God.[63] Fundamentally, creation and recreation do not differ, because both happen *ex nihilo*,[64] which means "without merits,"

---

[56] *WA* 5:537, 17-18.
[57] *WA* 5:537, 22-23; *WA* 5:537, 10-12; *WA* 5:547, 3-4.
[58] *WA* 5:257, 17-258, 2. Johannes Hilburg, op. cit. (note 6), 111.
[59] *WA* 5:281, 10-13.
[60] *WA* 5:63, 22-26.
[61] *WA* 5:425, 18. Not only faith itself but also endurance in faith and keeping purity in preaching and teaching are dependent on divine power. *WA* 5:382, 28-29.
[62] *WA* 5:543, 35-38
[63] *WA* 5:37, 25-27
[64] *WA* 5:544, 9-10. Cf. *WA* 5:162, 29-32.

but also "out of nothing" because on the cross, the sinner was reduced to nothing and only in this way can he return to God.[65]

Unbelief as the main sin is making God into a liar.[66] The converse is also valid:

> He who trusts God considers God to be truthful and ascribes all truth to God. He who hopes in God deems that God is powerful, wise and good, because he can receive help form God. In this way, one ascribes power to God because God can help; wisdom because God knows how to help; and goodness because God wants to help. This is what God is truthful means; and this is what it means to have God indeed.[67]

Faith is not a neutral attitude because the understanding of God's activity at a personal level, "for me" (*pro me*), belongs to the essence of faith.[68] A lengthy description of faith in "Operationes" appears in relation to Psalm 14:1. A personal aspect of faith is formulated as a firm trust in God's favor towards a repentant sinner: "In no circumstances is it faith if it is not a living and unquestionable conviction, through which the person is absolutely certain, that God is favorable to those who remit their deeds and intentions and that God is favorable in good and forgiving in evil."[69]

THE BELIEVER RESPONDS

In "Operationes," Luther taught that sinners are deaf to the Word of God. But that does not mean that they are mute. In faith, the Holy Spirit opens the ears to the Word of God. However, faith and unbelief can be articulated, expressed with words and doctrines. In the preceding chapter, how the Word of God, recorded in Scripture, is used in the form of sermons was discussed. In this chapter, how the believer answers in the form of prayer and meditation and doctrine will be analyzed.

Christians without philological expertise are not at a disadvantage with respect to theologians. They too can use the Word and search for its meaning. Luther calls this active approach to the Word that can be practiced by every Christian "meditation." He does not mean an inward-looking

---

[65] *WA* 5:168, 3-4; *WA* 5:176, 27-29.
[66] *WA* 5:104, 16-17.
[67] *WA* 5:104, 5-10; *WA* 5:459, 34-36. In exegesis of Psalm 8:2 Luther talks not only about faith, but also about hope and love (*WA* 5:253, 3-9).
[68] *WA* 5:49, 14-15.
[69] *WA* 5:395, 12-16; *WA* 5:444, 35-37; *WA* 5:543, 16-22. Luther's understanding of faith in Psalm 11 is worth reading. Cf. Beintker, op. cit. (note 6), 162.

contemplation. Rather, "it is the same as talking, arguing and using the words as they are said in Psalm 37:30."[70] The most special gift and capacity of human beings is the ability to speak. Luther accepted Augustine's translation of the verb "to meditate" in Psalm 1:2 as *garrire* (twitter), like birds do. Meditation comes close to prayer and is no less important than the sermon. It implies an active, constant and audible reflection on the meaning of the text, and in this form it resembles prayer.[71]

With regard to Psalm 3:2, Luther taught "Operationes" that Psalms are not only the "Words of God" (*verbum dei*), but also "song and teaching" (*canticum et eruditionem*), "the only prophecies revealed to a unique prophet through the Holy Spirit."[72] Psalms teach universal spiritual doctrines, for example, the exposition of Psalm 1:1. Richard Bucher specifies that the term *doctrina* was not commonly used in the Middle Ages. A more common term was *articulus fidei*, to which the opposite term was heresy.[73] For Luther, a doctrine should only be based on the Scriptures, because the Word of God is timeless and universal and therefore a doctrine should come from the Bible. The Holy Spirit does not make mistakes and Scripture expects us to believe the Holy Spirit (1 Thess 5:21). "Doctrine" is only such teaching that makes one a Christian, whereas the most important article of faith is the Gospel of Jesus Christ.

There is a close relationship between the Word of God and pure doctrine. A doctrine is based on the Word of God and is the fruit of faith. On the other hand, faith helps people to trust and understand the Word of God. Friedrich Beisser stated: "*Claritas scripturae* is a necessary precondition for *puritas doctrinae*."[74] This does not mean that it should suffice that the teaching be formally correct. It is important that the doctrine reflects the simple meaning of the Scripture (doctrine as a part of the believer's life). Preservation of pure doctrine forms the apostolic foundation of the church; its unity, sanctity and catholicity.

According to Oswald Bayer, "Where there is the Word of God, there is the church. Everything that Luther says about the church... is nothing

---

[70] *WA* 5:34, 3-4; *WA* 5:49, 7-8; *WA* 5:318, 28-30; *WA* 5:179, 34-37. Gerhard Ebeling: "Ja, Luther dehnt die Wortbedeutung von Gebet' auf den gesamten meditativen Umgang mit dem Worte Gottes überhaupt aus." Gerhard Ebeling, "Beten als Wahrnehmen der Wirklichkeit des Menschen, wie Luther es lehrte und lebte," in Helmar Junghans, *Lutherjahrbuch*, vol. 66 (Göttingen: Vandenhoeck Ruprecht, 1999), 151-66, here 165.

[71] *WA* 5:34, 4-8.

[72] *WA* 5:76, 13-16.

[73] Richard Bucher, *The Ecumenical Luther* (St. Louis: CPH, 2003), 21.

[74] Beisser, op. cit. (note 49), 175, see 173-80.

else than an elaboration of this fundamental thesis."[75] The Word remains; one can only either leave it or remain truthful to it.

An integral element coming from Luther's reading of Psalms is the notion that spiritual battles (*Anfechtungen*) are inevitable. They originate from people, the world, flesh, demons,[76] i.e., enemies of God, since these want to overturn the Word of God. Despite Horst Beintker's argument that we have to see God as the originator of the *Anfechtungen*,[77] we cannot neglect Luther's quote, "The basis of all false temptations is the false lie about divine activity, saying that 'God himself did all this'"[78] and similar affirmations. The goal of the enemy is to achieve a loss of faith in God. Spiritual tribulations belong in the realm of faith. The purity of the Word and teaching does not rest on what the eyes see at first sight. Paradoxically, it is hidden in the experience of temptation (*Anfechtung, tentatio*). Sinful humanity is humbled through the cross so that new life becomes possible. But after new life appears, a cross follows that threatens the loss of faith. Karl-Heinz zur Mühlen makes it clear that Luther does not search for "dialectics of suffering in some sort of spirituality," but is talking about the "essence of following Christ in the cross."[79] *Tentationes* appear where there is faith; they are not a victory of evil powers, but a "realm" where the *peccator* can lose and the *iustus* can arise. One must pray for deliverance from the reason for temptation—that is human sin—and not the removal of temptation. Luther does not aim at getting rid of the temptation but for the removal of unbelief.

The true *Sitz im Leben* of "Operations" was teaching in a lecture hall: "I see that it is not the one who knows and teaches a lot, but rather that the one who is learned in God's affairs who is a theologian."[80] Luther teaches us to view the cross Christologically, which is possible because of the Word of God. Between *vita activa* and *vita contemplativa*, there is a third way, *vita passiva*, which does not mean passivity but the beginning of careful listening to the preached word of God.

---

[75] "Wo das Wort Gottes ist, da ist Kirche. Alles was Luther sonst noch zu Kirche zu sagen hat ..., ist nichts anderes als eine Entfaltung dieses Grundsatzes." Oswald Bayer, *Martin Luthers Theologie* (Tübingen: Mohr Siebeck, 2003), 233.
[76] *WA* 5:385, 33–34.
[77] Beintker, op. cit. (note 6), 104. Cf. Aurelius, op. cit. (note 20), 93.
[78] *WA* 5:387, 9–11.
[79] Karl-Heinz Zur Mühlen, "Das Kreuz Jesu Christi und die Kreuzesnachfolge des Christen bei Martin Luther," in Athina Lexutt and Volkmar, Ortmann, *Reformatorische Prägungen* (Göttingen: Vandenhoeck Ruprecht, 2011), 124.
[80] *WA* 5:26, 18–20.

Conclusion

According to Luther, Psalms were written by the Holy Spirit. The word of the writer of the Psalms and the word of readers of Psalms need to be inspired by the Holy Spirit. There can be a timespan between the writing down of a Psalm and understanding it anew; therefore, the Book of Psalms can be used again in each period of time.

In "Operationes in Psalmos," Luther concentrates on the communicative process of God's actions through the Word in the world, in humans and in the church. An analysis of Luther's thought in this important phenomenal exegesis of the Book of Psalms provided a theology of the Word that revolves around a Trinitarian concept of the actions of all three persons of the Holy Trinity. The modes of God's action can be described as speaking by God the Father, revelation of God as Father in Words of God the Son, and a word of inspiration by the Holy Spirit.

The relational understanding of human essence existing in a relationship with the Triune God has major hamartiological implications on Luther's theology. Sin can be understood as a refusal of the Word, unbelief and "spiritual deafness" to the Word of God. Despite this, the deaf sinner does not remain silent. Even unbelief articulates its doctrine and teaches others in its ways. Hamartiology focused on an active God and not on impersonal law means that the true essence of sin does not rest in the negativity of deeds, but in the "heart" of the human being, who does not trust the Triune God. From 1517 on, Luther taught clearly that fundamental sin means breaking the first commandment and follows from a perverted thinking about God, God's words and deeds. In the final analysis, sin can be articulated as a lack of trust in God the Father, Son and Holy Spirit.

The renewed human being is delivered from spiritual "deafness by God's grace." In "Operationes," the emphasis rests on a complex "doctrine of salvation," not only on the "teaching of justification." In their images and concept, Psalms proclaim and teach in a comprehensive way what it means to be saved. Faith in Christ gives human beings the power to hear what they were not able to hear; it teaches them what they did not know, gives them power to say what they could not say and comforts them in spiritual tribulations. Luther spoke about *iustitia passiva*. He did not teach passivity with predestinarian conclusions, but a process of hearing in which the Word enters through the ear *merre passive* and touches the human heart. This happens in faith which comes from the Gospel of Christ.

According to Luther, there is no spiritual wisdom without the Word of God. Such a word creates faith; it is more than just information about Jesus. Likewise, it does not communicate Christ in an ontological manner. The Word gives human beings faith, not Christ himself. The Holy Spirit makes the justice of Christ and other spiritual blessings real—based on the proclamation of the gospel. Generally, the Word of God comes from outside, always *extra nos*. Renewed will in faith in Christ does not lead directly to heaven, but—characteristically for the theology of the cross—to Christ's death on the cross. In the expression that "only the cross, that is our theology," Luther wants to express that the exegesis of Psalms, the search for a single meaning of the Scriptures and theological "doctrine" cannot be separated from the experience of the cross: *sola autem experientia facit theologum*.[81] Luther does not think about a feeling or an emotional experience. A strong Christocentric explanation of Psalms is united with clear Christology. Christ is not an example that should be followed, but he is an exemplar—the medium through which God acts in this world. Psalms are inspired words. Divine actions in the medium of the Word, in sermons, meditation and prayer and the teaching of the church might seem too futile. In "Operationes," Luther taught that faith unites a person with the Word. The search for the meaning of the words of the Psalms is the search for the truth.

---

[81] *WATR* 1, 16, 13 (Nr. 46). For an analysis of the term *experientia*, as an experience of death, faith and salvation, see Hans Christian Knuth, *Zur Auslegungsgeschichte von Psalm 6* (Tübingen: Mohr Siebeck, 1971), 223-24.

VI. Contextual Approaches to the Psalms

Being 'Ādām: A Contextual Reading of the Psalms Today

Madipoane Masenya (ngwan'a Mphahlele)

Introduction

I am struggling hard to recall when in my ecclesiastical context I last heard a sermon based on a text from the Book of Psalms, or last prepared a sermon or Bible study teaching based on Psalms. Nonetheless, the Book of Psalms is familiar to my worshipping community and the Psalms are an integral part of the believers' "church" life as well as their daily lives. Within our ecclesiastical settings, it is not uncommon to "hear" some of the Psalms or texts derived from the Book of Psalms sung as hymns and/or choruses. The hymn *Ke na le Modisa, ke tla be ke hloka eng*, literally, "The Lord is my Shepherd, what (more) do I need?" springs to mind here. For instance, in times of distress, when the community mourns the loss of a loved one, the words of Psalm 23 help to soothe and reassure the bereft of God's care through (prayerful) songs. Within such settings, the Psalms constitute an important content of the believers' prayers and one could argue that, more than any other book in the Christian Scriptures, the Psalms live in the veins of many African Christians to whose lives the Bible is central. It is therefore not surprising that already during the days of slavery there was a notable connection between the psalms/music and the lives of people of African descent.

The words of Southern, as quoted by Murrell, are in order:

> The books were all very acceptable, but none more so than the Psalms and Hymns, which enable them [i.e., the slaves] to gratify their peculiar taste for psalmody. Sundry of them have lodged all night in my kitchen, and sometimes when I have awakened about two or three o'clock in the morning, a torrent of sacred harmony has poured into my chamber and carried my mind away to heaven....the Negroes, above all the Human Species that I ever knew, have an Ear for Musick and a kind

of extatic Delight in Psalmody; and there are no Books they learn so soon or take so much pleasure in, as those used in that heavenly Part of Divine Worship.[1]

In several of his works, Tuesday D. Adamo, a Nigerian Hebrew Bible scholar, illustrates how rooted the Book of Psalms is in African Christianity.

> African Indigenous Christians sought vigorously for that hidden treasure in the missionary religion that was not revealed to them. They sought it in the Bible, using their own cultural interpretive resources. Using Yoruba cultural hermeneutics to interpret the Bible, they found that there was (and is) a secret power in the Bible, especially in the Book of Psalms, if it is read and recited at the right time, in the right place and a certain number of times.[2]

Believers trust that the Psalm's potent words can for instance effect specific forms of healing, bring prosperity and offer protection. To a certain extent, Adamo justifies the use of such a hermeneutics by referring to the examples of Jesus and some of the Old Testament prophets.[3]

In order to promote healing, protection and success in life, they used potent words, prayers, touching, water and material means.[4] It is no won-

---

[1] Samuel Murrell, "Psalms," in Huge Page (ed.), *The Africana Bible: Reading Israel's Scriptures from Africa and the African Diaspora* (Minneapolis: Fortress, 2010), 220-29, here 221.

[2] Tuesday D. Adamo, "The Use of Psalms in African Indigenous Churches in Nigeria," in Gerald O. West and Musa W. Dube (eds), *The Bible in Africa: Transactions, Trajectories, and Trends*, (Leiden/Boston/Cologne: Brill, 2001), 337-49), here 339

[3] Tuesday D. Adamo, "Psalms," in Daniel Patte (ed.), *Global Bible Commentary* (Nashville: Abingdon Press, 2004), 151-62, here 161.

[4] Luther's interpretation of Psalm 8 within the context of the prophecies about Christ would perhaps make more sense to Adamo. See G. Sujin Pak, *Luther, Bucer and Calvin on Psalms 8 and 16: Confessional Formation and the Question of Jewish Exegesis*, at **www.ingentaconnect.com/content/brill/nakg/2005/00000085/F0040001/art00010?crawler=true**. Puk observes four common elements in Luther's interpretation of Psalm 8 and 16: First, that Luther reads each verse in the preceding Psalms as prophecies about the incarnation, death, resurrection and ascension of Christ. Second, Luther employs both of them to teach certain doctrines and in particular, the doctrines of the Trinity, that of Christ's two natures as well as that of the nature of Christ's kingdom. Third, in all of Luther's interpretation, the person of David does not feature at all. Lastly, we can consistently note an anti-Jewish rhetoric in Luther's exegeses of the Psalms. The latter makes sense in light of the interpretation of the Psalms as revealing something of Jesus' death given the fact that the latter has always been linked to the Jews. G. Sujin Pak, "Luther, Bucer, and Calvin on Psalms 8 and 16: Confessional Formation and the Question of Jewish Exegesis," in Wim Janse and Barbara Pitkin (eds), *The Formation of Clerical and Confessional Identities in Early Modern Europe* (Leiden: Brill, 2006), 169-86.

der then that elsewhere Adamo challenges outsiders to this African status quo to allow African Christianity to be shaped by the experiences of the African peoples.[5]

Within such contexts, any attempt to revisit Psalm 8 with its particular focus on humanity, not by way of a song and/or a prayer, might not be as appropriate as gospel artist Benjamin Dube's song based on parts of Psalms.[6] In light of the fact that scholars seem to invest more of their time to thinking, reading, writing and listening to speeches than to singing or listening to songs, I shall in the following present some thoughts on a contextual reading of Psalm 8. Before I engage the theme of "being 'ādām," as it is revealed in Psalm 8, a brief word about what it means to be a human being in African-South Africa is in order.

BEING A HUMAN BEING IN AFRICAN SOUTH AFRICA

The context into which I was born was and still is a complex one. A context riddled with inequities can only produce individuals with split identities. I grew up within a patriarchal African culture and, although apartheid culture was equally patriarchal, one could not immediately feel it as a child.

The Northern Sotho/Pedi word *motho* means human being and is used to designate all human beings, irrespective of their geographical background (urban/rural), gender, social class, age, etc. The word can also be used to denote "kindness" and it is therefore not uncommon to hear the expression *ke motho*, literally, "he/she is a human being," in contexts where someone's kindness is being commended. Its counterpart, *ntwe ga se motho*, literally "this thing is not a human being," may be heard in a context of hostility in which the object of scorn—a human being—behaves in an inhuman way. In that case, the noun class of objects *se* replaces the personal noun class *m/o*. In direct contrast to the view of the psalmist in Psalm 8:7 the human being is put on the level of animals. According to the African mentality, such a demotion reveals not only the lower status accorded to animals but also the

---

[5] In his advocacy for what he calls "Afrocentric methods of interpretation," he says, "Because Western methods of interpretation are not the only legitimate and universal methods, and since all interpretations are contextual (including Western interpretations), African biblical scholars should acknowledge the legitimacy of this type of African interpretation and encourage this interpretation with some possible modification." Adamo, op. cit. (note 3), 161–62; See Tuesday D. Adamo, "Psalms," in Hugh Page(ed.), *The Africana Bible: Reading Israel's Scriptures from Africa and the African Diaspora* (Fortress Press: Minneapolis, 2010), 230–36.

[6] I for one would be more at home with listening to Benjamin Dube's song than listening to a lecture on the Psalms (Benjamin Dube, CD, Song titled, "How Excellent is your Name...".

level of denigration which was accorded to some animals. Interestingly, the expression *motho wa Kgobe"* literally, "a human being who belongs to *Kgobe* (the deity)," is used in a euphemistic way to refer to a pregnant woman.

The category of "gender" clearly impacted the community's definition of what it means to be fully human. In biblical patriarchal cultures a boy was more highly prized than a girl. Although the latter was not categorized as a non-human, the way in which she was treated by virtue of her gender would persuade a (modern) politically conscious observer to conclude that a male child seems to have been viewed as being more human than a female one. Such low esteem influences the way in which each child is treated. In terms of provisions for education, a boy was given priority over a girl.[7] It is therefore hardly surprising that, in the past, when the birth of twins was still viewed as taboo within some of the African contexts, the female rather than the male twin would be killed.

At the national level, the policy of apartheid had another definition of what (normative) humanity entailed: a white male. Within the framework of apartheid, people of African descent came to be regarded as the least human compared to their human counterparts within the same context (whites, Indians and coloreds). The negative legacies of such problematic definitions of humanity continue to have an impact on us to this day. Could Steve Bantu Biko have been right when he argued that white folks tampered negatively with the minds of black folks? For Biko, the low self-esteem typical of South African Blacks was caused mainly by the damage done to their minds by white folks.[8] Could it be that the self-hate that was

---

[7] Such a gendered provision of education was based on the assumption that a girl child will eventually marry. Within traditional African communities, each human being, irrespective of gender, is expected to marry. In my view, the category of heterosexual marriage seems to determine the full humanity of human beings. In order for one to be viewed as fully human, one has to marry. Such a high esteem of marriage within African contexts is captured succinctly by Mercy Amba Oduyouye, "The language of marriage proverbs indicates that a wife only reflects the stage of the marriage and a man's competence as a husband...Society demands that she stays married, because a woman has no dignity outside marriage. Mercy A. Oduyoye, *Daughters of Anowa: African Women and Patriarchy* (Maryknoll: Orbis, 1995), 68 (author's own italics). John Mbiti also foregrounds the significance of marriage within African contexts. "To die without getting married and without children, is to be completely cut off from the human community...to become an outcast and to lose all links with mankind [sic]. Everybody therefore must get married and bear children: that is the greatest hope of the individual for himself [sic] and of the community for the individual." John S. Mbiti, *African Religions and Philosophy* (Oxford: Heinemann, 1989), 131.

[8] Cf Madipoane Masenya (ngwan'a Mphahlele), "An African-Conscious Female's Reading of Steve Biko," in Cornel du Toit (ed.), *The Legacy of Stephen Bantu Biko:*

instilled in us manifests itself in the atrocities typical of the present South African landscape?

Psalm 8 within the context of Psalms

While at face value Psalm 8 appears like a praise/hymn, a closer reading reveals that it is more of a meditation. Many scholars attest to the links between Psalm 8 and Genesis 1.[9] In its celebration of YHWH's greatness (Ps 8:1, 9), the praise that should be due to God's name (8:1, 9) and the celebration of God's works of creation (Ps 8:2-9), Psalm 8 reveals commonalities with other Psalms (cf. Ps19:1-7; 24; 33, 104, 145). The Psalm shares its view of the finite status of a human being with Psalm 103:14-16.

'Enôš/child of 'ādām, the subject of the psalmist's meditation

Human beings engage in innovative behavior such as "questioning, experimenting, observing, associating and networking."[10] Such behavior ought to be linked to an unending curiosity and willingness to take risks. The psalmist whose meditation almost two and half centuries ago is presented in Psalm 8 seems to have also been fascinated by *homo sapiens*. As he ruminated on the notion of *'enôš*, the child of *'ādām* / human being[11] in the

---

Theological Challenges (University of South Africa: Pretoria, 2008), 114-55.

[9] Walter Brueggemann, *Spirituality of the Psalms* (Minneapolis: Fortress Press, 2002); Dow W. Edgerton, "Asking about Who We Are," in *Theology Today*, vol. 50, no. 4 (1994): 557-66; Hans H. Spoer, "The Reconstruction of Psalm viii," in *Journal of Biblical Literature*, vol. 22, no. 1 (1903),75-84, at **www.jstor.org/stable/3268937**.

[10] **http://humanitiesplus.byu.edu/2011/08/humanities-and-innovation.html**

[11] The Hebrew word *'enôš*, as it appears mostly in the poetic sections of the Hebrew Bible, refers to "men"/"male human beings or generic "men" in the plural. It can also refer to a singular man as in *ben-'enôš*, literally, son of *'enôš*. Cf .William L. Holladay, *A Concise Hebrew and Aramaic Lexicon of the Old Testament* (Leiden: E.J. Brill, 1972), 22. It is important to note that the word *'enôš* has the connotation of "weakness," "wretchedness" and "mortality" resulting from the results of sin. Rudolph E Honsey, *Exegesis of Psalm 8:3-6 (4-7 in Hebrew)*, at **www.wlsessays.net/files/HonseyPsalm.pdf**, 8. Its use in Psalm 8:5 appears to depict a singular form as it appears in a synonymous pair with *ben-'ādām*, literally son of man. In line with the flow of the text in Psalm 8, I choose to translate the word as human being. Also, in line with Psalm 8's apparent reliance on the text of Genesis 1:26-27, as well as the psalmist's use of the designation *ben-'ādām*, I prefer to use the designation *'ādām* in the present essay to designate a human being irrespective of gender. See

context of the other major works within the household of God, the heavens, the moon and the stars, the psalmist could not but ask:

> what are human beings that you are mindful of them, mortals that you care for them? 5 Yet you have made them a little lower than God, and crowned them with glory and honor. 6 You have given them dominion over the works of your hands; you have put all things under their feet (Ps 8:4-6).

It may not be inaccurate to assume that within the Northern Sotho/Pedi culture, the suckling babes (cf. Ps 8:2) were also essentially regarded as human beings, perhaps human beings-in-the-making. Hence a different word, *lesea/ngwana* is used to refer to babies within the Northern Sotho/Pedi language. The observation that the psalmist questions the status of *'ādām*, from "outside" the immediate context of "babes" in the preceding verse, a verse which may appear as being misplaced, may also point in a similar direction. According to Pitkin, most pre-moderns (cf. Martin Luther in this category as well) understood the children referred to in the preceding verses as symbols of simple believers, those who are new to the Christian faith, or even disciples." In this regard, Luther argues:

> *2. Infants and sucklings* are not taken literally here, but they are those in the church who are more ignorant and weaker in their understanding of the faith [1 Peter 2:2]. Such were those children who praised the Lord in the temple, according to Matt. 21:15, concerning whom the Lord also cited this psalm verse against the Pharisees. They were not really sucklings and infants, because they were able to speak and to run. In a mystical sense, however, these are all the humble and those ignorant of boasting, but they are "infants" in the spirit (that is, in the spiritual will) and "sucklings" (that is, gentle and meek) like the Master Himself, who says, "I am meek and lowly of heart" (Matt. 11:29), that is, a "suckling," without the sharp teeth of anger, and an "infant," without the noise of boasting.[12]

In my view, Pitkin's understanding of the text makes sense, particularly if we not only choose to affirm the full humanity of babes and sucklings, but also if we believe that there is nothing too hard for God. In her view, "...the difficulty with traditional and modern readings of Ps 8:1-2 is that they implicitly view children as prolegomena to being human."[13] Consequently, the reference to "babes" or "suckling small human beings" in verses prior to the psalmist's

---

also James L. Mays. "What Is A Human Being? Reflections on Psalm 8," in *Theology Today* 50 (1994), 511-20, here 511.

[12] Martin Luther, "Psalm Eight," in *LW* 10, 87

[13] Barbara Pitkin, "Psalm 8:1-2," in *Interpretation* 55 (2001), 177-80.

meditation on the human being might also have been deliberate. Verse 2 might in fact be in synthetic parallelism with the following verses. Just as God can perform "military" wonders through *masea* (suckling babes)–powerless, dependent minute human beings–God lifts *'enôš* from their humble frail status to that of the divine. The age of a particular human being did not seem to count within the divine scheme of things. The Northern Sotho/Pedi proverb, *la hlogotšhweu le ka rutwa ke la hlogontsho maano,* literally, "the white-headed can also benefit from the wisdom of the black-headed," springs to mind here. Even children have something valuable to offer to the aged. At face value, the Sacred Other of the psalmist's portrayal appears not to have been complacent vis-à-vis the status quo, hence the portrayal of the reversals notable in his meditation. Just as God can use very small human beings to vanquish the enemy and the avenger through silencing, God can elevate a relatively small *'ādām* to the level of God.[14] In Psalm 8, all human beings, irrespective of age, gender, ethnicity, social class and geography, are included in the category of this god-like creature. Anderson thus makes sense when he argues that the psalmist's praise of YHWH does not lead to a theological confinement in Israel's history. Rather, it leads to a universalism that embraces all humankind and the whole cosmos: "Israel's faith is rooted, as we have seen, in the human situation in which all men [sic] are involved. Man [sic] is a historical being, who remembers the past, lives toward the future, and is called to decide and act responsibly in the present."[15] As already noted with Puk, Luther's opts for a Christological understanding of the Psalm. For him, the human being in question is a revelation of the incarnation (humiliation) and exaltation of Christ (cf. Paul's poem in Phil 2:5-11). He argues:

> Here the author seems to be changing his way of speaking and to be passing over from Christ, from one [human] nature to another, which nevertheless is one and

---

[14] Cf. Walter Brueggemann, *Spirituality of the Psalms* (Minneapolis: Augsburg Fortress, 2001). For Bruggemann, Psalm 8 reflects the opinions of the powerful. "God's acts of creation and maintenance offer theological and social certainties, and these Psalms both reflect and create that reality liturgically. These Psalms hence reflect the values of a powerful social class, and for them serve the purpose of dominance. For those dominated, these Psalms may however express hope, even eschatological expectations." Christo J.S.Lombaard, "Four Recent Books on Spirituality and the Psalms: Some Contextualizing, Analytical and Evaluative remarks," in *Verbum Et Ecclesia,* JRG 27 (3) (2006), 909-29, here 914-15. In my view, in affirming the humanity of all human beings—not only that of the powerful social class—Psalm 8, at least at face value, seem to offer hope to the less powerful not only in the *eschaton,* but already in the here and now.

[15] Bernhard W. Anderson, *Out of the Depths: The Psalms Speak for Us Today* (Philadelphia: The Westminster Press, 1974), 115-16.

the same. [So it is often done in the Scriptures, or by anticipation, speaking first of the man assumed rather than the Son of God made less.] *Than the angels*, namely, by the incarnation. "He emptied Himself, etc.," Phil. 2:7. And again he shifts to the other, namely, His exaltation, *glory*, etc.[16]

Although Luther's interpretation may make sense within the context of his own time, modern readers who might be affirmed by such a reading would basically be those of Christian persuasion. In my view, restricting the interpretation of "child of *'ādām*" only to Christ fails to take cognizance of the context of the production of the Psalms, most probably the post-exilic period in which the Jewish understanding of salvation and God's care for people was not as restricted as the pre-exilic one. The interpretation that understands the word *'ādām* as an average human being irrespective of age, gender, ethnicity, social class and geography, makes more sense (cf. particularly the close connections between Ps 8 and Gen 1).

In my view, the psalmist's meditation on the works of God's fingers as they are displayed in the heavens makes more sense in a nocturnal rural context. I can resonate with such a context. Having grown up in a rural village, surrounded by mountains, with a river gracefully providing a pillow for our homestead on the southern side, I am pretty aware of the close connection between (African) human beings and nature. The starry sky of the psalmist's meditation thus makes perfect sense. Coming from a context with relatively high summer temperatures, my nuclear family and I would spend some nights in the *lapa* (courtyard). There we would be treated to the night's cool air, the sight of the moon and the stars as we all drifted into sleep, deeply aware of mother earth. In fact, those of us who were female were more aware of earth than our male counterparts.[17] In light of this interaction and familiarity with nature, one cannot but agree that the child of *'ādām* seems almost like a grasshopper when located within the context of other major works of the Maker's creation.[18] However, argues

---

[16] Martin Luther, "Psalm Eight," in *LW* 10, 88.

[17] One example of how female biology was linked to nature is in order is the Northern Sotho/Pedi word for moon, *ngwedi/kgwedi*. The same word as in the expression go *ya kgweding(ngweding)*, literally to go to the moon, is used to refer to the menstruation cycle.

[18] Although the psalmists celebrate their position relative to God (cf. a little lower that Elohim/God/gods), they seem to him like grasshoppers within the context of the other major works of creation. "So" argues Mays ... "the psalmist does speak of the human species in its frailty and finitude, in its power and purpose to control its world, and its sense of dependence and destiny," at **www.pphf.hu/biblikum/ cikkek/Theology%20Today%20-%20Mays.htm**, 511-20

the psalmist, *'ādām* is an amazing creature. Small as she/he appears to be, *'ādām* has been created in the image of the Sacred Other (cf. Gen 1:26-27).

> The poet is looking back upon Gen. 1, man [sic] made in the image of God. In our passage the reference is not to the external appearance of man [sic], as Duhm believes, for that is just what created the doubt in the poet's mind, whether man [sic] could, so to speak, in any way compete with the praise of those grand manifestations of God's power in the heavens; but it is man [sic], the thinking and intelligent being, to whom the poet refers. By virtue of his[sic] mental superiority he [sic] stands far above all else, nearest to the Deity, and exercises a rule over the whole animate world (vs 82-9), and thereby reflects, in a far higher sense, the glory of him [sic] in whose image he [sic] was created.[19]

As insignificant as *'ādām* may appear to be in the context of the amazing works of YHWH's creation, *'ādām* is the apple of her/his Maker's eye (cf. Ps 8:4).

According to the poet, a human being is one who has been accorded the status of kinship/queenship, manifested in the responsibility given to *'ādām* to rule over other members of God's household: the sheep, the oxen, the beasts of the field, the birds of the air and the fish of the sea (Ps 8:6-7; cf. also Gen1:28). According to Limburg, *'ādām*, as she/he is presented in Psalm 8, belongs to royalty. To belong to royalty entails shouldering certain responsibilities. Limburg argues,

> The king is to be especially concerned for the poor and needy, the weak and powerless (Ps.72:12-14). Royalty are responsible for caring for the weakest, the least powerful, over whom they rule. Translated to the concern of Psalm 8, this means that humans, who are here identified as royalty, are to exercise care for earth and its creatures. They are asked to be responsible royalty. The same notion is developed on the first page of the Bible, in Genesis 1:26-28. In these times of ecological crisis, Psalm 8 is a call for humans to act as responsible royalty and to care for the fragile blue planet we call our home.[20]

Just like the Maker, who has dominion over God's creatures and yet still exercises care over them (Ps 8:4), the child of *'ādām* must do likewise. Exercising dominion over the other members of God's household has to happen within the context of care. As human beings exercise dominion over others, they should remember that the mandate given to them by the Royal One to have dominion over nature, to create and innovate must be carried out within the

---

[19] Spoer, op. cit. (note 9).
[20] James Limburg, *Psalms* (Louisville: Westminster John Knox Press, 2000), 26.

context of stewardship and not tyranny and greed. In view of the ecological crisis which stares us in the eye and whose impact is felt mainly by those who are at the margins of our communities and located in the less privileged parts of the globe we can no longer view issues pertaining to ecology as only the concern of the haves when it is the have-nots that are hardest hit.

Conclusion

A rereading of Psalm 8 and its portrayal of *'ādām* may lead to a marginalized reader, one whose humanity has been and continues to be contested (cf. the African-South African setting depicted earlier on in this essay) by those who think they are more human than him/her, feeling more affirmed. The impression one gets when one reads Psalm 8 is that all human beings are equal, that is, there is one, uniform, equally worthy creature called *'enôš* or *'ādām*. A creature who is so powerful over all other members of the Maker's creation. One who is very close to the divine, just a little lower that *'elōhîm*! In real life though, that is not the case. Even at the time when the Psalms were being produced[21] there was no unified understanding of humanity. Although the Israelites/Jews appeared to be more open toward non-Jews in the exilic and the post-exilic periods (cf. texts with universal tendencies such as Psalm 8 among others), the material conditions in Yehud for instance seem to have persuaded the members of the *Golah* community to claim that they were the ones who were truly human. Within the context of strife and inequality in Yehud, it is argued that Jewish men (cf. the members of the *Golah* community) whose concern was ethnic purity among others, struggled to handle women who dared to take control of their sexuality. In Camp's analysis of Woman Stranger in Proverbs 7 for example, she argues that we are not faced with a social reality of wanton wives but rather a socio-psychological reality of men who were threatened by a multiple stressed situation which included internal religio-political power struggles, economically oppressive foreign rule and the pressures

---

[21] In the view of Goldingay, "...the Psalster came into being in something like the form we know it sometime in the Second Temple period, in Persian or Early Greek times. From the beginning, it was presumably among the authoritative resources of the Jewish community, and in this sense the time it came into being is also the time when it became canonical." John Goldingay, *Psalms. Volume 1: Psalms1-41* (Grand Rapids: Baker Academic, 2006), 35.

of cultural assimilation. All these were projected onto the symbol of a woman, that is Woman Stranger.[22]

Some aspect of the language used by the psalmist in Psalm 8, reveals that the (sexist) translation of the word *'enôš* by Holladay[23] actually makes sense if today's readers of the text choose to read guided by the grain of the text. Is it any wonder then that the immediate quality of a human being as connected to the Creator would be that of one who had the prerogative to have control over others? The language of royalty/kingship only makes sense within the context of those who had the prerogative to rule over other human beings. Such a language was naturally projected onto the image of the deity being praised. Such a masculine depiction of the deity cannot be helpful in the affirmation of the female hearers of the Psalm, then and today.

The call to worship and praise YHWH for YHWH's great acts (cf. Ps 8:1, 9) could basically only be carried out by those who had the legitimate right to do so. We need to remember that not all male human beings had the prerogative to be kings and priests. So, even within a patriarchal set-up, not everyone was equal.

In light of the above one could argue that if read from the perspective of those at the margins Psalm 8 challenges the unequal status quo. The psalmist affirms the common humanity of all irrespective of age, belonging or non-belonging to the *Golah* community, irrespective of whether they had experienced the exile or not, location and gender because we derive from the one common source and have a common mandate to care for mother earth. Understood in the preceding sense, all humans, including those of African descent, can whole-heartedly agree with the psalmist's affirmation of the majesty of YHWH's name.

---

[22] Claudia V. Camp, "What is so Strange about the Strange Woman," in Norman K. Gottwald, David Jobling, Peggy Lynne Day, and Gerald T. Sheppard, *The Bible and the Politics of Exegesis: Essays in Honor of Norman K. Gottwald on his Sixty-fifth Birthday* (Cleveland: Pilgrim Press, 1991), 29.
[23] Holladay, op. cit. (note 11), 22.

The Wounds of War: Engaging the Psalms of Lament in Pastoral Care with Veterans Against the Background of Martin Luther's Hermeneutics

Andrea Bieler

At various stages of his life, Martin Luther engaged with the Psalms. Throughout his academic career at the University of Wittenberg, he gave three cycles of lectures on the Psalms.[1] In addition, he was a meticulous translator of the Psalter and his interpretation was an endeavor of deep hermeneutical reflection.[2] Luther also composed hymns that were based on the lyrics of the Psalms, and he was fervently convinced that the Psalms were not only to be read aloud in worship but should also be sung by the entire assembly. Luther found that the reading and singing of Psalms had an edifying, consoling and uplifting effect on the worshipper. We can assume that his enthusiastic appreciation of the Psalter had its roots in his Augustinian spirituality. As an Augustinian monk, he had regularly engaged the Psalter liturgically during mass as well as in the liturgy of the Hours.[3]

---

[1] Luther gave the first set of lectures on the Psalter "Dictata Super Psalterium" between 1513 and 1515 treating the entire Psalter. The second group of lectures (1518-1521) "Operationes in Psalmos," entails a theological commentary on Psalms 1 through 22. The third set of lectures given between 1532-1535 presents a choice of Psalms, such as Psalm 2, 51, 45, 90 and 120-134. See Andreas Mikoteit, *Theologie und Gebet bei Luther: Untersuchungen zur Psalmenvorlesung 1532-1535* (Berlin and New York: Walter de Gruyter, 2004), 2-3.

[2] On Luther's philosophy of translation which gave room for fairly literal translations as well as freer interpretations for the sake of vernacular intelligibility, see Vítor Westhelle's essay in this volume.

[3] On Luther's spiritual life as a monk and the importance of the Psalms in daily prayer practice, see Otto Scheel, *Martin Luther, Vom Katholizismus zur Reformation: Im Kloster*, 4th ed., vol. 2 (Tübingen: Mohr Siebeck 1930), 27-48.

By valuing the performative significance and the practice of Psalm singing and reading, Luther appears as a theologian who had an imminent interest in the Psalter as a transformative force for troubled human beings. In the following, I shall first outline how this insight was essential for Luther's hermeneutics of the Psalms before moving into the present time by exploring how Psalms are currently employed in pastoral care settings attending to veterans in the USA. Finally, I will explore how the Psalms offer imaginative spaces of deliverance that can support humans who struggle with trauma.

Martin Luther on the transformative power of Psalms

In the introductory remarks to his translation of the Psalter, Martin Luther suggests how to read the Psalms not just as historical artifacts but as prayers that help believers to enter more deeply into the Christian imagination.[4] This imagination has a twofold drive: In his Christological reading of the Psalms, Luther discovers the witness to Christ's death and resurrection. In that sense, he calls the Book of Psalms *eine kleine biblia*, a small Bible, as it essentially covers the main parts of the story of redemption.[5] Simultaneously, the Psalms are tremendously significant for the believer since they amplify the human condition before God. Luther argues that the Psalms do not just tell stories about the saints but share immediate ways in which believers speak directly with God. This ability to communicate distinguishes the human person from the rest of the created world.[6]

The words uttered in such speech, so Luther, are not just words that hover on the surface of the mind; rather, they lead to an inward journey that reveals what is hidden in the heart as well as the treasure of the soul of the one who prays. The heart can be the place of tumultuous emotions. He compares it to a ship, rocking back and forth on a wild ocean, buffeted by winds that blow from different directions. The emotional turmoil is directed toward the past as sorrow and sadness as well as toward the future as hope and joy:

> Denn ein menschlich Hertz ist wie ein Schiff auff eim wilden Meer /welchs die Sturmwinde von den vier örtern der Welt treiben. Hie stösset her / furcht vnd sorge fur zukünftigem Vnfall. Dort feret gremen her vnd traurigkeit /von gegenwertigem

---

[4] See Martin Luther, "Vorrede auff den Psalter," in Hans Volz (ed.), *Die gantze Heilige Schrift, Deudsch* (Darmstadt: Wissenschaftliche Buchgesellschaft, 1972), vol. 1, 964-68.
[5] See "Vorrede," ibid., 964, 36.
[6] See ibid., 965, 2-19.

> V bel. Hie webt hoffnung vnd vermessenheit/von zukünfftigem Glück. Dort bleset her sicherheit vnd freude in gegenwertigen Gütern. ... Solch Sturmwinde aber leren mit Ernst redden und das hertz öffenen ynd den grund eraus schütten. ... Was ist aber das meiste im Psalter / denn solch ernstlich reden / in allerley solchen Sturmwinden?[7]

The relationship with God that is expressed in the Psalms ranges from hopeful deliverance, the plea for divine attentiveness, to a struggle that comes to terms with the experience of divine anger or even absence. These prayers oscillate back and forth, directed toward and against God.

Especially the Psalms reflect the communication with God in such a tempest; they delve deeply into the sadness of the heart in its most desperate regions. The Psalms of praise lead into a brightness in which pure joy can be expressed. And most captivatingly, in the Psalms of lament sadness and hope intermingle, they seem to relate to each other; they depend on each other. The fullness of such emotions can apparently only be expressed when the relationship between hope and despair is not disconnected.

According to Luther, this introspective journey is not the only spiritual pathway the Psalter inspires; the reading and singing of the Psalms also reestablishes community. If so used, the Psalms inspire a sense of belonging in the individual, since all the facets of joy and sorrow the Psalms depict have also been experienced by the saints. In that vein, the Psalms establish a space of resonance in which the individual person is connected to myriads of believers. They promote a sense of synchronicity; they teach to be of the same mind as those who went before and those contemporaries who suffer and express delight in similar ways.[8] This is not just a cognitive insight but about profound consolation.

Martin Luther is therefore not concerned with the Psalms as historical artifacts but as living texts that establish a journey which entails the expression of self *coram deo* by means of introspection and reintegration into community. His multifaceted approach exposes the prayers' potential for pastoral care. His hermeneutics of the Psalms can be an inspiration for present contexts as pastoral counselors seek to attend to people who are entangled in life-shattering experiences.

From a practical theological perspective it is of particular interest to explore how the Psalter has been and is currently being used by communities and in pastoral care settings in which people struggle communally and individually with the tempests of the heart. Not only in the Lutheran worshipping community, but worldwide, Christians pray with the Psalms each Sunday morning in public liturgies. Yet, people also pray with the Psalms and use them in more intimate pastoral care settings.

---

[7] See ibid., 966, 1-121.
[8] See ibid., 967, 22-26.

Pastoral care contexts: Veterans suffering from posttraumatic stress disorder (PTSD) and moral injury

In the following I shall explore how working with the Psalms of lament creates an imaginative space for veterans who have to attend to the lasting psychosomatic scars left by war. The example to be presented leads us to pastoral care settings in veteran hospitals in the USA. Veterans, who have served in the US forces, have been trained not just to kill soldiers in combat but civilians. And many of them did kill women and children whom they perceived as enemies. As a result, these soldiers experienced the constant stress of their lives being threatened. They witnessed the violence wreaked against them and their comrades and it is estimated that about twenty-five percent of female soldiers have experienced sexual assault through fellow combatants. In the lives of these veterans the line between perpetrator and victim is often blurred. Attending to these highly ambiguous experiences is a challenge for veterans and chaplains.

Veterans who have returned from the wars in Iraq and Afghanistan frequently suffer from PTSD. Since 1990, over 1.6 million men and women affected by PTSD have been treated in veteran centers. The numbers include veterans from the Vietnam War, the Gulf War and the military activities in Iraq and Afghanistan. PTSD occurs in people who were confronted with life-threatening experiences in which they had to face the risk of serious physical injury or death threats pertaining to their own lives or that of others. Such exposure to a traumatic event can lead to flashbacks which include frequent, upsetting dreams, disjointed reoccurrence of the traumatic event(s), or intense destructive psychological or physiological response to any recall. The Department of Veteran Affairs offers the following description:

> Posttraumatic stress disorder (PTSD) is a clinically significant condition with symptoms continuing more than one month after exposure to a trauma that has caused significant distress or impairment in social, occupational, or other important areas of functioning. Patients with PTSD may exhibit persistent re-experiencing of the traumatic event(s), persistent avoidance of stimuli associated with the trauma, numbing of general responsiveness (not present before the trauma), and persistent symptoms of increased arousal (not present before the trauma). PTSD can also have a delayed onset, which is described as a clinically significant presentation of symptoms (causing significant distress or impairment in social, occupational, or other important areas of functioning) at least 6 months after exposure to trauma.[9]

---

[9] Department of Veterans Affairs and Department of Defense, *Clinical Practice Guideline for Management of Post-Traumatic Stress Version 2.0*, (2010), at **www.healthquality.va.gov/ptsd/cpg_PTSD-FULL-201011612.pdf**.

A serious indicator and symptom of PTSD are tenacious signs of increased arousal that have been unfamiliar to the patient before as well as physiological response issues, such as sleep deprivation, uncontrolled outbursts of anger, lack of concentration, or hyper vigilance. Additional symptoms include irritability, angry outbursts, increased startled response and concentration or sleep problems. Acute stress disorder or injury (in order to avoid a derogative, pathologizing connotation that comes with the term disorder) is diagnosed when such symptoms arise for more than one month and lead to severe anguish or impairment of major areas of life.

An extensive study released in February 2013 by the Department of Veterans Affairs on suicide among military veterans reveals disturbing numbers: on average twenty-two veterans a day commit suicide—or one every sixty-five minutes. The study was released a few days after the US military had admitted that suicides hit a record high in 2012, outnumbering combat deaths, with 349 active-duty suicides—almost one a day.[10] Although, undeniably, the treatment of PTSD has lessened suffering and enabled many service members returning from combat to transition to civilian life, the suicide rate for veterans under thirty is on the increase.[11]

Various forms of psychotherapy have been promoted for trauma-related problems such as PTSD. Scientific research into the effectiveness of particular therapies has reached differing conclusions. An agreed upon entry point for therapies however is the assumption that it is essential for psychotherapeutic interventions to create the condition for and provision of safety and support and to offer basic education about PTSD. Most controversial are the so-called exposure therapies that seek to create a reencounter with the traumatic event as an essential step in the healing process. Other therapeutic settings such as cognitive behavioral therapy (CBT) seek to change the way a trauma victim feels and acts by changing the patterns of thinking or behavior, or both, responsible for negative emotions. In CBT, individuals learn to identify thoughts that frighten or upset them and replace them with less distressing thoughts. The goal is to reduce the anxiety symptoms that are a major cause of suffering.

Not only psychotherapy but also a social network of support seem to be invaluable in the coping process and this is where the responsibility not only of families and friends comes in but also of congregations. Churches are challenged to develop programs of support that deal in a more comprehensive

---

[10] See Peter Cooney (ed.), "U.S. military veteran suicides rise, one dies every 65 minutes," *Reuters*, 1 February 2013, **www.reuters.com/article/2013/02/02/us-usa-veterans-suicide-idUSBRE9101E320130202**

[11] On this topic, see Penny Coleman, *Flashback. Posttraumatic Stress Disorder, Suicide, and the Lessons of War* (Boston: Beacon Press, 2006).

way with the psychological damage, the economic marginalization and the social disintegration veterans need to come to terms with. Many veterans have to face long-term unemployment, homelessness and the deterioration of relationships and families. The psychosomatic phenomenon of trauma thus corresponds to social, political and cultural issues. Some veterans express that they feel like walking dead or ghosts in a society which no longer supports them or is ambivalent toward wars that were waged in the past.

In addition, many veterans suffer from moral injuries caused by an employment that also included the potential killing of civilians. In December 2009, Veteran's Administration (VA) mental health professionals described, for the first time, a war wound they call moral injury. The VA defines it as the extreme distress brought about by "perpetrating, failing to prevent, or bearing witness to acts that transgress deeply held moral beliefs and expectations."[12] The VA suggests that it contributes significantly to clinical depression, addiction, aggressive behavior and suicide and that it may sometimes precipitate or intensify PTSD. Moral injury needs to be distinguished from PTSD, since it points to a particular moral conflict between the intent to protect freedom and liberty and the experienced senseless killing. Addressing moral injury is a task that politicians, civilians and also congregations need to follow up on; it is not only the responsibility of specialized therapists and counselors. Church leaders are challenged to offer spiritual guidance and theological and ethical reflection. Moral injury cannot be considered merely as a personal problem that returning soldiers have to grapple with. It is a challenge to a society that considers warfare an appropriate means of foreign policy.

> Moral injury is an inner conflict based on a moral evaluation of having inflicted harm, a judgment grounded in a sense of personal agency. It results from a capacity for both empathy and self-reflection. Judgments pertain not only to active behavior, such as killing, but also to passive behavior, such as failing to prevent harm or witnessing a close friend being slain. Moral injury can also involve feeling betrayed by persons in authority. Even when an action may have saved someone's life or felt right at the time, a veteran may come to feel remorse or guilt for having had to inflict harm that violates his or her inner values. Just having to view and handle human remains can sometimes cause moral injury.[13]

---

[12] Shira Maguen and Brett Litz, "Moral Injury in Veterans of War," in *PTSD Research Quarterly* 23/1 (2012), 1.

[13] Herman Keizer Jr., "I'll be home for Christmas," at **http://worship.calvin.edu/resources/resource-library/i-ll-be-home-for-christmas**.

Feelings such as shame, grief, worthlessness and remorse point to acts of transgression that have violated core moral values. They are symptomatic of the profound crisis that moral injury presents.

Regarding the interpretative schemes, those who suffer from trauma question the world in a way that is based on causal attributions or meaning attributions and that often addresses a sense of cognitive dissonance. In the realm of causal attributions such questions as, Why did this event happen? Who is to blame—myself? Others? God? Did my reactions help or hurt others? Is this event fair, just, right? are frequently asked. Meaning attributions can engender the following questions: Can I trust people? Am I still safe? What does this say about me? Can I control my future? Am I worthwhile? What lessons have I learned? What does this mean for my future? Cognitive dissonance relates to the question how the event fits into my previous view of the world. Can I hold the event alongside my core assumptions without tension? Since I cannot change trauma–how do my thoughts and beliefs have to change?[14] The work of chaplains is about reframing the meaning attributions. It is in this turmoil of questions and insecurities that the work of chaplains who work in veterans' hospitals and accompany veterans on their journey can be situated. Chaplains are most often not therapists but intend to support the therapeutic processes by focusing on the religious or spiritual questions that arise for patients.

Reassembling some broken pieces:
The creation of the Psalms of lament

The Spiritual Care Handbook on PTSD discusses a variety of interventions that chaplains might employ in pastoral care settings. These include: the use of prayer, healing rituals that are appropriate to a person's own religious background, confession, guilt and forgiveness work, spiritual autobiography work, Scripture paralleling, reframing God assumptions and, finally, encouraging the connection with a spiritual community.[15] The variety of spiritual interventions seeks to address the complex psychosomatic wounds that

---

[14] See Kent Drescher, "Suggestions for Including Spirituality in Coping with Stress," at **http://uwf.edu/cap/HCWMS/materials/Drescher%20-%20Suggestions%20 for%20Including%20Spirituality%20in%20Coping%20with%20Stress%20 and%20Trauma.pdf**

[15] Rev. Brian Hughes, BCC and the Rev. George Handzo, BCC, *Spiritual Care Handbook on PTSD/TBI. The Handbook on Best Practices for the Provision of Spiritual Care to Persons with Post Traumatic Stress Disorder and Traumatic Brain Injury*, at **www.healthcarechaplaincy.org/userimages/Spiritual%20Care%20PTSD%20 Handbook1.pdf**.

veterans experience. Such interventions need to be grounded in a spiritual presence that counselors provide which is non-anxious and non-judgmental.

In what follows, I shall concentrate on two examples in which Psalms of lament are used in different ways. Chaplain Brian Kimball offers Bible studies in which he suggests reading Psalm 55 in the voice of a soldier wounded by combat stress, by identifying combat stressors and combat stress reactions in the text:

combat stressors:
    v.2: (physical) restless
    v.3: (mental) pressure
    v.4: (mental) terror
    v.5: (mental) fear
    v.13: (spiritual) betrayal
    v.15: (spiritual) anger toward injustice

combat stress reactions:
    v.2: (physical) restless
    v.5: (physical) trembling
    v.2: (mental) distracted
    v.4: (emotional) anxiety
    v.5: (emotional) overwhelmed
    v.6-8: (emotional) desire to escape
    v.1-2a: invocation of God
    v.2b-8: the psalmist's distress
    v.9-11: plea for judgment of the enemy
    v.12-14: the faithless friend
    v.15: renewed call for judgment
    v.16-19: statement of confidence
    v.20-21: faithless friend reprise
    v.22-23: confident trust in God.[16]

Kimball prompts veterans to see their own woundedness reflected in this Psalm. He motivates them to discuss such questions as,

> Does it surprise you that David experienced combat stress? What are some of the obstacles a veteran must overcome in order to depend upon God as David did? In light of today's war, how does Psalm 55 apply to those returning from combat? How did God sustain you during your combat tour?[17]

---

[16] Ibid., 75.
[17] Ibid., 75.

In Martin Luther's words, this way of interpreting the Psalms might help veterans to find their own tempests of the heart being expressed in the words of Psalm 55. In that sense a journey of introspection is fostered. Yet, there is also the communal aspect that such reading might inspire. Through such an interpretation a connection to the communities that pray with these words is engendered and a web of laments is depicted in which the veterans are encouraged to find their own voice. Read in this way, the Psalm describes a trust in God that is accompanied by passionate struggle. Counselors ought to encourage such expressions of faith.

The second example reflects the work of a chaplain at a VA medical center in the Mid-West. The chaplain uses practices of lament to assist those dealing with PTSD to reframe the experience of trauma and to create an environment in which the veterans are enabled to express their relationship with God.[18] This practice has been adopted in other veterans hospitals around the country. The following example does not rely on material images of lament and hope that the Psalms provide. It is rather the structure of the Psalms of lament that is chosen to generate an imaginative space that is clearly framed. A creative writing process is stimulated by sharing a formula with the following questions and tasks:

- How do you get God's attention?
- What are your complaints?
- Expression of trust
- What do you want?
- Expression of certainty that you have been heard
- Expression of praise.

A veteran participated in this writing group offers the following:

> Dear God, Great Gaia, King of Kings, Heavenly Father, Savior, Hey You up there, Lord our Father, J.C. Jehovah, YHWH,
> You don't listen!!! Why did this happen? ... to ME? Why am I here? Where are you? Where were you? What did I do wrong? Are You even listening / do you care? Why did it take so long for me to find out about my problem? Are you even there? Why do you let me suffer? Why don't you just take me ou? Why is there war? When will the pain stop? ... or will it? Don't mean nuttin'

---

[18] I am grateful to Wade Meyers who introduced me to this work during a class on Practices of Remembering at the Graduate Theological Union in spring of 2010. He gave me permission to share the example.

> I shot myself in the chest and I am still fuckin' here. I don't want to trust in You but the fact that I am here says something. I'don so many things that should've taken me ... We've contemplated suicide, many of us have tried suicide, but here we are ...
> I want answers ... sanity ... peace ... serenity. I want to be loved. I want to sleep – all through the night with no nightmares, sweats, without startling awake not knowin' where I am. I want to be able to love ... trust... find forgiveness within myself for myself first, and then for others. I want to be "normal." I want to be able to sit with no one at my back for protection. I want to be able to relax in a crowd and enjoy myself. I want to understand myself and find understanding in others for me. I want to move ahead, get on with things ... cope.
> When I get answers to my prayers I know I've been heard. That the group exists... shows me you care. I keep getting so many rules from others about 'how to pray.' I want to trust that you hear my prayers ... no matter how they come to you... I want to pray to You ... any time ... anywhere.
> I thank you every morning for being here ... I thank you for another day. ..... Amen.[19]

This practice of lament loosely follows the form of Psalms of lament which have been recognized by Hebrew Bible scholars such as Claus Westermann. He identifies the following aspects: A Psalm of lament usually begins with an invocation, an urgent plea to God for attention. The lament itself is often threefold: the lament against the enemies expresses the threats that have been experienced. The lament in the I-voice describes the suffering of the one who prays, the God-lament articulates concerns about divine involvement in the suffering, often times in the form of a complaint. These lamentations are contrasted with sentences of trust, the recall of experiences of security and support. This finally flows into the urgent plea for rescue.[20]

We can see a significant modification by the chaplain who adapts the above described sequence. It does not include an explicit invitation to share the original experience that could be attached to the complaints about the enemy. Rather, it speaks more broadly about complaints. The frame of the lament offers a stabilizing structure. It begins with an address to God and thus establishes a relationship. This is not about a free fall into the horror, but about a truth telling that is finally geared towards a future which promises an expression of trust in God. This exercise of creating Psalms of lament might be called an anticipating practice. It might not be fully in sync with the momentary state of emotions, yet it trusts that the structure of Psalms of lamentation offer an opportunity to speak oneself into a reality which is not entirely realized yet.

---

[19] Wade Meyers, Handout.
[20] See Claus Westermann, *Lob und Klage in den Psalmen,* 6th ed. (Göttingen: Vandenhoeck & Ruprecht, 1983).

The example at hand offers in its invocations a wide range of names for the divine, most of them reside in a metaphorical world that hint at a God who is all powerful (King of Kings, heavenly Father). It is mixed with names that are used in neo-pagan circles in the US such as Great Spirit and Gaia.

The first complaint immediately leads into a dispute about God's involvement in this situation. As an immediate address it challenges God's ability to be compassionate. The questions struggle with the experience of divine absence: You don't listen? Where are you? The questions simultaneously contemplate a God who causes such suffering. The paradox between the claim of divine agency in the suffering and divine absence is refined by creating this litany of questions.

In the next paragraph, a failed suicide attempt is mentioned. The person who writes the lament hints at the larger situation that many veterans who struggle with PTSD have to go through. He/she immediately creates a counterpoint that sounds almost stubborn, "I am still fuckin' here" and later: "but here we are..." The expression of trust that the formula calls for comes at this point only in tentative terms: "the fact that I am here, says something."

It is by answering the question, What do you want? that a sense of trust arises. First, the overarching things of profound well-being are expressed: sanity, serenity, peace and love, the ability to love and to be loved by others, the desire to receive forgiveness and the ability to forgive others. The desire to live that is expressed here has intimate, social, religious, psychological as well as physical dimensions. It manifests itself in the yearning to be liberated from the symptoms PTSD unleashes such as nightmares, sweats and the inability to sleep. Stages of hyper arousal as well as numbness in relationships are articulated. All of these things are to be named in the struggle that unfolds in the practice of lament.

The expression of certainty that the praying person has been heard is expressed again in tentative terms in form of a wish: I want to trust you; I want to pray to you. The statement that relates to some sense of steadfast trust relates to the support group: That the group exists ... shows me you care. The closing expression of praise relates to the experience of divine presence in the here and now: I thank you every morning for being here.

The invitation to articulate a complaint creates an opening to focus on the here and now and not to recall the past horrors in an immediate way. It is not about seeking to return to the original wounds or mentally to engage in depth the flashbacks and the terrorizing memory pieces. The question invites attentiveness in the writing process in which the current symptoms are taken seriously, yet they do not have to have the final word. Such creative writing inspires a sense of agency that is directed towards healing such wounds.

Working with Psalms of lament in the ways described above can be a meaningful aspect in pastoral care. While it opens up the dimension of victimization, it obviously cannot address transgressions that torment many veterans. The spiritual work of coming to terms with the depth of ambiguous experiences also needs to engage the complicated dimensions of guilt. Coming to terms with committed transgressions, with the entanglement in immoral and cruel behavior during times of deployment one cannot justify in hindsight are challenges pastoral caregivers need to leave room for. Karl Marlantes, for instance, describes the struggle of what it means to come to terms with the experience of having killed another person.[21] He claims that the Marine Corps trained him to lose the inhibition to kill another person, yet no one prepared him for what happens in the aftermath—spiritually, morally and emotionally—when conscience strikes. The Vietnam veteran and philosopher Camillo Bica captures the issue in a poem called *The Warrior's Dance* (Tai Chi Chuan) that he wrote while being deployed in Vietnam:

> I fear I am no longer alien to this horror
> I am, I am, I am the horror.
> I have lost my humanity.
> And have embraced the insanity of war.
> The monster and I are one ...
> The blood of innocents forever stains my soul.
> The transformation is complete,
> And I can never return.
> Mea culpa, mea culpa, mea maxima culpa.[22]

This dimension of remorse cannot be addressed by working with Psalms of lament. In order to respond to the magnitude of guilt and shame different interventions are needed. This might include a close look at the sense of guilt that people carry and how it is accompanied by auto-aggressive and hurtful meaning attributions in order to reframe these.

This insight does not take away from the significance of working with Psalms but rather it helps to distinguish different dimensions in the pastoral care process.

---

[21] See Karl Marlantes, *What it is Like to Go to War* (New York: Atlantic Monthly Press, 2012).
[22] Published in Rita Nakashima Brock and Gabriella Lettini, *Soul Repair: Recovering from Moral Injury after War* (Boston: Beacon Press 2012), 29–30.

Psalms as Resources in Pastoral Care with Trauma Patients

It is remarkable that the basic structure of Psalms of lament coincide with insights from cognitive therapies that proceed from the intent to create a balance between addressing the horrific experiences and engendering helpful resources that support the drive towards life. It is pivotal not to allow negative images and feelings to overwhelm the person. It is rather about the ability to create a sense of resourcefulness and resilience in which hopeful images and a sense of future can emerge despite the horror that people have experienced.

German trauma therapist Luise Reddemann stresses that it is pivotal to create this balance. In her approach to trauma therapy she proposes a sequence of interventions that fosters a sense of inner stability, a feeling of being at home in one's body, facing the terror and finally accepting and integrating one's personal history.[23]

During all stages of this sequence, the enabling of imagination plays a key role. According to Reddemann it is essential to enter the therapeutic process by focusing on resources for healing that already exist within the patient. This entails identifying a list of seemingly ordinary skills which are available to solve everyday life problems. Another exercise consists in packing a "toolbox"—imagining a box or suitcase which can be filled with anything that has been helpful in other difficult situations—memories and pictures of friends, music, physical activities. Strengthening one's resourceful imagination is crucial for the therapeutic process. I would like to suggest that images from the Psalms that entice beauty, awe, security and love of oneself could find their place in such an imaginary toolbox as well. Psalms speak abundantly of the beauty of creation and how awesome the human person has been made.

Besides the toolbox exercise Reddemann proposes to work with the imagination of the inner shelter. This is an exercise in spatial imagination where the patient is invited to envision a place of comfort and safety. The patient decides who should inhabit this inner shelter and what it should

---

[23] See Luise Reddemann, *Imagination als heilsame Kraft: Zur Behandlung von Traumafolgen mit ressourceorientierten Verfahren* (Stuttgart: Klett-Cotta, 2001). For a discussion of religious aspects in Reddemann's work, see Kristina Augst, *Auf dem Weg zu einer traumagerechten Theologie. Religiöse Aspekte in der Traumatherapie–Elemente heilsamer religiöser Praxis* (Stuttgart: Kohlhammer 2012), 89–118. For a reception of Reddemann's work in the context of pastoral care, see also Hans-Martin Gutmann, "After Violence: Narratives of Grace in the Midst of Trauma," in Andrea Bieler, Christian Bingel, and Hans-Martin Gutmann (eds), *After Violence. Religion, Trauma, and Reconciliation* (Leipzig: Evangelische Verlagsanstalt, 2011), 138–48.

look like.[24] Such mental images are created with the intent to counterbalance and constrain horrifying intrusions that are connected with places of trauma. It is interesting to see that many Psalms invite spatial imagination as well. Many Psalms carve out an imaginative space of rescue and shelter in the midst of tremendous threat. Psalm 55, which was already mentioned, articulates the voice of a traumatized self that finds the possibility of departure from the threat of death in the city, which has become an unsafe place, by unfolding the image of the dove that flies away into the wilderness as a place of rescue and of rest, away from the gust of the wind.[25] The wilderness, which in the Hebrew Bible is a very ambiguous dwelling as it refers to experiences of danger and loss of control, is also depicted here as the place of rescue. It is offered as an alternative space to the violent city that does not provide any protection (see vv. 11ff). Another example is Psalm 23, which can be read in the voice of a person seeking refuge and asylum. The spatial imagination Psalm 23 hints at is the dark valley (v. 4) which is juxtaposed with green pastures and still waters that restore the soul as the place that God provides. In Psalm 27:4–5 it is Adonaj's temple and Adonaj's tent which are depicted as places of divine rescue. Many Psalms are grounded in this dynamic of creating a shelter, a place of refuge in the midst of surrounding enemies.

Furthermore, Reddemann describes how one gets acquainted with the "inner observer" within the therapeutic context.[26] It is oftentimes a breakthrough experience to realize that one is not simply indistinguishable from one's feelings and reactions, but that there exists the possibility of momentary detachment from the effects of trauma by observing oneself and by entering into an inner dialogue with haunting memories. In this kind of inner dialogue the feeling of absorption—I am the horror—as depicted in the poem by Camillo Bica would be confronted. Raising the voice of the inner observer would mean to persevere in asking the nightmares, What do you want to teach me?

This exercise can be of tremendous significance, since it helps to restores a sense of agency against the experience of overwhelming helplessness that occurs when one suffers from PTSD.

Within the Psalms the voice of lament of the inner self is frequently established; it describes the violence that surrounds the person in the

---

[24] See Reddemann, ibid., 42–46.
[25] For a detailed exegesis, see Ulrike Bail, *Gegen das Schweigen klagen. Eine intertextuelle Studie zu den Klagepsalmen Ps 6 und Ps 55 und der Erzählung von der Vergewaltigung Tamars* (Gütersloh: Gütersloher Verlagshaus 1998), 160–213.
[26] See Reddemann, op. cit. (note 23), 115–27.

outside environment and it attends to the inner states, to the dreadful emotions of horror and fear of being overwhelmed. See again Psalm 55:2ff:

> I am troubled in my complaint. I am distraught by the noise of the enemy, because of the clamor of the wicked. For they bring trouble upon me, and in anger they cherish enmity against me. My heart is in anguish within me, the terrors of death have fallen upon me. Fear and trembling come upon me, and horror overwhelms me.

At first sight it might appear as if this prayer witnesses to the loss of self. Restlessness, despair and confusion are evoked. A top-down spatial orientation is induced through the repetitive use of the term "upon me." Following Ulrike Bail's interpretation, I would like to suggest that the articulation of the voice in the first person singular is a first step toward creating a sense of agency. This way of lamenting can be interpreted as the recognition of violence and its effects by constraining its power at the same time. The I-voice can be understood in a similar way as inner observer, as a voice that is able to enter into a dialogue with the experiences at hand without becoming overwhelmed.

Psalms read in such ways can support processes of resourceful imagination, which feed alternative images of a stronger inner self—the inner shelter, as well as the inner observer. These imaginings are couched as prayers that express faith in God, who is not detached from human suffering, but who provides shelter for those who are most vulnerable. Psalms of lament can be a powerful resource since they open up spaces in which veterans can borrow images in order to express their own turmoil and at the same time develop a language of hope that is geared toward trust in God and toward the work of soul repair.

Luther's Poetic Reading of Psalms

Dorothea Erbele-Küster

When reading and listening to Martin Luther's interpretation of Psalms, one is affected not only by the Psalms themselves but, likewise, by his poetic interpretation of them. This concurs with Luther's appreciation of singing and music. He stresses the "experience" and that the Psalms move the senses (*movere affectus*).[1] His interpretation of Psalm 23 may serve as an example of how the senses are involved in the reception of a Psalm: one is intoxicated by the grace and Word of God.[2] This intoxication puts the reader in a convivial mood. Luther's vivid evocation of how God prepares the festive table matches the emphasis in his theology on God's grace and on the beneficial effect of God's Word. God invites us to the table. The sensual aspects of tasting God and God's Word—rather like tasting delicious food—are emphasized.

Poetic and rhetorical analysis accompanies Luther's contextual interpretations. He uses images to relate the Psalms to the context of his readers and listeners and, sometimes, to highlight certain topics in a polemical manner. Such topics include Jews and Jewish communities, people associated with the Pope and women. The implicit warning with regard to my own interest in aesthetics and rhetoric is to be attentive to the misuse of poetic talk. However, my argument, as captured in the expression "po/et(h)ics," is that aesthetics can lead us to ethics.[3] It conveys the idea that the poetic is intrinsically ethical. Po/et(h)hics is not, however, meant to replace either ethics,[4] the concern for the good, by aesthetics/poetics, the

---

[1] Cf. Martin Luther's use of *"movere affectusi"* as discussed by Gerhard Hammer, *Historisch-Theologische Einleitung zu den Operationes in Psalmos* (Köln/Wien: Böhlau, 1991), 390.
[2] Cf. Luther's interpretation of Psalm 23: *WA* 51: 268, 23-29; 288, 3-27; 291, 27-292, 7; 292, 33-294, 13.
[3] Cf. Ruben Zimmermann, "The etho-poetic of the parable of the good Samaritan (Lk 10:25-37). The ethics of seeing in a culture of looking the other way," in *Verbum et ecclesia* 29 (1008), 269-92. Berhard Greiner and Maria Moog-Grünewald (eds), *Etho-Poietik. Ethik und Ästhetik im Dialog: Erwartungen, Forderungen, Abgrenzungen* (Bonn: Bouvier 1998). Wolfgang Welsch, "Ästhet/hik. Ethische Implikationen und Konsequenzen der Ästhetik," in Christoph Wulf, Dietmar Kamper and Ulrich Gumbrecht (eds), *Ethik der Ästhetik* (Berlin: Akademie Verlag, 1994), 3-22.
[4] Cf. Martin Seel, *Ethisch-Ästhetische Studien*, stw 1249 (Frankfurt: Suhrkamp Verlag, 1996).

concern for the beautiful or the senses, but to highlight the ethical moments within aesthetics.

I use po/et(h)hics in a broad sense interchangeably with aesthetics in reference to the Greek word *aesthesis*: perception, sense, etc. Po/et(h)ics implies that (right) perception leads to the (right) judgment, hence aesthetics to ethics. The conjunction of the beautiful and the good likewise finds expression in the Hebrew word *tov*. This is clearly expressed in Genesis 1, where God perceives and declares the created works to be good and beautiful.

At a methodological level, po/et(h)ics comes to the fore at various levels, beginning with the level of the text itself, as I consider those Psalms which have the beauty (of God) as their topic. Secondly, I shall investigate the aesthetic experiences induced by these texts, basing my arguments on poetic structure and language. I am interested in the est(h)etical interplay between text and reader(s).[5] The aesthetics of reception, which focus on the aesthetic and sensual experiences of reading and writing and not on the poetic quality of a text as such, provide the theoretical framework. Hence, this article pursues the question of how reading becomes an aesthetic and ethical process with transformative power. To this end, Psalm 27 will be investigated as an example. I shall focus on how the (perception of the) beauty of God transforms the speaker, whose longing to see God implies the realization of justice. As a second step, I shall make some general remarks on how po/et(h)ics enhance our understanding of the Psalms.

Rereading Psalm 27 in the light of po/et(h)ics

Psalm 27[6]

Of David
Eternal, my illumination and my saving liberation, whom shall I fear?
The Eternal is the stronghold of my life; of whom shall I be frightened?
When evildoers draw near to me to devour my flesh,
my adversaries and my enemies stumble and fall.
If an army takes up arms against me, my heart shall not fear;
If a war should rise up against me, yet will I be confident.

---

[5] Cf. Dorothea Erbele-Küster, *Lesen als Akt des Betens. Eine Rezeptionsästhetik der Psalmen*, WMANT 87 (Neukirchen-Vluyn: Neukirchener, 2001; reprint by Eugene/Origon: Wipf & Stock, 2013).

[6] All translations of the Psalms are the author's own. I would like to thank the students of the Protestant Faculty of Theology in Brussels for the discussions on this Psalm during the spring term of 2013.

> One thing I demand from the Eternal, I desire only this: that
> I shall live in the house of the Eternal all the days of my life
> to gaze upon the loveliness of the Eternal and to contemplate God´s temple.
> For God will hide me in a shelter on the day of trouble
> and conceal me under the cover of his tent, set me high on a rock.
> Now—my head is lifted up above my enemies all around me,
> and I shall offer in his tent offerings of joyful shouts;
> I shall sing and make a melody to the Eternal.
> Hear my voice Eternal when I cry,
> Show your grace to me and answer me!
> For to you speaks my heart: see my face.
> Eternal I seek your face.
> Do not hide your face from me!
> Do not turn your servant away in anger!
> You who have been my help
> Do not cast me off, do not abandon me,
> God of my saving liberation!
> If my father and mother abandon me
> the Eternal will take me up.
> Teach me your way Eternal
> and lead me on a level path because of my enemies.
> Do not give me up to the voracity of my adversaries
> for false witnesses have risen against me
> and they are breathing out violence.
> What would be if I would not dare to hope to see
> the beautiful goodness of the Eternal in the land of the living?
> Put your expectations in the Eternal!
> Be steadfast and your heart may show that it is firm.
> Put your expectations in the Eternal!

Psalm 27 opens up in illumination. In a dense nominal phrase, the I-speaker describes the close relationship between God and her-/himself:[7] "Eternal my illumination and my saving liberation" (v. 1a). In the rest of the Psalm, we can trace how the light, indeed God's enlightenment, brightens the perception of the I. The affirmation in verse 1a is followed by a question, of whom

---

[7] In the German Luther Bible edition (*Die Bibel oder die Heilige Schrift des Alten und Neuen Testaments nach der Übersetzung Martin Luthers*, Stuttgart: Deutsche Bibelgesellschaft, 1982) with which I grew up the following sentence was written in bold: Der HERR ist mein Licht und mein Heil; vor wem sollte ich mich fürchten? Der HERR ist meines Lebens Kraft; vor wem sollte mir grauen? [The Lord is my light and my salvation; whom shall I fear? The Lord is the stronghold of my life; of whom shall I be afraid.

shall I be afraid? Even though rhetorical, the question evokes the possibility of fear. This builds up a kind of antithesis—oscillating between confidence and fear—within the first part of the verse. The wordplay and the alliteration between the two Hebrew words *ori* (my light) and *ira* (fear) hold both together.

The very first word of the prayer (Psalm) and the very last one as well is the name of God. The four Hebrew consonants *jod he waw he* (the Tetragrammaton) designate the name of God in the Hebrew Bible. As a name, it is untranslatable. In our translation, it is transliterated with "Eternal." A proper name allows communication and through it, one can directly address the other. On the level of the Psalm's structure, the name of God encompasses everything. It has an inclusive function. Whereas this opening announcement addresses God directly by crying out God's un-pronounceable name, the I admonishes her-/himself at the end of the Psalm to trust the Eternal one. Beyond this admonishment, the Psalm ends with the I-speaker crying out the name of God which embraces everything.

The speaker goes on to describe situations of trouble (vv 2-3), of being offended and surrounded by evildoers in which s/he nevertheless feels safe and confident. Speaking of an army camp, the verse uses military metaphors. Rereading the Psalm aloud, the sound emphasizes the emotion: similarly harsh consonants are repeated in this verse: *chet teht he mem*.[8] In the midst of this life-threatening situation, the I-speaker utters the plea (v. 4):

> One thing I demand from the Eternal,
> I desire only this that
> I shall live in the house of the Eternal all days of my life
> to gaze upon the loveliness of the Eternal
> and to contemplate God's temple.

The verb "to gaze" (*hzh*) in combination with the preposition "upon" stresses the closeness to the object. This construction expresses a participatory act. The loveliness of God stands parallel to the temple and is therefore perceived as space. The speaker is obsessed with a single desire: to contemplate the loveliness of the Eternal (v. 4).[9] The Hebrew radix *noam* is

---

[8] Günther Bader, *Psalterspiel: Skizze einer Theologie des Psalters* (Tübingen: Mohr Siebeck, 2009), 230, speaks of "alliterierende Paronomasie" [alliterative paronomasia].
[9] The form-critical literature deals with the expression in the context of the question of whether it is to be understood as a reflection of a cultic "Sitz im Leben." However, just labeling the Psalm with the so-called motif of hearing in the morning (*Morgenmotiv*) does not highlight either the aesthetic or the bodily experience of God. Cf. Frank-Lothar Hossfeld and Erich Zenger, *Die Psalmen. Psalm 1–50*, NEB. AT 29 (Würzburg: Echter Verlag, 1993), 172.

used in the context of physical beauty (Song of Songs 1:16; 7:1; 2 Sam 23:1). In 2 Samuel 1:23; 26, it also expresses the closeness and delightfulness of a friend. It stands parallel to *tov* (good and beautiful) that describes the name of God in Psalm 135:3 (cf. Ps 147:1).

In his Bible translation (1545), Martin Luther refrains from the visual and concrete image of God. Translating it by the "beautiful service of the Lord," the aesthetic aspect is applied to the service of God that humans perform. However, the Hebrew Bible speaks of the delightfulness and beauty of God, and Luther also paraphrases it in his first lecture on the Psalms 1513-1515:[10] "the sweetness and joy in the Lord."

The sight of the I-speaker in Psalm 27 is absorbed by the beauty and resplendence or radiance of the Eternal. S/he begs for face-to-face contact, crying out (v. 8):

> For to you speaks my heart:
> Address my face
> Eternal I seek your face.

The I exposes him-/herself before the face of God. S/he goes on: "Do not hide your face!" (v. 9a). This expresses the striving for a relationship of mutual recognition: to see (vv 4; 8) and be seen (v. 9). The face of the Other reflects mine and mine reflects the face of the Other. In this sense, God is enlightenment. This light shall lead the speaker on a just and even path (v. 11).

The I asks for directions, i.e., for ethos; s/he wants to know how to live in the light of God. To see God's saving beauty and to stand up against evildoers go hand in hand. Aesthetics may highlight the precariousness of life. We could call this an aesthetic justice which is open to a perception of the unseen. Towards the end of the Psalm, the I expresses the wish to see God (v. 13) for the second time.

> What would be if I would not dare to hope to see the goodness of the Eternal in the land of the living?

The fragile hope of tasting the grace and goodness of the Eternal is expressed in a (negated) question. In the Hebrew word *tov*, goodness and beauty conflate, as mentioned above. It can stand parallel with *ifa* beautiful (1 Sam 16:12). Objects designed as *tov* are attractive.[11] Here, the

---

[10] *WA* 3:147–50.

[11] Cf. I. Höver-Johag, "Tov," in G. Johannes Botterweck and Helmut Ringgren (eds), *Theologisches Wörterbuch zum Alten Testament*, vol. III (Stuttgart: Kohlhammer, 1986), 315–39; 318.

designation includes the ethical and aesthetic stance of God's grace. The I of the Psalm takes refuge in this hope and ends her/his prayer in this vein (cf. Ps 31:25). In the final verse the speaker tries to reassure her/himself with admonitions at the beginning and the end of the verse "Put your expectations in the Eternal!." At a formal level the repetition of this line creates an inclusion that highlights and embraces the appeal to her/his own heart in the middle of the verse: Be steadfast and your heart may show that it is firm. The heart, center of thought and decision, will show that it is firm. By its repetitive occurrence, the double admonishment ("Put your expectations in the Eternal") expresses reassurance. The poetic and rhetorical structure of the verse indicates firmness—the I is grounded in his/her orientation towards God.

Martin Luther describes this verse in two different ways. In terms of editorial criticism *avant la lettre*, it is described as a secondary verse. Theologically speaking, it functions on the poetic and anthropological levels as a conclusion with affirmative power: "This verse is like a small chaplet."[12]

Psalm 27 vibrates from beginning to the end with the longing to participate in the beauteousness and splendor of God. The eyes of the speaker are wearied by all the evil s/he sees. S/he finds herself/himself surrounded by people who try to devour her/him, to take her body. And yet, s/he states that if there is a war against her/him, s/he would not be afraid. The person desires to see afresh, that is, to see in the light of the goodness of the Eternal. The gaze becomes brightened by God's radiance and goodness. Indeed, Psalm 27 unfolds how our perception changes in the light of beauty and loveliness; seeing beatific loveliness sheds light on violence. As a critique of unjust situations, the awesome beauty of God destabilizes the worldly order.

As we have seen, this relation between aesthetics and justice is likewise underlined in Psalm 17 which opens with a series of pleas:

Listen, Eternal, oh justice, decipher my crying, listen carefully to my prayer.

The noun "justice" is the third word. It stands alone in the middle of the plea (v.1a). The first translators stumbled and tried to smooth over the eruption of justice by linking it grammatically directly with God. The theme of the striving for justice pervades the Psalm. The Psalm employs justice as a relational term: God's justice illuminates mine (vv 2;14). The

---

[12] In a sermon (*WA* 49: 269-70) he calls the verse first a "Glosse" adding that it makes a round structure (Kränzlein). Cf. Erwin Mühlhaupt (ed.), *D Martin Luthers Psalmenauslegungen, Psalm 26-90*, vol. 2 (Göttingen: Vandenhoeck & Ruprecht, 1962), 17.

I-speaker confirms, "From your face goes out my righteousness" (v. 2). Further corporality is linked to this theme, as justice is related to one's aesthetic experiences (v. 15):[13]

> In righteousness (justice) I will see your face;
> When I wake up, I will be satisfied with seeing your likeness.

When the senses awaken in the morning, the image of God saturates the I-speaker. His/her whole human being is affected. Finally, by seeing God's face, the body is saturated. Whereas in the beginning of the Psalm, s/he asks for a just judgment from God (vv 2; 3), at the end of the Psalm s/he states that s/he is now centered in justice (v. 17a). Justice as a relational term is realized in the uniqueness of the event. Taking up a term from Kryszof Ziarek, one could call this po/et(h)ic "justice":[14] "Quite distinct from the legal and ethical senses of justice, this 'justice' is eminently poetic, calling for a measure which displaces and decisively reorients the debates about justice." According to Psalm 27 and the just alluded to Psalm 17, po/et(h)ics reveals itself in acting over against those who perform unjust and treacherous deeds.

GOD'S PO/ET(H)ICS AFFECTING OURS

In a second and final step, some general features of po/et(h)ical and contextual readings of the Psalms shall be highlighted. Martin Luther's readings serve as impulse for our Psalter hermeneutics from a Lutheran perspective.

When reading the Psalms the issue at stake is the role of aesthetic perception, thus aesthetics for ethics. As has been suggested by Brian Brock, "Luther's ethics is not one of prescription but of perception and affection" implying that the manner in which he reads the Psalms renews his ethics.[15]

According to Greek philosophy, aesthetic experiences are threefold: *poiesis* refers to the productive and creative aspect of aesthetic experience; *aisthesis* refers to the receptive experience; while *catharsis* refers to the

---

[13] Cf. Erbele-Küster, op. cit. (note 5), 187.
[14] Cf. Kryzysztof Ziarek, "Poetic 'justice,'" in Oren Ben-Dor (ed.), *Law and Art. Justice, Ethics and Aesthetics* (New York: Abingdon, 2011), 33–44; 43. A "justice" which "is to signal that neither law nor ethics, and certainly not imperial power/command, will serve here as the determining perspective," 34.
[15] Brian Bock in this publication. Cf. also Brian Brock, *Singing the Ethos of God: On the Place of Christian Ethics in Scripture: On the Place of Scripture in Christian Ethics* (Grand Rapids: Eerdmans, 2007).

transformative and liberating one.[16] This tripartite model shows that a dualistic confrontation between an active and passive part in the reading of Psalms is a misleading shortcut. All three dimensions are at the core. Reception and production is intertwined.

Likewise, Psalm 40:4 in the Hebrew text (in most English translations it corresponds to verse 3) describes this interconnectedness between the poetics of God and our productive work: "And God gives in my mouth a new song, a psalm song of our God." This song emanates from God and flows back to God. In situations where one is desperate and lacks words, God provides new words. The song of the I-reader is God's song and, vice versa, the song of God is the song of the I-reader. God's beauty affects the speaker. In this effect lies a transformative ethical power. Poetics makes the Psalm writer and reader sing poetically. As we have seen in our interpretation of Psalm 27 and others, God's poetics affects the I-speaker and the exegete. In a sense, both coincide, a prominent example being Martin Luther.

Lutheran po/et(h)ics

Martin Luther's language is picturesque and he himself becomes a poet; in his interpretation, he employs concrete images. He is rather explicit, almost graphic, in his descriptions. Martin Luther's poetic readings and rewritings of Psalms serve as a stimulus for our poetic creativity. When poetry (poetics) affects us viscerally, then reading itself may become an act with transformative ethical power. Luther calls this simply "the word," implying its effective and formative power. In his praxis, exegesis and enactment of the Psalms were interrelated. Interpreting the Psalms leads to singing and rewriting Psalms and vice versa if we are sensitive to the poetic and aesthetic structure. Reading Psalms in the light of Luther becomes what might be called committed reading and performing.

The introductory Psalm to the Psalter (Ps 1:3) uses an onomatopoetic word (*hgh*) for this activity of studying the Torah/Psalms. The sound of the word is felt in the throat, referring to a "desire in the throat" like the roaring of lions (Isa 31:4) and the cooing of pigeons (Isa 38:14). Studying the Psalms is thus not quite like the Latin translation *meditari* (to meditate) might suggest. According to the former monk Luther, it is (no longer) an exercise done by monks behind closed doors in silence, but a hilarious act in public: singing and speaking of the word.[17] In "Operationes in Psalmos"

---

[16] Cf. Hans Robert Jauß, *Ästhetische Erfahrung und literarische Hermeneutik* (München: Fink, 1977), 62f.

[17] Cf. Luther in his sermon "Die Lust am Gesetz," in Erwin Mühlhaupt (ed.), *D Martin Luthers Psalmenauslegungen, Psalm 1-25*, vol. 1 (Göttingen: Vandenhoeck

(1519-1521), Luther likewise underlines this beautiful metaphor when he calls the verb referring to Augustine's interpretation in the sense of the Latin word *garrire*, to twitter and chatter, as an exercise of hilarious birds.[18]

(LUTHER'S) TRANSLATION AS CONTEXTUALIZATION

Translators move between cultures and languages. Martin Luther spent a lot of time and energy on this activity. His translations of the Psalms and the Bible as a whole into the vernacular still inspire us today. In his afterword in the revised Psalter edition, Luther stresses his wish to be closer to the German, the language into which he translated the Psalms. They should sound like songs in the mother tongue and in the language of the context.[19] Indeed, as Georg Steiner phrases it, "The translator invades, extracts and brings home."[20] This idea is already reflected in the title of his edition of Luther's translated Psalter: "Psalter Deutsch" (German Psalter).

This goes hand in hand with the contextual uses of the Psalter in Reformation times. Most songs of the Reformation were first printed as broadsheets.[21] Whereas in the Reformed tradition from the times of Calvin onwards, the same Psalter Song Book has been in use throughout the ages, within the Lutheran tradition, the rewriting of Psalms and the composition of new Psalms became popular. The well-known hymn "Eine feste Burg ist unser Gott" is an outstanding example of this.[22] In a letter to Georg Burkhardt (1523), Luther asked if he would be like Heman, Asaph or Yedutun,

---

& Ruprecht, 1959), 20: "Es geht nicht nur ums Meditieren, man muss (mit dem Wort) umgehen, gern davon reden und singen." (WA 49:223-32).

[18] Cf. Gerhard Hammer and Manfred Biersack (eds), *D. Martin Luther, Operationes in Psalmos, Teil II: Psalm 1-10* (Archiv zur Weimarer Ausgabe, Bd. 2) (Köln/Wien: Böhlau 1981), 42, Psalmum primum 1,2; See Lubomir Batka's essay in this publication.

[19] Cf. Luther, "Nachwort 1531," *WA.DB* 10/1,590,45f: "wie man mit Dolmetschen neher vnd neher kompt," and cf. "Summarien über die Psalmen und Ursachen des Dolmetschens" [Summary on the Psalms and Reasons for the Translation] 1531/33, *WA* 38:9-21.

[20] Georg Steiner, *After Babel. Aspects of Language & Translation* (Oxford: Oxford University Press, ³1998), 314.

[21] Cf. Inka Bach and Helmut Galle, *Deutsche Psalmdichtung vom 16. bis 20. Jahrhundert. Untersuchungen zur Geschichte einer lyrischen Gattung* (Quellen und Forschungen zur Sprach- und Kulturgeschichte der germanischen Völker 95) (Berlin/New York: De Gruyter, 1989).

[22] Roger Wanke (in this publication) referred to the contextual reading of Psalm 94 as a consolation in times of distress and a postwar situation in 1526. Being hosted close to the Wartburg, and after having made a kind of pilgrimage on foot up to the castle during the consultation, we were able to grasp Luther's rewriting of the Psalm.

meaning like one of the members of the Psalm guilds creating Psalms.[23] All these efforts to create vernacular songs lead to an empowerment of the community. In this vein, I would like to stress the necessity of "new" Psalms and the need for translations that are consistent with the hermeneutical presuppositions of one's own (community). Taking up the initial question of criteria against the misuse of Psalms they may be identified in the Psalm's contextual rootedness linked with poetic justice. Psalm 17 and 27 link the beauty of God to God's justice. The poetic and aesthetic senses thus make us aware of the beauty of the Other.

---

[23] Cf. *WAB* 3, 220.

Authors

Batka, Ľubomír, Dr, Dean, Evangelical Lutheran Theological Faculty, Comenius University Bratislava, Solvakia

Bieler, Andrea, Prof. Dr, Professor of Practical Theology, Kirchliche Hochschule Wuppertal/Bethel, Germany

Brock, Brian, Dr, Reader in Moral and Practical Theology, University of Aberdeen, United Kingdom

Dicke, Klaus, Prof. Dr, Rector and Professor of Political Science and the History of Ideas, Friedrich-Schiller-University of Jena, Germany

Erbele-Küster, Dorothea, Dr, Lecturer, University of Mainz, Germany

Grosshans, Hans-Peter, Prof. Dr, Professor of Systematic and Ecumenical Theology, Faculty of Protestant Theology, University of Muenster, Germany

Hausmann, Jutta, Prof. Dr, Chair, Old Testament Studies, Lutheran Theological University, Budapest, Hungary

Hentschel, Anni, Dr, Research Associate, Johann Wolfgang Goethe-Universität, Frankfurt a. M., Germany

Hossfeld, Frank-Lothar, Prof. Dr, Professor emeritus of Old Testament, Catholic Faculty, University of Bonn, Germany

Junge, Martin, Rev., General Secretary, The Lutheran World Federation, Geneva, Switzerland

Koester, Craig R., Rev. Dr, The Asher O. and Carrie Nasby Professor of New Testament, Luther Seminary, Saint Paul, Minnesota, USA

Körting, Corinna, Prof. Dr, Professor of Old Testament Studies and Ancient Near Eastern Religion, Department of Theology, University of Hamburg, Germany

Masenya, Madipoane J., Prof. Dr, Professor of Old Testament Studies, University of South Africa, South Africa

Melanchthon, Monica Jyotsna, Dr, Associate Professor of Old Testament, University of Divinity, Melbourne, Australia

Mtata, Kenneth, Rev. Dr, Secretary for Lutheran Theology, Practice and Formation, The Lutheran World Federation, Geneva, Switzerland

Niebuhr, Karl-Wilhelm, Prof. Dr, Professor of New Testament Studies, Theological Faculty, Friedrich-Schiller-University of Jena, Jena, Germany

Nõmmik, Urmas, Dr, Senior Lecturer Old Testament and Semitic Studies, Faculty of Theology, University of Tartu, Estonia

Rose, Miriam, Prof. Dr, Professor of Systematic Theology, Friedrich-Schiller-University of Jena, Germany

Wanke, Roger Marcel, Dr, Docent for Old Testament Studies, Faculdade Luterana de Teologia, São Bento do Sul, Brazil

Westhelle, Vítor, Rev. Prof. Dr, Professor of Systematic Theology, Lutheran School of Theology at Chicago, USA